THE
EVERYTHING®
KETOGENIC DIET
COOKBOOK

Dear Reader,

If you're one of the people who followed a low-fat diet and failed to lose weight, or failed to see any other major health improvements, don't worry; you're in the company of millions. When the popularity of the low-fat diet surged, many followers found themselves gaining more weight. Removing fat from your diet was supposed to make you thinner and healthier, but it did just the opposite. When people started replacing fats with carbohydrates and low-fat alternatives, the incidences of diabetes and obesity began to skyrocket. Could the beloved low-fat diet be to blame? Absolutely.

Consumers thought they were making good choices, but instead they were removing a healthy nutrient from their diet based on bad science. As fat was removed from the diet, it was replaced with lots of carbohydrates, especially in the form of sugar. This led to hormone troubles, brain fog, weight gain, fatigue, and just plain not feeling good.

Whether you've stumbled across this book by accident or you're a ketogenic pro, welcome. You're going to learn all you can about fat and why it's not the nutritional nemesis it was made out to be. After you have a good understanding of why fat is your friend and why you should be including more of it in your diet, you'll be given the tools to create a ketogenic diet of your own. I've made the process even easier by including three hundred recipes that will kick you into ketosis and turn you into a lean, mean, fat-burning machine.

Whether you choose to fully immerse yourself in the ketogenic diet or you just want to learn something new, I commend you for picking up this book and I wish you all the best.

Lindsay Boyers, CHNC

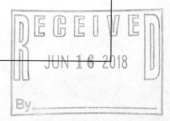

Welcome to the EVERYTHING® Series!

These handy, accessible books give you all you need to tackle a difficult project, gain a new hobby, comprehend a fascinating topic, prepare for an exam, or even brush up on something you learned back in school but have since forgotten.

You can choose to read an Everything® book from cover to cover or just pick out the information you want from our four useful boxes: e-questions, e-facts, e-alerts, and e-ssentials.

We give you everything you need to know on the subject, but throw in a lot of fun stuff along the way too.

We now have more than 400 Everything® books in print, spanning such wide-ranging categories as weddings, pregnancy, cooking, music instruction, foreign language, crafts, pets, New Age, and so much more. When you're done reading them all, you can finally say you know Everything®!

QUESTION

Answers to
common questions

FACT

Important snippets
of information

ALERT

Urgent
warnings

ESSENTIAL

Quick
handy tips

PUBLISHER Karen Cooper

MANAGING EDITOR Lisa Laing

COPY CHIEF Casey Ebert

ASSISTANT PRODUCTION EDITOR Jo-Anne Duhamel

ACQUISITIONS EDITOR Lisa Laing

DEVELOPMENT EDITORS Zander Hatch and Khelsea Purvis

EVERYTHING® SERIES COVER DESIGNER Erin Alexander

THE
EVERYTHING®
KETOGENIC DIET
COOKBOOK

Lindsay Boyers, CHNC

Adams Media

New York London Toronto Sydney New Delhi

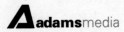

Adams Media
An Imprint of Simon & Schuster, Inc.
57 Littlefield Street
Avon, Massachusetts 02322

An Everything® Series Book.
Everything® and everything.com® are registered trademarks of Simon & Schuster, Inc.

First Adams Media trade paperback edition DECEMBER 2017

ADAMS MEDIA and colophon are trademarks of Simon and Schuster.

For information about special discounts for bulk purchases, please contact Simon & Schuster Special Sales at 1-866-506-1949 or business@simonandschuster.com.

The Simon & Schuster Speakers Bureau can bring authors to your live event. For more information or to book an event contact the Simon & Schuster Speakers Bureau at 1-866-248-3049 or visit our website at www.simonspeakers.com.

Nutritional statistics by Melinda Boyd

Manufactured in the United States of America

10 9 8 7 6 5 4 3 2 1

Library of Congress Cataloging-in-Publication Data
Boyers, Lindsay, author.
The everything ketogenic diet cookbook / Lindsay
Boyers, CHNC.
Avon, Massachusetts: Adams Media, 2017.
Series: Everything.
Includes index.
LCCN 2017037357 (print) | LCCN 2017040825 (ebook) | ISBN 9781507206263 (pb) | ISBN 9781507206270 (ebook)
LCSH: Ketogenic diet--Recipes. | Reducing diets--Recipes. | Low-carbohydrate diet--Recipes. | Weight loss. | BISAC: COOKING / Health & Healing / Low Carbohydrate. | COOKING / Health & Healing / Weight Control. | COOKING / General. | LCGFT: Cookbooks.
LCC RM222.2 (ebook) | LCC RM222.2 .B64825 2017 (print) | DDC 641.5/6383--dc23
LC record available at https://lccn.loc.gov/2017037357

ISBN 978-1-5072-0626-3
ISBN 978-1-5072-0627-0 (ebook)

Always follow safety and commonsense cooking protocols while using kitchen utensils, operating ovens and stoves, and handling uncooked food. If children are assisting in the preparation of any recipe, they should always be supervised by an adult.

The information in this book should not be used for diagnosing or treating any health problem. Not all diet and exercise plans suit everyone. You should always consult a trained medical professional before starting a diet, taking any form of medication, or embarking on any fitness or weight-training program. The author and publisher disclaim any liability arising directly or indirectly from the use of this book.

Contains material adapted from the following titles published by Adams Media, an Imprint of Simon & Schuster, Inc.: *The Everything® Guide to the Ketogenic Diet* by Lindsay Boyers, CHNC, copyright © 2015, ISBN 978-1-4405-8691-0, and *The Everything® Big Book of Fat Bombs* by Vivica Menegaz, CTWFN, copyright © 2016, ISBN 978-1-4405-9675-9.

For my dad, Scott. I love you. Nice.

Acknowledgments

Thank you to my family—my mom, Lola, who is always my biggest supporter; my dad, Scott, who always encourages me to do better; and my sister, Tiffany, who always has my back. I feel like the luckiest person in the world to have a family like you.

Contents

Introduction

IN THE 1990s, with the rise of the low-fat diet craze, fat was given the title of the nutritional bad guy. All of the world's weight and heart problems were blamed on the nutrient (even though the rates of obesity skyrocketed at the same time low-fat diets became popular), and things haven't been the same since. Even though science has backtracked on this issue—there are many studies showing that fat doesn't cause heart disease or high cholesterol—the damage has been done. Fat was given a lasting reputation that's proven to be increasingly difficult to break. People are wary of fat, worrying that it's the major cause of weight gain and heart disease and insisting that it has no place in a healthy diet, but that couldn't be further from the truth.

Sure, like anything, if you overdo it, too much fat can cause weight gain, but it's not the scary monster you might think it is. In fact, it's the opposite. Dietary fat is an absolute necessity. Eating fat can help you lose weight and build muscle; it also increases mental clarity, gives you energy, improves mood, contributes to glowing skin and better eye health, boosts your immune system, and leads to better brain function. And here's a big shocker: fat has been shown to improve cholesterol ratio and reduce heart disease risk. That's right: eating fat is actually linked with a healthier heart and lower cholesterol levels!

Here's something else that might surprise you, especially since these foods are often glorified for their supposed health benefits: it's carbohydrates (especially sugar) and processed vegetable oils, like canola, corn, and soybean, that are largely responsible for weight gain and the increasing rates of chronic health conditions, like heart disease, diabetes, and autoimmune disorders. Limiting carbohydrates and sugars and replacing them with both saturated and unsaturated fats—the basis of the ketogenic diet—can help you lose weight today as well as keep you healthy for years to come.

Although it's been gaining a lot more attention recently, largely thanks to social media, the ketogenic diet is not a new trend or a fad. The high-fat, low-carbohydrate diet has been around since the 1920s, when it was used for nearly two decades as the main treatment method for difficult-to-control epilepsy in young children. Although the diet worked remarkably well, eventually it fell by the wayside when antiseizure medications became more readily available. People preferred a quick fix even if that fix meant the potential for more side effects. Today more and more people are following a nutritional ketogenic diet and reporting a wide range of wonderful health benefits.

The ketogenic diet encourages that you get most of your calories—around 75 percent—from fat, only 5–10 percent from carbohydrates, and the rest from high-quality proteins. This may be a far cry from the nutritional recommendations most are used to hearing, and, sure, it takes some getting used to, but as you'll come to find out, change is a good thing.

CHAPTER 1

Understanding the Ketogenic Diet

Your body is highly intelligent. It knows exactly what it wants and what it needs to do to get what it wants, and what it wants is energy. Without energy you could not survive. Your cells would starve and all of the physiological processes in your body would cease. So what is energy exactly and where does it come from? Your body uses several different metabolic pathways to convert the food you eat into useable energy. The default metabolic pathway uses the glucose from carbohydrates as fuel. As long as you provide your body with carbohydrates, it will use them as energy, storing fat in the process. When you deny your body carbohydrates, it has to turn somewhere else to get the energy it needs to live.

Why Fat Is Your Friend

Fat is an integral part of every cell in your body. This macronutrient is a major component of your cell membranes, which hold each cell together. Every single cell in your body, from the cells in your brain to the cells in your heart to the cells in your lungs, is dependent on fat for survival. Fat is especially important for your brain, which is made up of 60 percent fat and cholesterol.

Fat and cholesterol are used as building blocks for many hormones, which help regulate metabolism, control growth and development, and maintain bone and muscle mass, among many other things. Fat is vital for proper immune function, helps regulate body temperature, and serves as a source of protection for your major organs, surrounding all of your vital organs to provide a sort of cushion for protection against falls and trauma. It also helps boost metabolic function and plays a role in keeping you lean.

Fat is classified as an essential nutrient, which means that you need to ingest it through the foods you eat because the body cannot make what it needs on its own. Fat is composed of individual molecules called fatty acids. Two of these fatty acids, omega-3 fatty acids and omega-6 fatty acids, are absolutely essential for good health. Omega-3 fatty acids play a crucial role in brain function and growth and development, while omega-6 fatty acids help regulate metabolism and maintain bone health. Fat also allows you to absorb and digest other essential nutrients, such as vitamins A, D, E, and K and beta-carotene. Without enough fat in your diet, you wouldn't be able to absorb any of these nutrients and you would eventually develop nutritional deficiencies.

Fat is also a major source of energy for your body. Because each gram contains 9 calories, fat is a compact source of energy that your body can use easily and efficiently. Unlike with carbohydrates, which your body can only store in limited amounts, your body has an unlimited ability to store fat for later use. When food intake falls short, such as between meals or while you're sleeping, your body calls on its fat reservoirs for energy. This physiological process is what the entire ketogenic diet is based upon.

How Your Body Obtains Energy

Energy cannot be created. It can only be converted from one form to another. Because of this, your body needs to get energy from somewhere. It uses the food, and the macronutrients from the food, that you eat. The biochemical process of obtaining energy is a complicated one, but it's important to understand the basics so you can get a feel for how ketosis works on a cellular level.

Energy from Carbohydrates

Although your body is adept at using any food that's available for energy, it always turns to carbohydrates first. When you eat carbohydrates, they are ultimately broken down or converted into glucose, which is absorbed through the walls of the small intestine. From the small intestine, glucose enters into your bloodstream, which naturally causes your blood glucose levels to rise. As soon as the glucose enters your blood, your pancreas sends out insulin to pick it up and carry it to your cells so they can use it as energy.

Once your cells have used all the glucose they need at that time, much of the remaining glucose is converted into glycogen (the storage form of glucose), which is then stored in the liver and muscles. The liver has a limited ability to store glycogen, though; it can only store enough glycogen to provide you with energy for about twenty-four hours. All the extra glucose that can't be stored is converted into triglycerides, the storage form of fat, and stored in your fat cells.

FACT

A healthy adult can store about 500 grams (2,000 calories worth) of carbohydrates. Approximately 400 grams are stored as glycogen in your muscles, 90–110 grams are stored as glycogen in the liver, and 25 grams circulate throughout the bloodstream as glucose. The body has an unlimited ability to store fat.

When you don't eat for a few hours and your blood sugar starts to drop, your body will call on the glycogen stored in the liver and muscles for energy before anything else. The pancreas releases a hormone called glucagon, which triggers the release of glucose from the glycogen stored in your liver to help raise your blood sugar levels. This process is called glycogenolysis. The glycogen stored in your liver is used exclusively to increase your blood glucose levels, while the glycogen stored in your muscles is used strictly as fuel for your muscles. When you eat carbohydrates again, your body uses the glucose it gets from them to replenish those glycogen stores. If you regularly eat carbohydrates, your body never has a problem getting access to glucose for energy and the stored fat stays where it is—in your fat cells.

Energy from Protein

Protein is the body's least favorite macronutrient to use as energy. This is because protein serves so many other functions in the body. Protein provides structural support to every cell in your body and helps maintain your body tissues. Proteins act as enzymes that play a role in all of the chemical reactions in your body. Without these enzymes, these chemical reactions would be so slow that your body wouldn't be able to carry out basic processes like digestion and metabolism and you wouldn't be able to survive. Proteins also help maintain fluid and acid-base balance, help transport substances such as oxygen through the body and waste out of the body, and act as antibodies to keep your immune system strong and help fight off illness.

ESSENTIAL

This process of using protein for energy is what makes extreme calorie restriction dangerous. When your diet doesn't provide enough calories, your body begins to break down the protein in your muscles for energy, which can lead to muscle loss or muscle wasting in addition to nutritional deficiencies.

Proteins are made up of amino acids. When you eat proteins, your body breaks them down into their individual amino acids, which are then converted into sugars through a process called deamination. Your body can use these protein-turned-sugars as a form of energy, but that means your body isn't using the amino acids for those other important functions. It's best to avoid forcing the body to use protein for energy, and you do that by providing it with the other nutrients it needs.

Energy from Fat

In the absence of carbohydrates, your body turns to fat for energy. The fat from the food you eat is broken down into molecules called fatty acids, which enter the bloodstream through the walls of the small intestine. Most of your cells can directly use fatty acids for energy, but some specialized cells, such as the cells in your brain and your muscles, can't run on fatty acids as they are. To appease these cells and give them the energy they need, your body uses fatty acids to make ketones.

What Is Ketosis?

In order to convert fat into useable energy, the liver breaks it down into fatty acids and then breaks down these fatty acids into energy-rich substances called ketones or ketone bodies. The presence of ketone bodies in the blood is called ketosis. The goal of a ketogenic diet is to kick your body into long-term ketosis, essentially turning it into a fat-burning machine.

The Creation of Ketones

When following a ketogenic diet, fat is taken to the liver where it is broken down into glycerol and fatty acids through a process called beta-oxidation. The fatty-acid molecules are further broken down through a process called ketogenesis, and a specific ketone body called acetoacetate is formed.

Over time, as your body becomes adapted to using ketones as fuel, your muscles convert acetoacetate into beta-hydroxybutyrate, or BHB, which is the preferred ketogenic source of energy for your brain, and acetone, most of which is expelled from the body as waste.

The glycerol created during beta-oxidation goes through a process called gluconeogenesis. During gluconeogenesis, the body converts glycerol into glucose that your body can use for energy. Your body can also convert excess protein into glucose. Your body does need some glucose to function, but it doesn't need carbohydrates to get it because it does a good job of converting whatever it can into the simple sugar.

Ketosis and Weight Loss

Now that you understand how your body creates energy and how ketones are formed, you may be left wondering how this translates into weight loss. When you eat a lot of carbohydrates, your body happily burns them for energy and stores any excess as glycogen in your liver or as triglycerides in your fat cells. When you take carbohydrates out of the equation, your body depletes its glycogen stores in the liver and muscles and then turns to fat for energy. Your body obtains energy from the fat in the food you eat, but it also uses the triglycerides, or fats, stored in your fat cells. When your body starts burning stored fat, your fat cells shrink and you begin to lose weight and become leaner.

ESSENTIAL

Triglycerides are the storage form of fat in your body and the food you eat. When you eat more food than your body needs for energy, those extra calories are converted into triglycerides and stored in your fat cells for later use.

How to Induce Ketosis

The first step in inducing ketosis is to severely limit carbohydrate consumption, but that's not enough. You must limit your protein consumption as well. Traditional low-carbohydrate diets don't induce ketosis because they allow a high intake of protein. Because your body is able to convert excess protein into glucose, your body never switches over to burning fat as fuel. You can induce ketosis by following a high-fat diet that allows moderate amounts of protein and only a small amount of carbohydrates—or what is called a ketogenic diet.

The exact percentage of each macronutrient you need to kick your body into ketosis may vary from person to person, but in general the macronutrient ratio falls into the following ranges:

- 60–75 percent of calories from fat
- 15–30 percent of calories from protein
- 5–10 percent of calories from carbohydrates

Once you're in ketosis, you have to continue with the high-fat, low-carbohydrate, moderate-protein plan. Eating too many carbohydrates or too much protein can kick you out of ketosis at any time by providing your body with enough glucose to stop using fat as fuel.

Signs That You Are in Ketosis

Signs that you're in ketosis may start appearing after only one week of following a true ketogenic diet, but for some people it can take longer—as much as three months. When signs do start to show, they are pretty similar across the board. Signs of ketosis typically include:

- Bad breath
- Decreased appetite and nausea
- Cold hands and feet
- Increased urinary frequency
- Difficulty sleeping
- Metallic taste in the mouth
- Dry mouth
- Increased thirst

And eventually:

- Increased energy
- Improved mental focus and clarity

Keto "Flu"

"Keto flu," or "low-carb flu," commonly affects people in the first few days of starting a ketogenic diet. Of course, the ketogenic diet doesn't actually cause the flu, but the phenomenon is given the term because its symptoms closely resemble that of the flu. It would be more accurate to refer to this stage as a carbohydrate withdrawal, because that's really what it is. When you take carbohydrates away, it causes altered hormonal states and electrolyte imbalances that are responsible for the associated symptoms. The basic symptoms include headaches, nausea, upset stomach, sleepiness, fatigue, abdominal cramps, diarrhea, and lack of mental clarity, or what is commonly referred to as "brain fog."

FACT

Carbohydrate addiction is a real thing. Some research shows that carbohydrates activate certain stimuli in the brain that can be dependence forming and cause addiction. Carbohydrate addicts have uncontrollable cravings for carbohydrates, and when they do eat them, they tend to binge. In a carbohydrate addict, the removal of carbohydrates can cause withdrawal symptoms such as dizziness, irritability, and intense cravings.

The duration of symptoms varies—it depends on you as an individual, but typically a "keto flu" lasts anywhere from a couple of days to a week. In rare cases it can last up to two weeks. Some of the symptoms of the "keto flu" are associated with dehydration, because in the beginning stages of ketosis you lose a lot of water weight, and with that lost fluid you also lose electrolytes. You can replenish these electrolytes by drinking enhanced waters (but make sure they are not sweetened) and drinking lots of homemade bone broth. This may help lessen the severity of the symptoms.

Although these signs are common among many people who follow a ketogenic diet, your experience may be different. Every body is unique, so it's impossible to say exactly what your personal experience will be. Keep in mind that in the early stages of ketosis your symptoms may be unpleasant, but as your body adapts you will begin to experience the benefits of following a ketogenic diet plan.

The Skinny on Fat

If you're still on the fence about consuming so much fat, read this next sentence carefully and really let it sink in: fat is not your enemy; sugar is. And that applies to all forms of sugar, not only the granulated stuff that you put in your coffee in the morning. Sure, the sugar in fruit is packaged with vitamin C, potassium, fiber, and other valuable nutrients, which makes it a far superior choice over white sugar, but overdoing it can actually hinder weight loss efforts and set you up for other health problems, particularly if you have blood sugar issues. But before delving too deeply into sugar, it's important to spend some time debunking the myths that have surrounded the word "fat" for years.

Eating Fat Makes You Fat

On the surface, the theory that eating fat makes you fat seems like a no-brainer. Of the three macronutrients—protein, carbohydrates, and fat—fat contains the most calories per gram. Protein and carbohydrates have 4 calories per gram, while fat contains 9 calories per gram. It would make sense that if you cut out fat or replace fat with protein or carbohydrates at each meal, you would be saving yourself calories throughout the course of the day, and while technically this is true, it doesn't lead to sustainable weight loss.

In order to understand why fat doesn't make you fat, you have to understand how you gain weight in the first place. Here's a simple explanation: You start thinking about food and your body secretes insulin in response. The insulin triggers your body to store fatty acids instead of using them for energy, so you get hungry. When you get hungry, you eat. If you're on a low-fat diet, your lunch may consist of two slices of whole-wheat toast with a couple of slices of turkey—no cheese, no mayo—and an apple on the side. If you've subscribed to the low-fat diet theory, this looks like a healthy meal, but in reality it's loaded with carbohydrates that pass through your digestive system quickly, causing significant spikes in blood sugar.

ESSENTIAL

Carbohydrates are a fast-acting source of energy for your body, but they don't do a lot to fill you up. Even carbohydrates that are loaded with fiber are far less satiating than either protein or fat. If you want your meal to be truly satisfying, make sure it contains plenty of fat.

Your body quickly breaks down your high-carbohydrate meal, which sends a rush of glucose into your bloodstream. Your body responds to this glucose by secreting more insulin, which carries the glucose out of your blood and into your cells. Once the glucose levels drop, you get hungry again, your body secretes more insulin, and the cycle starts over.

Now here's where you'll want to pay close attention. Your body's main regulator of fat metabolism is insulin. Insulin controls lipoprotein lipase, or LPL, an enzyme that pulls fat into your cells. The higher your insulin levels, the more fat LPL pulls into your cells. Translation: when insulin levels increase, you store fat. When insulin levels drop, you burn fat for energy. The main thing that affects insulin levels is carbohydrates, not fat. So when you eat a lot of carbohydrates, your insulin levels increase, which increases your LPL levels, which increases your storage of fat. The goal is to avoid surges and crashes in glucose and insulin and to keep your levels consistent and steady throughout the day. When you do this, your body is better able to handle both glucose and insulin over the long term.

It's important to remember that overdoing it on any of the nutrients will lead to weight gain. Regularly exceeding your caloric needs will cause weight gain regardless of whether you do it with carbohydrates, protein, or fat—but fat is not, and never has been, the major culprit.

Cholesterol Causes Heart Disease

The cholesterol you eat actually has very little impact on your blood cholesterol levels for two reasons. The first reason is that your body doesn't absorb dietary cholesterol very efficiently. Most of the cholesterol you eat goes right through your digestive tract and never even enters your bloodstream. The second reason is that the amount of cholesterol in your blood is tightly controlled by your body. When you eat a lot of dietary cholesterol, your body shuts down its own production of cholesterol to compensate. There is a percentage of the population, however, that is hypersensitive to dietary cholesterol. For these people—about 25 percent of the population—dietary cholesterol does cause modest increases in both LDL (low-density lipoprotein) and HDL (high-density lipoprotein) levels, but even so, contrary to popular belief, the increased cholesterol levels do not increase the risk of heart disease. In fact, both the Framingham Heart Study and the Honolulu Heart Program found the opposite to be true: low cholesterol levels were actually associated with increased risk of death. A separate study published in the *Journal of the American Medical Association* reported findings that neither high LDL ("bad" cholesterol) levels nor low HDL ("good" cholesterol) levels were important risk factors for death from coronary artery disease or heart attack.

Cholesterol is absolutely essential for your survival. This lipoprotein, as it is physiologically classified, performs three major functions: it makes up the bile acids that help you digest food, it allows the body to make vitamin D and other essential hormones such as estrogen and testosterone, and it is a component of the outer coating of every one of your cells. Without cholesterol, your body would literally crumble.

Now that's not to say that you should throw all caution out the window when it comes to cholesterol, but you need to pay attention to the right thing, and that's the size of the cholesterol particles in your bloodstream rather than the total numbers. Cholesterol comes in two forms: large particles that "bounce" off the arterial walls and small, dense particles that stick to the walls of your arteries and contribute to arterial blockage, which can eventually lead to heart disease. The problem is that so much focus is placed on the total numbers that many people fail to pay attention to cholesterol particle size.

According to Dr. Mark Hyman, a functional medicine doctor and founder and medical director at The UltraWellness Center in Lenox, Massachusetts, it's not fat that causes the accumulation of small, dense cholesterol particles in your blood; it's sugar in any form, including refined carbohydrates. Sugar decreases the amount of the large cholesterol particles in your blood; creates the small, damaging cholesterol particles; increases triglyceride levels; and contributes to prediabetes.

Saturated Fat Causes Heart Disease

The other widespread belief is that eating saturated fat causes an increase in the amount of cholesterol in your blood, which in turn causes heart disease or increases your risk of heart disease. This theory was developed from some human and animal studies that were done decades ago. However, more recent research calls these theories into question.

ESSENTIAL

The idea that eating cholesterol causes heart disease is called the diet-heart hypothesis. The theory that high cholesterol levels in the blood cause heart disease is called the lipid hypothesis. Both of these hypotheses are so widely accepted that most healthcare professionals and consumers don't even question them, although more recent research has shown that cholesterol and heart disease may not be as interconnected as previously believed.

In 2010 the *American Journal of Clinical Nutrition* did a meta-analysis of several studies that investigated the relationship between saturated fat and heart disease and concluded that there is no significant evidence to make the claim that dietary saturated fat is associated with increased risk of coronary heart disease or cardiovascular disease, in general. In fact, several of the studies the journal investigated showed a positive inverse relationship, which means that a higher intake of saturated fat was actually associated with a lower incidence of heart disease.

Researchers went even further to suggest that more analysis be done to determine whether the nutrients that replaced saturated fat actually had more of an influence on the risk of developing heart disease. After all, the nutrient that was used to replace saturated fat on low-fat diets was carbohydrates.

Designing Your Ketogenic Diet Plan

The first thing you need to do to design your ketogenic diet is figure out how many calories you need each day. From there you'll be able to calculate your macronutrient ratio—or the best breakdown of fat, protein, and carbohydrates for you. There are several online calculators that can calculate this number for you, but to do it yourself, you can use a method called the Mifflin-St. Jeor formula, which looks like this:

- Men: $10 \times$ weight (kg) $+ 6.25 \times$ height (cm) $- 5 \times$ age (y) $+ 5$
- Women: $10 \times$ weight (kg) $+ 6.25 \times$ height (cm) $- 5 \times$ age (y) $- 161$

To make this explanation easier, let's try using the equation with a 30-year-old, 160-pound (72.7 kg) woman who is 5 feet 5 inches (165.1 cm) tall. When you plug this woman's statistics into the Mifflin-St. Jeor formula, you can see that she should be eating 1,448 calories per day. Now you'll use the estimated macronutrient percentages to calculate how much of each nutrient she needs to consume in order to follow a successful ketogenic diet plan.

Carbohydrates

On a ketogenic diet, carbohydrates should provide only 5–10 percent of the calories you consume. Many ketogenic dieters stay at the low end of 5 percent, but the exact amount you need depends on your body. Unfortunately there is no one-size-fits-all approach to this, so you'll have to do a little trial and error. You can pick a percentage that feels right for you and try that out for a couple of weeks. If you don't see the results you want, you'll have to adjust your nutrient ratios and calculate them again. Getting 7 percent of your calories from carbohydrates is a good place to start.

FACT

When counting carbohydrates on a ketogenic diet plan, you want to pay attention to net carbohydrates, not total carbohydrates. Net carbohydrates are the amount of carbohydrates left over after you subtract grams of fiber from total grams of carbohydrates. If a particular food contains 10 grams of carbohydrates, but 7 grams come from fiber, the total number of net carbohydrates is 3 grams. You count the 3 grams toward your daily total rather than the 10 grams.

To convert this percentage into grams, multiply 7 percent by the total number of calories, which, in the earlier example, is 1,448, and then divide by 4 (since carbohydrates contain 4 calories per gram). The number you're left with—25 in this example—is the amount of carbohydrates in grams you should eat per day.

Fat

Next up is fat. Again, the exact amount you'll need depends on you as an individual, but consuming 75 percent of your calories from fat is a good place to start. To figure out the amount of fat you need in grams, multiply the amount of calories you need (in this example, 1,448) by 75 percent and then divide by 9 (since fat contains 9 calories per gram). The number you're left with is the total grams of fat you need for the day. In this example it's 121 grams.

Protein

Once you've calculated carbohydrates and fat, protein is easy. The remainder of your calories, which equates to 18 percent, should come from protein. To figure out this number in grams, multiply the total number of calories by 18 percent and then divide by 4 (since protein contains 4 calories per gram). The number you're left with is the total grams of protein you need for the day. In this example it's 65 grams.

Foods to Eat and Avoid

When following a ketogenic diet, some foods are strictly off-limits, while others fall into a sort of gray area. Regardless of whether foods are "allowed," you still have to make sure that you're staying within your macronutrient ratios. Just because a food is technically allowed doesn't mean you can eat as much of it as you want. Use these recommendations as a guideline, but always make sure that you're staying within your calculated macronutrient ratios.

A Word on Quality

The quality of your food matters, especially when it comes to fat and protein sources. Ideally you want to choose meats that are organic, grass-fed, and pasture raised. Eggs should come from your local farmer or from pasture-raised hens whenever possible. Choose grass-fed butter and organic creams, cheese, fruits, and vegetables. Eating conventional foods won't prevent you from entering a ketogenic state, but high-quality foods are better for your body in general. After all, you are what you eat. Do your best to get the highest-quality food you can find and/or afford.

Fats and Oils

Fats and oils provide the basis of your ketogenic diet, so you'll want to make sure you're eating plenty of them. The ketogenic diet is not just a fat free-for-all, though. While following a ketogenic diet, there are certain fats that are better for you than others, although which ones fall into which category may surprise you. On the ketogenic diet you should eat plenty of saturated fats in the form of meat, poultry, eggs, butter, and coconut; monounsaturated fats such as olive oil, nuts, nut butters, and avocado; and natural polyunsaturated fats such as tuna, salmon, and mackerel. Avoid highly processed polyunsaturated fats such as canola oil, vegetable oil, and soybean oil. Homemade mayonnaise is also an easy way to add a dose of fat to every meal.

Proteins

Many of the fat sources mentioned previously—meat, poultry, eggs, butter, nuts, nut butters, and fish—are also loaded with protein and should be your main protein sources when following a ketogenic diet. Bacon and sausage are other sources of protein that also provide a significant dose of fat, so keep that in mind when including them in your ketogenic diet. When eating protein make sure to stay within your recommended grams for the day, since your body turns excess protein into glucose, which can kick you out of ketosis.

Fruits and Vegetables

On a ketogenic diet most fruits fall onto the "do not eat" list because even though the sugars are natural, they still raise your blood glucose levels significantly and can kick you out of ketosis. There's not a hard rule—that fruit isn't allowed on a ketogenic diet—but you do need to limit your intake. When you do eat fruit, choose fruits that are high in fiber and lower in carbohydrates, such as berries, and limit your portions.

Vegetables are extremely important on a ketogenic diet. They provide the vitamins and minerals that you need to stay healthy and help fill you up without contributing a lot of calories to your day. You do have to be choosy about which vegetables you eat, though, since some are loaded with carbohydrates. As a general rule, choose dark green or leafy green vegetables, such as spinach, broccoli, cucumbers, green beans, lettuce, and asparagus. Cauliflower and mushrooms are also good choices for a ketogenic diet. Avoid starchy vegetables like white potatoes, sweet potatoes, yams, and corn.

Dairy

Full-fat dairy products are a staple on the ketogenic diet. You can use butter, heavy cream, sour cream, cream cheese, hard cheese, and cottage cheese to help meet your fat needs. Avoid low-fat dairy products and flavored dairy products, such as fruit yogurt, which is full of sugar; serving for serving, some versions contain as much sugar and carbohydrates as soda. It's especially important to pay attention to quality when choosing dairy products. Dairy from grass-fed cows and raw cheeses are best.

Beverages

As with any diet plan, when it comes to beverages, water is the ideal choice. Make sure to drink at least half of your body weight in ounces. Coffee and tea are also permitted on a ketogenic diet, but they must be unsweetened or sweetened with an approved sweetener, such as stevia or erythritol. Avoid sodas, flavored waters, sweetened teas, sweetened lemonade, and fruit juices. You can infuse plain water with fresh herbs, such as mint or basil, to give yourself a little variety.

Grains and Sugars

Avoid grains and sugars in all of their forms on the ketogenic diet. Grains include wheat, barley, rice, rye, sorghum, and anything made from these products. That means no breads, no pasta, no crackers, and no rice. Sugar, and anything that contains sugar, is also not allowed on a ketogenic diet. This includes white sugar, brown sugar, honey, maple syrup, corn syrup, and brown rice syrup. There are many names for sugar on ingredient lists; it's extremely beneficial to familiarize yourself with these names so you'll know when a product contains sugar in any form.

When the Ketogenic Diet Should Not Be Used

While the ketogenic diet is safe for most individuals, there are some people who should not follow the diet plan. If you have certain metabolic conditions or health conditions, talk to your doctor before starting a ketogenic diet.

Contraindicated health conditions include:

- Gallbladder disease
- Impaired fat digestion
- History of pancreatitis
- Kidney disease
- Impaired liver function
- Poor nutritional status
- Previous gastric bypass surgery
- Type 1 diabetes
- Impaired insulin production
- Excessive alcohol use
- Carnitine deficiency
- Porphyria

Pregnancy

If you're pregnant or trying to become pregnant, a ketogenic diet may not be right for you. A woman is the most fertile when her body feels satisfied and well nourished. Because ketosis is essentially a starvation state, it's a gamble for women attempting to become pregnant to try this diet. A high level of ketones in the blood may also pose a risk to a developing fetus. While traditional low-carbohydrate diets are okay during pregnancy, you should not limit your carbohydrates to the point of ketosis if you're pregnant.

Achieving success on a ketogenic diet may take some trial and error and a little bit of practice (and patience), but once you get into the routine and reach a state of optimal ketosis your body will adjust accordingly. If you experience any uncomfortable symptoms or hit any roadblocks, contact a functional medicine doctor or a functional nutritionist who can help you troubleshoot and overcome any hurdles.

CHAPTER 2

Breakfast

Spicy Sausage Egg Cups

If you don't like spice, omit or use less of the red pepper flakes.
You could also substitute with garlic powder.

Versatile Zucchini

Zucchini is a good source of vitamin C and vitamin B_6, and at only 2.5 net grams of carbohydrates per cup, it makes a great addition to any ketogenic meal. Because zucchini is extremely mild tasting, you can add it to any meal without significantly changing the flavor.

1. Preheat oven to 350°F.

2. Heat a large skillet over medium heat and add ground pork, sage, salt, black pepper, and red pepper flakes. Cook until meat is no longer pink. Remove pork mixture with a slotted spoon and set aside. Add onion and zucchini to pan and sauté until tender, about 4 minutes. Add cooked onion and zucchini to pork mixture in a medium bowl.

3. Add eggs to pork mixture and stir until combined. Oil each well of a 12-cup muffin tin with a small amount of coconut oil and pour mixture evenly into each well.

4. Bake for 30 minutes or until egg is cooked through.

5. Top each egg cup with a few pieces of avocado.

PER SERVING Calories: 227 | Fat: 13.1g | Protein: 20.3g | Sodium: 357mg | Fiber: 1.8g | Carbohydrates: 3.5g | Sugar: 0.8g

Bacon-Wrapped Egg Cups

To give this recipe a little kick, replace the Cheddar cheese with pepper jack and add a pinch of red pepper flakes to the eggs while you're whisking.

INGREDIENTS | SERVES 12

12 slices sugar-free bacon

12 large eggs

½ cup heavy cream

½ teaspoon salt

¼ teaspoon black pepper

½ cup shredded Cheddar cheese

2 cups chopped and steamed broccoli

Be Choosy with Bacon

Like commercially prepared sausage, bacon often contains added sugar in the form of maple syrup or brown sugar. Look for uncured varieties at the supermarket or ask your local butcher to track down some sugar-free bacon for you.

1. Preheat oven to 350°F.

2. Grease each well of a 12-cup muffin tin with butter or coconut oil.

3. Cook bacon in a medium skillet over medium heat until almost crisp. When bacon is fully cooked, quickly line each well of the muffin tin with a piece of bacon.

4. Whisk eggs, heavy cream, salt, and pepper together in a large mixing bowl. Add cheese and chopped broccoli and stir.

5. Pour an equal amount of mixture into each well of the muffin tin.

6. Bake for 20 minutes or until lightly browned on top and firm throughout.

7. Allow to cool for 10 minutes and then remove egg cups from muffin tins. Store in refrigerator.

PER SERVING Calories: 187 | Fat: 13.1g | Protein: 12.5g | Sodium: 398mg | Fiber: 0.9g | Carbohydrates: 2.6g | Sugar: 0.9g

Western Scrambled Eggs

You can increase the fat content of this recipe by adding chopped avocado to the scrambled eggs once you remove them from the heat.

INGREDIENTS | SERVES 4

8 large eggs

¼ cup heavy cream

1 teaspoon salt

½ teaspoon black pepper

1 tablespoon unsalted butter

½ cup diced sugar-free ham

½ cup chopped onion

½ cup chopped red and green peppers

1 cup shredded Cheddar cheese

Chopped scallions for garnish

1. Whisk eggs, cream, salt, and black pepper together in a large mixing bowl.

2. Melt butter in a medium skillet over medium heat. Add egg mixture and stir. When eggs start to scramble, add ham, onion, and peppers. Continue to stir until eggs are almost cooked. Add cheese and stir until cooked.

3. Garnish with scallions.

PER SERVING Calories: 373 | Fat: 25.8g | Protein: 24.5g | Sodium: 1,144mg | Fiber: 0.7g | Carbohydrates: 4.4g | Sugar: 2.2g

Eggs Benedict

Traditional Eggs Benedict calls for Canadian bacon, but you can use sugar-free bacon, sugar-free sausage, or prosciutto in place of the Canadian bacon.

INGREDIENTS | SERVES 2

1 tablespoon unsalted butter

4 large eggs

4 slices sugar-free Canadian bacon

½ large avocado, cut into 4 slices

1 cup Hollandaise Sauce (see recipe in Chapter 5)

1. Heat up a medium skillet over medium-high heat and add the butter. Crack eggs into pan. Cook for 2 minutes and then flip eggs, using care not to break yolks. Cook for another 2 minutes or until white is completely cooked, but yolk is still runny. Transfer eggs to a plate.

2. Top each egg with a slice of Canadian bacon and a slice of avocado. Pour ¼ cup of the sauce mixture onto each egg.

PER SERVING Calories: 1,370 | Fat: 125.3g | Protein: 36.5g | Sodium: 1,205mg | Fiber: 2.3g | Carbohydrates: 7.9g | Sugar: 1.3g

Almond Butter Muffins

For some variation, replace the almond butter in this recipe with another one of your favorite nut butters. Cashew butter, peanut butter, and sunflower seed butter work well.

INGREDIENTS | SERVES 12

⅔ cup almond flour

¼ cup granulated erythritol

1 teaspoon ground cinnamon

¼ cup unsweetened almond butter

2 tablespoons butter

1 tablespoon coconut oil

1 teaspoon vanilla extract

4 large eggs

¼ cup heavy cream

Learning about Erythritol

Erythritol is a naturally derived sugar substitute that looks and tastes like sugar but has almost no calories and a low glycemic load, which means it doesn't significantly affect your blood sugar levels. Erythritol comes in two forms, granulated and powdered, and can be used in place of sugar in any recipe, although it is only 70 percent as sweet.

1. Preheat oven to 350°F.

2. Mix together almond flour, erythritol, and cinnamon in a medium mixing bowl.

3. In a separate bowl, beat almond butter, butter, coconut oil, vanilla extract, eggs, and heavy cream together until smooth.

4. Add almond flour mixture to almond butter mixture and stir until smooth.

5. Put a paper cupcake liner in each well of a 12-cup muffin tin. Fill each paper cup with batter.

6. Bake for 20 minutes or until a toothpick inserted in the center comes out clean.

7. Remove from muffin tin and allow to cool before serving.

PER SERVING Calories: 112 | Fat: 9.4g | Protein: 3.4g | Sodium: 42mg | Fiber: 1.5g | Carbohydrates: 7.0g | Sugar: 0.4g | Sugar alcohol: 4.0g

Bacon Hash

Turn this into a complete meal by adding a couple of poached or over-easy eggs on top. You can also mix this bacon hash into some scrambled eggs.

INGREDIENTS | SERVES 4

6 slices sugar-free bacon

2 cups chopped cauliflower

1 medium onion, diced

2 cloves garlic, minced

½ teaspoon salt

½ teaspoon black pepper

½ teaspoon garlic powder

1. Cook bacon in a medium skillet over medium heat until crispy, about 10 minutes. Remove from pan and let cool, then dice.

2. Add cauliflower, onion, and garlic to the skillet. Cook 5 minutes over medium heat, or until cauliflower starts to brown. Add salt, black pepper, garlic powder, and diced bacon. Stir until combined.

3. Remove from heat and serve.

PER SERVING Calories: 107 | Fat: 5.9g | Protein: 7.3g | Sodium: 597mg | Fiber: 1.6g | Carbohydrates: 6.2g | Sugar: 2.1g

Scrambled Eggs with Bacon

This is a simple recipe, but it's a staple for a ketogenic diet. Scrambled eggs and bacon are typically thought of as breakfast food, but you can eat this whenever you need a quick dose of protein and fat.

INGREDIENTS | SERVES 2

4 slices sugar-free bacon

6 large eggs

¼ cup heavy cream

¼ teaspoon salt

¼ teaspoon black pepper

1. Cook bacon in a medium skillet over medium heat until crispy, about 10 minutes. Remove bacon from pan and dice.

2. Crack eggs into a medium bowl and whisk together with heavy cream, salt, and pepper. Add egg mixture to bacon grease in pan and stir until scrambled. Add diced bacon to eggs and stir.

3. Remove from heat and serve immediately.

PER SERVING Calories: 425 | Fat: 31.2g | Protein: 27.3g | Sodium: 901mg | Fiber: 0.1g | Carbohydrates: 2.5g | Sugar: 1.4g

Sausage Quiche

This quiche holds up well in the fridge, so it's a good choice when meal planning. You can prepare the quiche on Sunday, put each serving in a plastic container in the fridge, and eat it for breakfast all week.

INGREDIENTS | SERVES 12

12 large eggs
¼ cup heavy cream
½ teaspoon salt
¼ teaspoon black pepper
12 ounces sugar-free breakfast sausage
2 cups shredded Cheddar cheese

1. Preheat oven to 375°F.

2. Whisk eggs, heavy cream, salt, and pepper together in a large bowl.

3. Add breakfast sausage and Cheddar cheese.

4. Pour mixture into a greased 9" × 13" casserole dish.

5. Bake for 25 minutes. Cut into 12 squares and serve.

PER SERVING Calories: 262 | Fat: 18.9g | Protein: 16.3g | Sodium: 633mg | Fiber: 0.0g | Carbohydrates: 2.0g | Sugar: 0.6g

Ham, Cheese, and Egg Casserole

Mozzarella and Cheddar cheese give this dish a mild cheesy flavor, but you can use any type of shredded cheese you want.

INGREDIENTS | SERVES 6

4 cups broccoli florets
12 large eggs
2 cups cooked diced sugar-free ham
½ cup shredded mozzarella cheese
½ cup shredded Cheddar cheese
¼ cup chopped scallions

1. Preheat oven to 375°F.

2. Fill a large pot with water and bring to a boil. Blanch broccoli by putting in boiling water for 2–3 minutes.

3. Put eggs, ham, mozzarella, Cheddar, and scallions in a large bowl and whisk until combined. Add broccoli.

4. Pour into a 9" × 13" baking dish and cook for 35 minutes or until eggs are cooked through.

PER SERVING Calories: 296 | Fat: 15.8g | Protein: 30.1g | Sodium: 893mg | Fiber: 0.1g | Carbohydrates: 3.8g | Sugar: 0.6g

Bunches of Broccoli

One cup of chopped broccoli contains only 6 grams of carbohydrates, half of which come from fiber. In addition to being low in carbohydrates, broccoli is high in vitamin C, a nutrient that you definitely need when following a ketogenic diet.

Spinach and Mozzarella Egg Bake

Use only the green stalks of the scallions for this recipe, but don't throw the white parts out! Save them to use in other recipes.

INGREDIENTS | SERVES 4

1 tablespoon olive oil
4 cups baby spinach
¾ cup shredded mozzarella cheese
¾ cup shredded Colby jack cheese
¼ cup chopped scallions, green tops only
8 large eggs
½ teaspoon salt
½ teaspoon black pepper

1. Preheat oven to 375°F.

2. Heat olive oil in a medium skillet over medium heat and add spinach. Sauté until wilted. Transfer spinach to a 9" × 9" baking dish.

3. Put remaining ingredients in a medium bowl and whisk until combined. Pour egg mixture on top of spinach.

4. Bake for 30 minutes or until eggs are no longer runny. Serve warm.

PER SERVING Calories: 342 | Fat: 23.9g | Protein: 24.1g | Sodium: 737mg | Fiber: 0.9g | Carbohydrates: 3.6g | Sugar: 1.0g

Bacon-and-Egg-Stuffed Avocados

Take these stuffed avocados out of the oven as soon as the egg is cooked through. If you cook an avocado too long, it develops a bitter, unpleasant taste.

INGREDIENTS | SERVES 2

2 large avocados
4 strips cooked sugar-free bacon, crumbled
4 large eggs
¼ teaspoon sea salt
¼ teaspoon black pepper

A for Avocado

Avocados are the ketogenic dieter's dream. A single avocado contains almost 30 grams of fat and only 3 grams of net carbohydrates. You can easily increase the fat content of any meal by adding a few slices of avocado.

1. Preheat oven to 400°F.

2. Cut avocados in half lengthwise and remove the pit. Scoop some avocado out of each half to create a well.

3. Sprinkle 1 strip crumbled bacon into each avocado well. Crack 1 egg directly into each avocado half. Season with salt and black pepper. Place avocados on a baking sheet.

4. Bake for 15 minutes or until egg is cooked to desired doneness.

PER SERVING Calories: 478 | Fat: 35.1g | Protein: 23.1g | Sodium: 830mg | Fiber: 9.3g | Carbohydrates: 13.1g | Sugar: 0.8g

Mediterranean Rollups

Olives and sun-dried tomatoes are the flavors of the Mediterranean Sea. From Italy to Greece, the tastes of hot summer days include ripe tomatoes and fresh olive oil, and the scent of beautiful olive groves. This recipe will take you there!

INGREDIENTS | MAKES 2 FAT BOMBS

1 large egg
1 tablespoon extra-virgin olive oil
⅛ teaspoon sea salt
6 large kalamata olives, pitted
1 ounce sun-dried tomatoes in oil
⅛ teaspoon red chili flakes
⅛ teaspoon parsley flakes

1. In a small bowl, combine egg, olive oil, and salt and whisk until foamy.

2. Heat a small nonstick skillet over high heat and pour in egg mixture, spreading evenly so it forms a thin, even layer.

3. Once the first side is cooked, about 1 minute, flip frittata with the aid of a plate or a lid. Cook until golden on bottom, about 2 more minutes.

4. Remove frittata to a plate.

5. In a small food processor, mix olives, tomatoes, chili flakes, and parsley flakes until well chopped and blended, about 30 seconds.

6. Spread olive paste on top of frittata in an even layer.

7. Roll frittata into a tight roll, cut into 2 pieces, and serve immediately.

PER 1 FAT BOMB Calories: 155 | Fat: 12.6g | Protein: 3.9g | Sodium: 502mg | Fiber: 1.9g | Carbohydrates: 4.9g | Sugar: 0.1g

Quattro Formaggi Rollups

Have you ever had quattro formaggi pizza? Can anyone resist this delicious blend of melted cheese? The kids will love it too.

INGREDIENTS | MAKES 2 FAT BOMBS

1 large egg
1 tablespoon grated Parmesan cheese
1 tablespoon crumbled blue cheese
1 teaspoon butter
1 tablespoon mascarpone cheese
1 ounce thinly sliced Brie cheese

1. In a small bowl, whisk egg, Parmesan, and blue cheese until foamy.

2. Heat a small nonstick skillet over high heat and melt butter.

3. Pour in egg mixture, spreading evenly so it forms a thin, even layer.

4. Once the first side is cooked, about 1 minute, flip frittata with the aid of a plate or a lid.

5. Spread mascarpone on top of frittata, then place Brie slices in the middle and cover with a lid.

6. Cook until golden on bottom, about 2 more minutes.

7. Remove frittata to a plate.

8. Roll frittata into a tight roll, cut into 2 pieces, and serve immediately while hot.

PER 1 FAT BOMB Calories: 156 | Fat: 12.6g | Protein: 8.2g | Sodium: 221mg | Fiber: 0.0g | Carbohydrates: 0.8g | Sugar: 0.2g

Baked Avocado with Egg and Brie

A classic baked avocado and egg with a French twist!

INGREDIENTS | MAKES 2 FAT BOMBS

1 medium avocado, halved and pitted, skin on

2 large egg yolks

1 ounce coarsely chopped Brie cheese

¼ teaspoon freshly ground black pepper

1. Preheat oven to 350°F.

2. Place avocado halves hole-side up in a shallow ramekin or ovenproof dish just large enough to hold them.

3. Place 1 egg yolk into each avocado cavity. Divide Brie in half and place gently on top of egg yolks without breaking them. Season with pepper.

4. Bake 20 minutes. Serve hot.

PER 1 FAT BOMB Calories: 215 | Fat: 17.4g | Protein: 7.0g | Sodium: 102mg | Fiber: 4.7g | Carbohydrates: 6.7g | Sugar: 0.4g

Smoked Salmon and Brie Baked Avocado

Smoked salmon and Brie are a classic combination. These avocados are great served cold, but are so much better when hot and melted!

INGREDIENTS | MAKES 2 FAT BOMBS

1 medium avocado, halved and pitted, skin on

1½ ounces wild-caught smoked salmon, coarsely chopped

1 tablespoon plus 1 teaspoon Brie cheese

¼ teaspoon freshly ground black pepper

1. Preheat oven to 350°F.

2. Place avocado halves hole-side up in a shallow ramekin or ovenproof dish just large enough to hold them.

3. Mix salmon, Brie, and pepper in a small bowl, then scoop ½ mixture into each avocado cavity.

4. Bake 20 minutes. Serve hot.

PER 1 FAT BOMB Calories: 158 | Fat: 11.7g | Protein: 6.5g | Sodium: 184mg | Fiber: 4.7g | Carbohydrates: 6.1g | Sugar: 0.2g

Egg, Sausage, and Chorizo Bacon Cups

These classic flavors combine to make a portable, low-carbohydrate breakfast bowl. This bowl is a truly filling meal for any pork lover on the run.

INGREDIENTS | MAKES 6 FAT BOMBS

12 slices regular-cut bacon, 6 cut in half
4 large eggs
½ teaspoon salt
2 tablespoons freshly chopped cilantro
4 ounces raw breakfast sausage
2 ounces chorizo, diced
¼ small yellow onion, peeled and diced

1. Preheat oven to 400°F.

2. In a standard-sized muffin tin, place half-strips bacon in an X shape in the bottom of 6 cups.

3. Line those same cups with a full slice of bacon along the inside of the cup vertically.

4. Place a cookie sheet underneath muffin tin and bake cups 8–10 minutes until they're a little pliable.

5. While cups are precooking, whisk eggs with salt and cilantro in a medium bowl. Set aside.

6. Combine breakfast sausage, chorizo, and onions in small mixing bowl.

7. Take cups out of oven and divide chorizo and sausage mixture equally between cups.

8. Pour egg mixture over sausage mixture and return cups to oven.

9. Bake cups 12–15 minutes more until eggs set. Serve warm.

PER 1 FAT BOMB Calories: 258 | Fat: 18.6g | Protein: 16.7g | Sodium: 901mg | Fiber: 0.1g | Carbohydrates: 1.4g | Sugar: 0.5g

Egg, Sour Cream, and Chive Bacon Cups

Sour cream is an excellent way to add extra fat to your fat bombs, and to make scrambled eggs taste even creamier. Chives enhance the flavor to make this cup even better than a potato chip with a similar name.

INGREDIENTS | MAKES 6 FAT BOMBS

12 slices regular-cut bacon, 6 cut in half
4 large eggs
½ teaspoon salt
¼ teaspoon freshly ground black pepper
2 tablespoons diced chives
2 tablespoons sour cream

1. Preheat oven to 400°F.

2. In a standard-sized muffin tin, place half-strips in an X shape in the bottom of 6 cups. Line those same cups with 1 full slice bacon along the inside of the cup vertically.

3. Place a cookie sheet underneath muffin tin and bake cups 8–10 minutes until they're a little pliable.

4. While cups are precooking, whisk eggs with remaining ingredients in a medium bowl. Set aside.

5. Take cups out of oven and divide egg mixture equally between cups.

6. Bake cups 8–10 minutes more until eggs set. Serve warm.

PER 1 FAT BOMB Calories: 163 | Fat: 11.3g | Protein: 12.1g | Sodium: 533mg | Fiber: 0.5g | Carbohydrates: 0.9g | Sugar: 0.3g

Smoked Salmon Mousse Bacon Cups

The salty crunch of bacon surrounding a luscious, creamy salmon mousse is the definition of decadence. Intensifying the flavor with fresh herbs only adds to the gourmet taste of this fantastic finger food.

INGREDIENTS | MAKES 6 FAT BOMBS

12 slices regular-cut bacon, 6 cut in half
6 ounces smoked salmon
4 ounces cream cheese, softened
1 tablespoon heavy whipping cream
⅛ teaspoon freshly ground black pepper
1 teaspoon fresh dill, plus 6 sprigs for garnish

A Little Lox Lesson

While lox is generally a salted, not smoked, salmon, it is a popular way to serve salmon with cream cheese. Salted salmon, also known as lox, became a popular staple with Jewish immigrants in the late 1800s in America, but the mystery of when it was first combined with cream cheese, capers, red onion, and a bagel still remains.

1. Preheat oven to 400°F.

2. In a standard-sized muffin tin, place half-strips bacon in an X shape in the bottom of 6 cups.

3. Line those same cups with 1 full slice bacon along the inside of the cup vertically.

4. Place a cookie sheet underneath muffin tin and bake cups 12–15 minutes until slightly browned and crisp.

5. While cups are baking, combine remaining ingredients except for the sprigs of dill in a food processor and pulse until smooth. Cover and set in refrigerator to chill.

6. After bacon cups have cooled, fill with mousse mixture and serve with a fresh sprig of dill on top.

PER 1 FAT BOMB Calories: 214 | Fat: 15.3g | Protein: 14.2g | Sodium: 647mg | Fiber: 0.1g | Carbohydrates: 1.5g | Sugar: 0.7g

Savory-Sweet Baked Avocado with Pecans and Coconut

This is another recipe that mixes savory and sweet. This one has a subtle sweetness but no added sugar.

INGREDIENTS | MAKES 2 FAT BOMBS

1 medium avocado, halved and pitted, skin on

2 tablespoons grated unsweetened coconut

2 tablespoons coconut oil

6 pecan halves

Taste Enhancer!

You will find that once you reduce the amount of sugar you consume, your taste buds will reset. You'll start enjoying much wider nuances of flavor!

1. Preheat oven to 350°F.

2. Place avocado halves hole-side up in a shallow ramekin or ovenproof dish just large enough to hold them.

3. Mix grated coconut with coconut oil in a small bowl and scoop into each avocado cavity.

4. Place 3 pecans on top of each avocado half, gently nudging them in.

5. Bake 20 minutes. Serve hot or cold.

PER 1 FAT BOMB Calories: 285 | Fat: 27.7g | Protein: 2.0g | Sodium: 6mg | Fiber: 5.5g | Carbohydrates: 7.5g | Sugar: 0.6g

Lunch

"Mac" 'n' Cheese

You can make this "Mac" 'n' Cheese into a vegetarian option by simply omitting the crushed pork rinds.

INGREDIENTS | SERVES 6

6 cups cauliflower florets
3 ounces cream cheese
1 cup heavy cream
1½ cups shredded Cheddar cheese, divided
½ teaspoon black pepper
¼ teaspoon garlic powder
¼ teaspoon salt
1 ounce crushed pork rinds

1. Preheat oven to 375°F.

2. Fill a double boiler with water and bring water to a boil. Cut cauliflower into small pieces and place in the top portion of the double boiler. Steam until tender, about 5 minutes.

3. Remove cauliflower from double boiler and place in a strainer.

4. Melt cream cheese in a medium saucepan over medium heat. Add heavy cream and whisk until combined. Whisk in 1 cup of Cheddar cheese, pepper, garlic powder, and salt. Once cheese has melted, remove from heat.

5. Transfer strained cauliflower to a 9" × 9" baking dish. Pour in cheese mixture and toss to coat cauliflower. Sprinkle remaining ½ cup of cheese and pork rinds on top. Bake until bubbly, about 20 minutes.

PER SERVING Calories: 352 | Fat: 27.9g | Protein: 13.4g | Sodium: 463mg | Fiber: 2.2g | Carbohydrates: 7.6g | Sugar: 3.7g

Tuna and Egg Salad

This tuna and egg salad keeps well in the refrigerator for a week. Save time during the week by doubling or tripling the recipe and having it for lunch all week.

INGREDIENTS | SERVES 2

2 large hard-boiled eggs

2 (5-ounce) cans water-packed tuna

¼ cup Homemade Mayonnaise (see recipe in Chapter 5)

¼ cup diced white onion

¼ cup sugar-free relish

¼ teaspoon salt

¼ teaspoon black pepper

Put eggs in a medium mixing bowl and mash with a fork. Add tuna and mayonnaise and mash together until ingredients are combined. Stir in onion, relish, salt, and pepper.

PER SERVING Calories: 482 | Fat: 29.4g | Protein: 39.8g | Sodium: 1,330mg | Fiber: 0.9g | Carbohydrates: 9.8g | Sugar: 1.1g

Chicken and Avocado Salad

Precooked canned chicken makes this recipe a cinch to whip up, but if you have extra time, you can cook some boneless, skinless chicken breasts, shred them, and use that instead.

INGREDIENTS | SERVES 2

1 (12.5-ounce) can shredded chicken breast

1 medium avocado, cubed

¼ cup Homemade Mayonnaise (see recipe in Chapter 5)

2 tablespoons sliced black olives

¼ teaspoon garlic salt

¼ teaspoon black pepper

⅛ teaspoon paprika

1 teaspoon fresh lemon juice

1 teaspoon olive oil

Put all ingredients in a medium mixing bowl and mash with a fork until combined.

PER SERVING Calories: 471 | Fat: 37.5g | Protein: 22.4g | Sodium: 1,092mg | Fiber: 5.0g | Carbohydrates: 7.1g | Sugar: 0.4g

Ham and Cheese Casserole

Allow the cream cheese to reach room temperature before starting this recipe. Softened cream cheese is much easier to work with than cream cheese fresh from the fridge.

INGREDIENTS | SERVES 6

6 cups cauliflower florets
½ cup cream cheese, softened
½ cup heavy cream
¼ cup coconut cream
2½ cups cooked cubed sugar-free ham
1 cup shredded Cheddar cheese
1½ tablespoons grated Parmesan cheese
¼ cup chopped scallions
½ teaspoon salt
¼ teaspoon black pepper

Corralling Coconut Cream

Coconut cream is the solid portion of the coconut milk you buy in a can. You can easily separate the cream from the milk by refrigerating a can of full-fat milk for a few hours. When it's chilled, open the can and scoop out the solid part on top—this is the coconut cream and the part that contains most of the fat. Save the milk that's left at the bottom for a smoothie or use it in another recipe.

1. Preheat oven to 350°F. Bring a large pot of water to a boil and add cauliflower. Boil until cauliflower is fork tender, about 5–10 minutes. Strain cauliflower and return to pot.

2. Put cream cheese, heavy cream, and coconut cream in a medium mixing bowl and beat with a handheld beater until smooth. Transfer cream cheese mixture to cauliflower pot and stir until cauliflower is coated. Add in ham, Cheddar cheese, Parmesan cheese, scallions, salt, and pepper and stir until combined.

3. Transfer mixture to a 9" × 9" baking dish and bake until cheese is melted and casserole is bubbly, about 30 minutes. Serve hot.

PER SERVING Calories: 355 | Fat: 23.6g | Protein: 23.2g | Sodium: 1,223mg | Fiber: 2.3g | Carbohydrates: 7.8g | Sugar: 3.7g

Deli Rollups

Instead of purchasing prepared chive cream cheese, you can make your own by combining plain cream cheese with minced onions and dried chives.

INGREDIENTS | SERVES 2

8 ounces sugar-free deli ham, sliced

½ cup chive cream cheese

1 cup chopped baby spinach

1 red bell pepper, sliced

Check Your Labels!

Many hams contain cane sugar, brown sugar, maple syrup, or honey. When choosing a ham, read your labels carefully and stay away from any that contain added sugars, which will up the carbohydrate content of this meal significantly.

1. Lay out each slice of ham flat. Take 1 tablespoon of cream cheese and spread it on a slice of ham. Repeat for the remaining slices.

2. Put 2 tablespoons of chopped spinach on top of the cream cheese on each slice.

3. Divide bell pepper into 8 equal portions and put each portion on top of spinach.

4. Roll up the ham and secure with a toothpick. Eat immediately or refrigerate until ready to serve.

PER SERVING Calories: 302 | Fat: 19.7g | Protein: 24.1g | Sodium: 1,723mg | Fiber: 0.8g | Carbohydrates: 5.2g | Sugar: 3.2g

Stuffed Avocados

Choose avocados that are ripe but still firm for this recipe—dark and slightly soft, but not mushy.

INGREDIENTS | SERVES 2

1 large avocado

1 (6-ounce) can tuna

2 tablespoons Homemade Mayonnaise (see recipe in Chapter 5)

½ medium green bell pepper, chopped

¼ teaspoon dried minced onion

⅛ teaspoon garlic salt

⅛ teaspoon black pepper

1. Cut avocado in half lengthwise and remove the pit. Set aside.

2. Put tuna, mayonnaise, bell pepper, dried onion, garlic salt, and black pepper in a medium mixing bowl and mash together with a fork until combined.

3. Scoop half of the mixture into each half of the avocado.

PER SERVING Calories: 304 | Fat: 21.8g | Protein: 17.9g | Sodium: 445mg | Fiber: 5.0g | Carbohydrates: 7.0g | Sugar: 0.7g

Meatball "Sub"

For another variation of this recipe, use sliced mozzarella cheese in place of provolone and ½ pound of lamb instead of pork.

INGREDIENTS | SERVES 6 (18 MEATBALLS)

1 pound ground beef
½ pound ground pork
2 tablespoons grated Parmesan cheese
2 large eggs
¼ cup chopped fresh basil
2 tablespoons minced fresh parsley
1 tablespoon minced garlic
1 teaspoon salt
½ teaspoon black pepper
6 slices provolone cheese
1 cup Marinara Sauce (see recipe in Chapter 5)

1. Preheat oven to 325°F.

2. Mix beef, pork, Parmesan cheese, eggs, basil, parsley, garlic, salt, and pepper in a large mixing bowl until well combined.

3. Roll meat mixture into 1" balls and place about 1" apart on a baking sheet. Bake until cooked through, about 15 minutes. Remove meatballs from the oven and set aside to cool for a few minutes.

4. Place 1 slice of provolone cheese flat on a plate and put 3 meatballs on one side of it. Pour ⅙ of the marinara sauce over the meatballs. Fold the other side of the cheese over the meatballs.

PER SERVING Calories: 322 | Fat: 17.9g | Protein: 30.7g | Sodium: 884mg | Fiber: 1.0g | Carbohydrates: 4.5g | Sugar: 1.9g

Roast Beef Lettuce Wraps

These lettuce wraps are incredibly easy to take with you on the go. When you're in a rush or have a busy day, prepare a few in the morning and pack them away for lunch later in the day.

INGREDIENTS | SERVES 4

8 large iceberg lettuce leaves

8 (1-ounce) slices rare roast beef

¼ cup Homemade Mayonnaise (see recipe in Chapter 5)

8 slices provolone cheese

1 cup baby spinach

Iceberg Lettuce

The iceberg lettuce in this recipe serves mainly as a vehicle for the meat, since it contains very few nutrients, aside from being high in water. You can use romaine lettuce in place of iceberg, but iceberg tends to hold its shape better.

1. Wash lettuce leaves and pat them dry, being careful not to rip them.

2. Place 1 slice of roast beef in each lettuce wrap.

3. Spread ½ tablespoon of mayonnaise on each piece of roast beef.

4. Top mayonnaise with 1 slice of provolone cheese and ⅛ cup of baby spinach.

5. Roll lettuce up around toppings. Serve immediately.

PER SERVING Calories: 438 | Fat: 33.2g | Protein: 29.1g | Sodium: 603mg | Fiber: 0.5g | Carbohydrates: 2.5g | Sugar: 1.0g

Spicy Chicken and Avocado Casserole

You can replace the chicken in this recipe with canned tuna, ground beef or pork, or diced chunks of ham.

INGREDIENTS | SERVES 6

2 large avocados, roughly chopped

2 tablespoons coconut oil

1 small onion, diced

1 medium green bell pepper, diced

3 (12.5-ounce) cans shredded chicken breast

½ cup sour cream

½ cup Homemade Mayonnaise (see recipe in Chapter 5)

1½ cups shredded Cheddar cheese, divided

⅛ teaspoon red pepper flakes

¼ teaspoon salt

¼ teaspoon black pepper

Go Crazy for Coconut Oil

Coconut oil is a staple in the ketogenic diet. The oil is resistant to high heat, so unlike olive oil, it doesn't oxidize with high temperatures. Coconut oil also contains medium-chain triglycerides, a type of fat that can help boost metabolism.

1. Preheat oven to 350°F.

2. Spread chopped avocados along the bottom of a 9" × 13" baking pan.

3. Heat coconut oil in a medium skillet over medium-high heat. Add onions and cook until lightly browned, about 3 minutes. Add bell pepper to pan and cook until soft, another 3 minutes. Remove from heat.

4. Place chicken, sour cream, mayonnaise, 1 cup of Cheddar cheese, red pepper flakes, salt, and black pepper in a medium mixing bowl and stir until combined. Add onions and bell peppers.

5. Spoon mixture over avocados. Top with remaining ½ cup of Cheddar cheese.

6. Bake for 20 minutes, or until cheese is slightly browned and casserole is bubbling.

7. Allow to cool slightly before serving.

PER SERVING Calories: 533 | Fat: 40.1g | Protein: 29.0g | Sodium: 1,031mg | Fiber: 3.5g | Carbohydrates: 6.7g | Sugar: 1.6g

Fried Chicken

If you want extra-crispy fried chicken, dip the chicken breasts in pork rind mixture, then egg mixture, then pork rind mixture again. This will create a thick coating and really crisp it up.

INGREDIENTS | SERVES 4

1.5 ounces crushed pork rinds

¼ cup grated Parmesan cheese

½ teaspoon garlic powder

½ teaspoon onion powder

½ teaspoon dried minced onion

¼ teaspoon salt

½ teaspoon black pepper

2 large eggs

4 (4-ounce) boneless, skinless chicken breasts

2 tablespoons coconut oil

Picking Pork Rinds

All pork rinds are not created equal. When choosing pork rinds, read the ingredient list and choose one that contains only pork skin and pork fat or pork skin and salt. You want to avoid pork rinds that are cooked in processed lard.

1. Put pork rinds, Parmesan cheese, garlic powder, onion powder, minced onion, salt, and black pepper in a large mixing bowl and stir until well mixed.

2. Crack eggs into a separate bowl and whisk.

3. Dip each chicken breast into eggs and then coat in pork rind mixture, making sure the chicken is completely covered.

4. Heat coconut oil in a skillet over medium-high heat. When coconut oil is hot, place chicken breasts into pan. Let cook for 5–7 minutes or until pork rind crust is browned. Flip chicken over and let cook for another 5–7 minutes until cooked through.

5. Serve hot.

PER SERVING Calories: 316 | Fat: 15.7g | Protein: 36.9g | Sodium: 546mg | Fiber: 0.2g | Carbohydrates: 1.9g | Sugar: 0.2g

Pepperoni Pizza Casserole

Instead of pepperoni, you can use salami or prosciutto in this recipe. Just read the ingredients and make sure that the cured meats don't contain any added sugar.

INGREDIENTS | SERVES 6

6 cups cauliflower florets

2 tablespoons unsalted butter

¼ cup heavy cream

2 tablespoons grated Parmesan cheese

1 teaspoon Italian seasoning

1 cup mozzarella cheese, divided

½ cup Marinara Sauce (see recipe in Chapter 5)

12 slices sugar-free pepperoni

1. Preheat oven to 375°F. Bring a large pot of water to a boil and add cauliflower florets. Boil until fork tender, about 5–7 minutes.

2. Strain cauliflower and put into a food processor or blender. While cauliflower is still hot, add butter and heavy cream, and process or blend until smooth. Add Parmesan cheese, Italian seasoning, and ¼ cup mozzarella cheese and process until smooth.

3. Pour cauliflower mixture into a 9" × 9" pan and spread it out evenly. Pour marinara sauce over cauliflower mixture.

4. Top with remaining mozzarella cheese and pepperoni. Bake for 20 minutes, or until cheese is slightly browned and casserole is bubbling.

PER SERVING Calories: 191 | Fat: 13.7g | Protein: 8.1g | Sodium: 321mg | Fiber: 2.6g | Carbohydrates: 7.7g | Sugar: 3.4g

Turkey Avocado Rolls

Lemon pepper has a strong taste, so in this recipe, a little goes a long way. If you don't like the zing of lemon, try garlic pepper in place of the lemon pepper or just omit the spice blend completely.

INGREDIENTS | SERVES 4

12 (1-ounce) slices turkey breast

12 slices Swiss cheese

3 cups baby spinach

1 large avocado, cut into 12 slices

¼ cup Homemade Mayonnaise (see recipe in Chapter 5)

¼ teaspoon lemon pepper

Check Your Spices

It may come as a surprise, but many commercial spices contain sugar or hydrogenated fats. Don't assume that an ingredient, such as lemon pepper, is free of carbohydrates until you check the label. If it contains sugar, ditch it and find one that doesn't. When it comes to herbs and spices, there are plenty of sugar-free options out there.

1. Lay out the slices of turkey breast flat and place a slice of Swiss cheese on top of each one.

2. Top each slice with ¼ cup baby spinach and 1 slice of avocado. Drizzle with 1 teaspoon of mayonnaise.

3. Sprinkle each "sandwich" with lemon pepper. Roll up sandwiches and secure with toothpicks. Serve immediately or refrigerate until ready to serve.

PER SERVING Calories: 689 | Fat: 49.3g | Protein: 47.6g | Sodium: 424mg | Fiber: 2.8g | Carbohydrates: 8.6g | Sugar: 1.4g

Breadless BLT

When cooking the tomato for this recipe, you just want to char it slightly, not cook it through. If it gets too soft, it won't hold up as well.

INGREDIENTS | SERVES 2

6 slices sugar-free bacon
1 large tomato, cut into 4 equal slices
4 leaves romaine lettuce
½ large avocado, sliced
2 tablespoons Homemade Mayonnaise (see recipe in Chapter 5)

1. Cook bacon in a medium skillet over medium heat until crisp. Remove bacon and return bacon fat to heat.

2. Place each tomato slice in bacon fat and cook for 1 minute. Remove from pan and set aside.

3. Top each of 2 tomato slices with 2 slices of romaine lettuce, 3 strips of bacon, ¼ of avocado, and 1 tablespoon mayonnaise.

4. Cover with remaining tomato slices.

PER SERVING Calories: 401 | Fat: 33.3g | Protein: 14.2g | Sodium: 662mg | Fiber: 4.6g | Carbohydrates: 9.1g | Sugar: 3.2g

Smoked Salmon and Crème Fraîche Rollups

If you love a bagel and lox for breakfast or Sunday brunch, try this fat-bomb recipe instead. It will be just as satisfying and more rewarding as it helps you stay on track with the ketogenic way of eating.

INGREDIENTS | MAKES 3 FAT BOMBS

3 ounces crème fraîche
⅛ teaspoon fresh lemon zest
3 slices smoked salmon, about 1 ounce each

1. In a small bowl, mix crème fraîche and lemon zest.

2. Spread ⅓ mixture on top of each salmon slice.

3. Roll slices into individual rolls and secure with a toothpick.

4. Serve immediately.

PER 1 FAT BOMB Calories: 134 | Fat: 12.3g | Protein: 6.2g | Sodium: 576mg | Fiber: 0.0g | Carbohydrates: 1.0g | Sugar: 1.0g

Crème Fraîche

Crème fraîche is the French version of sour cream. Just like sour cream, it is a cultured cream, but it has lower acidity and higher fat content, which makes it the perfect ingredient for fat bombs!

Portobello Pizzas

This is a basic pizza combination, but you can use whatever combination of toppings you want. Try sausage and green peppers or prosciutto and mushrooms.

INGREDIENTS | SERVES 4

4 large portobello mushrooms

4 teaspoons olive oil

1 cup Marinara Sauce (see recipe in Chapter 5)

1 cup shredded mozzarella cheese

12 slices sugar-free pepperoni

The Versatile Portobello

Portobello mushrooms are larger, more mature versions of the common white mushroom. The portobello mushroom has a rich, meaty flavor and texture and, because of this, it's often used as a substitute for meat in vegetarian recipes.

1. Preheat oven to 375°F.

2. Remove stems from mushrooms and brush each cap inside and outside with 1 teaspoon olive oil. Place on a foil-lined baking sheet and bake stem side down for 10 minutes.

3. Remove mushrooms from oven and fill each cap with ¼ cup marinara sauce, ¼ cup mozzarella cheese, and 3 slices of pepperoni.

4. Return to oven and cook for another 10 minutes or until cheese is lightly browned and bubbly. Serve hot.

PER SERVING Calories: 212 | Fat: 14.9g | Protein: 10.3g | Sodium: 493mg | Fiber: 2.3g | Carbohydrates: 8.2g | Sugar: 4.9g

Chicken Cordon Bleu Casserole

Traditional chicken cordon bleu contains ham, chicken, and Swiss cheese, but if you're not a fan of Swiss cheese, swap it out for a cheese with a milder flavor, such as provolone or mozzarella.

INGREDIENTS | SERVES 4

2 cups cooked chopped chicken breast

1 cup cooked diced sugar-free ham

1 cup cubed Swiss cheese

½ cup heavy cream

½ cup sour cream

½ cup cream cheese

½ teaspoon granulated garlic

½ teaspoon granulated onion

¼ teaspoon salt

¼ teaspoon black pepper

1 ounce crushed pork rinds

1. Preheat oven to 350°F.

2. Mix chicken and ham and spread out in the bottom of a 9" × 13" baking dish.

3. Sprinkle Swiss cheese on top of chicken and ham.

4. Put heavy cream, sour cream, and cream cheese in a medium saucepan and heat over medium heat until cream cheese is melted and mixture is smooth. Add garlic, onion, salt, and pepper. Pour mixture over chicken, ham, and Swiss cheese.

5. Sprinkle pork rinds across casserole. Bake for 30 minutes, or until slightly browned and cheese is bubbly.

PER SERVING Calories: 584 | Fat: 38.9g | Protein: 44.0g | Sodium: 927mg | Fiber: 0.1g | Carbohydrates: 5.2g | Sugar: 3.1g

Creamy Rosemary and Prosciutto Baked Avocado

Have you ever tried the combination of rosemary and prosciutto? It's a perfect blend of savory flavors that will delight your taste buds and stimulate digestion.

INGREDIENTS | MAKES 2 FAT BOMBS

1 medium avocado, halved and pitted, skin on

1 ounce cream cheese

1 tablespoon finely chopped fresh rosemary

1 ounce cooked prosciutto, crumbled

1. Preheat oven to 350°F.

2. Place avocado halves hole-side up in a shallow ramekin or ovenproof dish just large enough to hold them.

3. In a small bowl, mix cream cheese with rosemary and prosciutto.

4. Place ½ mixture into each avocado cavity.

5. Bake 20 minutes. Serve hot.

PER 1 FAT BOMB Calories: 195 | Fat: 15.4g | Protein: 5.7g | Sodium: 344mg | Fiber: 5.3g | Carbohydrates: 7.5g | Sugar: 0.7g

Crab and Avocado Endive Cups

Crab can be tasty in many different ways, not just in crab cakes.

INGREDIENTS | MAKES 4 FAT BOMBS

1 ounce canned crabmeat, drained

1 ounce avocado pulp

1 teaspoon finely chopped cilantro

1 tablespoon chopped green onion

1 teaspoon fresh lime juice

1 tablespoon coconut oil

⅛ teaspoon sea salt

⅛ teaspoon freshly ground black pepper

4 Belgian endive leaves, washed and dried

1. In a small food processor, mix all ingredients except endive until well blended.

2. Scoop 1 tablespoon crab mix onto each endive cup.

3. Serve immediately.

PER 1 FAT BOMB Calories: 48 | Fat: 4.2g | Protein: 1.5g | Sodium: 186mg | Fiber: 1g | Carbohydrates: 1.1g | Sugar: 0.1g

Creamy Tuna Endive Cups

A super-simple, super-quick recipe that can save your lunch in a moment.

INGREDIENTS | MAKES 4 FAT BOMBS

1 ounce canned tuna in olive oil, drained

1 ounce cream cheese

4 Belgian endive leaves, washed and dried

2 tablespoons hemp hearts

1. In a small food processor, mix tuna and cream cheese until well blended.

2. Scoop 1 tablespoon tuna cream onto each endive cup.

3. Sprinkle ½ tablespoon hemp hearts over each endive cup. Serve immediately.

PER 1 FAT BOMB Calories: 67 | Fat: 4.9g | Protein: 4.2g | Sodium: 55mg | Fiber: 0.4g | Carbohydrates: 0.8g | Sugar: 0.2g

CHAPTER 4

Dinner

Stuffed Chicken Breast

You can use frozen spinach in place of the fresh spinach for this recipe. Just make sure it's completely thawed and drained before use or the filling will be runny.

INGREDIENTS | SERVES 4

1 pound (4 individual) boneless, skinless chicken breasts

¼ cup cream cheese, softened

¼ cup sour cream

1 (10-ounce) package fresh spinach, chopped

⅓ cup chopped fresh basil

1 tablespoon minced green onions

½ cup shredded pepper jack cheese

2 cloves garlic, minced

¼ teaspoon salt

¼ teaspoon black pepper

1. Preheat oven to 375°F.

2. Cut a slit into the side of each chicken breast to create a pocket.

3. Combine all other ingredients in a medium bowl and beat until smooth.

4. Fill each chicken breast with ¼ of the mixture and secure pocket closed with toothpicks.

5. Place chicken breasts in a baking dish and cook for 35 minutes, or until chicken is no longer pink.

PER SERVING Calories: 271 | Fat: 12.7g | Protein: 30.8g | Sodium: 346mg | Fiber: 1.7g | Carbohydrates: 4.7g | Sugar: 1.3g

Baked Salmon with Garlic Aioli

Watch the clock when marinating this recipe. If you leave raw fish sitting in lemon juice too long, the fish will start to "cook." The citric acid in the lemon juice can change the proteins in the fish, turning the flesh firm and opaque, similar to how it would look and feel if it had been cooked with heat.

INGREDIENTS | SERVES 4

3 cloves garlic, minced

¼ cup extra-virgin olive oil

¼ cup melted butter

1 tablespoon lemon juice

½ teaspoon salt

½ teaspoon black pepper

1 teaspoon dried parsley

1 pound (4 individual) salmon fillets

½ cup Garlic Aioli (see recipe in Chapter 5)

Outstanding Omega-3s

A 4-ounce fillet of salmon contains just about 15 grams of fat. Most of this fat comes in the form of omega-3 fatty acids, which promote brain health and heart health and help protect against cancer and autoimmune diseases such as rheumatoid arthritis and lupus.

1. Combine garlic, olive oil, butter, lemon juice, salt, pepper, and parsley in a mixing bowl. Place salmon in a baking dish and pour marinade on top. Refrigerate for 1 hour.

2. Preheat oven to 350°F.

3. Put salmon in oven and bake for 35 minutes or until fish flakes easily with a fork.

4. Remove from oven and top each piece of salmon with ⅛ cup of garlic aioli.

PER SERVING Calories: 559 | Fat: 48.2g | Protein: 21.2g | Sodium: 369mg | Fiber: 0.7g | Carbohydrates: 2.3g | Sugar: 0.3g

Meatloaf

You don't need bread crumbs to hold meatloaf together. This recipe uses an egg instead, which keeps the carbohydrates low while also increasing fat and protein content.

INGREDIENTS | SERVES 4

2 tablespoons butter

1 large yellow onion

4 cloves garlic, minced

4 slices cooked sugar-free bacon

1 pound 85/15 lean ground beef

1 large egg

1 teaspoon dried thyme

1 teaspoon dried parsley

½ teaspoon dry mustard

½ teaspoon salt

¼ teaspoon black pepper

The Power of Parsley

Parsley isn't just a garnish. The herb is rich in vitamin C and vitamin A, so it helps keep your immune system, bones, and nervous system strong. Parsley also helps flush out excess water from the body and keeps your kidneys healthy.

1. Preheat oven to 350°F.

2. Heat butter in a large skillet over medium-high heat until melted. Add onions and garlic and sauté until softened, 3–4 minutes. Remove from heat and set aside to cool.

3. Chop bacon and put in a large mixing bowl. Add ground beef, egg, herbs, spices, and garlic and onion mixture and mix until evenly incorporated.

4. Transfer meat mixture to a 9" × 5" loaf pan.

5. Cook for 1 hour or until a meat thermometer inserted in the center reads 165°F.

PER SERVING Calories: 321 | Fat: 19.5g | Protein: 25.7g | Sodium: 566mg | Fiber: 0.8g | Carbohydrates: 4.7g | Sugar: 1.5g

Taco Bowls

If you prefer to mimic more traditional tacos, you can place the filling for this recipe into large leaves of iceberg lettuce and fold them up like tacos.

INGREDIENTS | SERVES 4

1 pound 85/15 lean ground beef

2 tablespoons taco seasoning

1 large avocado, chopped

1 cup shredded Cheddar cheese

1 cup sour cream

½ cup sliced black olives

Cilantro, chopped (optional)

Choosing Your Meats

Whenever possible, choose high-quality meats such as grass-fed beef and free-range, organic chicken. Animals that consume their natural diet are better for you nutritionally.

1. Brown ground beef in a large skillet over medium heat. Without draining fat, add taco seasoning and stir until liquid is absorbed and beef is covered with seasoning.

2. Put ¼ of the beef into each of four bowls. Top beef in each bowl with ¼ avocado, ¼ cup of Cheddar cheese, ¼ cup of sour cream, and ⅛ cup of sliced olives.

3. Garnish with cilantro, if desired.

PER SERVING Calories: 494 | Fat: 33.7g | Protein: 28.5g | Sodium: 704mg | Fiber: 3.4g | Carbohydrates: 8.5g | Sugar: 2.3g

Shrimp Scampi

This dish is easy to prepare and extremely versatile. Pour it over zucchini noodles or a plate of spinach. If you have room for some extra carbohydrates, try spooning it over spaghetti squash.

INGREDIENTS | SERVES 4

1 pound cooked medium shrimp

¾ cup unsalted butter

2 cloves garlic, minced

1 tablespoon lemon juice

Benefits of Shrimp

Shrimp is an unusually concentrated source of the carotenoid astaxanthin, which acts as an antioxidant and an anti-inflammatory agent. Shrimp is also an excellent source of the mineral selenium.

1. Remove tails from shrimp. Set shrimp aside.

2. Melt butter in a large skillet over medium heat. When butter is hot, add garlic and sauté until translucent, 3–4 minutes. Add lemon juice and shrimp and cook over medium heat until shrimp is hot, about 2 minutes. Serve shrimp with garlic butter poured on top.

PER SERVING Calories: 420 | Fat: 32.3g | Protein: 27.7g | Sodium: 130mg | Fiber: 0.0g | Carbohydrates: 1.0g | Sugar: 0.1g

Creamy Chicken Zoodles

This recipe calls for zucchini noodles or zoodles, which you can easily make with a vegetable spiralizer. You can find a spiralizer at most home stores. If you prefer, you can also make zucchini noodles by julienning the zucchini with a vegetable peeler.

INGREDIENTS | SERVES 4

2 large zucchini

3 tablespoons extra-virgin olive oil

1 pound boneless, skinless chicken breast, cut into cubes

½ teaspoon salt

½ teaspoon black pepper

8 ounces fresh spinach

½ cup cream cheese

2 tablespoons grated Parmesan cheese

2 tablespoons feta cheese crumbles

1. Cut zucchini in long strips with a vegetable peeler or a spiralizer. Set zucchini aside on a paper towel and allow to sweat.

2. Heat olive oil in medium skillet over medium heat. Season chicken cubes with salt and pepper and add to hot pan. Cook chicken until no longer pink, about 10 minutes.

3. Remove chicken from pan with slotted spoon and set aside.

4. Add spinach to hot pan and sauté until wilted. Add cream cheese, Parmesan cheese, and feta cheese, and stir until melted. Add chicken back to pan and toss until coated. Remove from heat and pour over zucchini noodles.

PER SERVING Calories: 383 | Fat: 22.8g | Protein: 31.8g | Sodium: 600mg | Fiber: 2.8g | Carbohydrates: 8.5g | Sugar: 5.0g

"Spaghetti" and Spicy Meatballs

When you taste this recipe, you won't even miss regular pasta noodles. The zucchini has a mild flavor that serves as the perfect vehicle for the sauce and meatballs.

INGREDIENTS | SERVES 4

2 large zucchini

2 tablespoons extra-virgin olive oil

1 cup chopped white onion

2 cloves garlic, minced

1 large egg

¼ cup shredded pepper jack cheese

½ teaspoon salt

¼ teaspoon black pepper

⅛ teaspoon red pepper flakes

½ pound 85/15 ground beef

½ pound ground pork

2 tablespoons butter

2 cups Marinara Sauce (see recipe in Chapter 5)

1. Preheat oven to 375°F.

2. Cut zucchini into long strips using a vegetable slicer or a spiralizer. Set aside onto a paper towel and allow to sweat.

3. Heat olive oil over medium-heat in a large skillet. Add onions and garlic and sauté until transparent, 3–4 minutes. Set aside and allow to cool.

4. Put egg, cheese, salt, black pepper, red pepper flakes, beef, and pork in a large mixing bowl. Add onions and garlic and mix until evenly incorporated.

5. Shape meat mixture into 12 meatballs. Place meatballs on a baking sheet and bake for 20 minutes or until internal temperature reaches 165°F.

6. Put butter in a skillet and heat over medium heat. Add zucchini noodles and sauté, stirring frequently, until softened but still firm, about 5 minutes. Remove from heat.

7. Divide zucchini up into 4 servings. Top each serving with 3 meatballs and ½ cup marinara sauce.

PER SERVING Calories: 442 | Fat: 27.0g | Protein: 29.0g | Sodium: 837mg | Fiber: 4.7g | Carbohydrates: 17.9g | Sugar: 10.4g

Stuffed Pork Tenderloin

Pork is so versatile that you can use this recipe as a basic template and change the fillings to anything you want. Try ham instead of prosciutto or Gorgonzola cheese instead of feta.

INGREDIENTS | SERVES 4

1 pound pork tenderloin

4 (0.5-ounce) slices prosciutto

4 slices cooked sugar-free bacon, chopped

½ teaspoon garlic powder

½ teaspoon ground sage

½ teaspoon black pepper

¼ teaspoon salt

½ teaspoon dry mustard

¼ cup cream cheese, softened

¼ cup feta cheese crumbles

1 cup frozen spinach, thawed

3 tablespoons extra-virgin olive oil

1. Preheat oven to 350°F.

2. Butterfly pork tenderloin and set aside.

3. Lay each slice of prosciutto down on the pork.

4. Put bacon, garlic powder, spices, cream cheese, feta cheese, and spinach in a medium mixing bowl and beat until smooth.

5. Spread filling over prosciutto and roll tenderloin closed. Secure pork with a kitchen string.

6. Heat olive oil in a large pan over medium-high heat. Sear pork for 2 minutes on each side, then place in a baking dish.

7. Bake for 30 minutes or until inside is no longer pink and thermometer reads 160°F.

PER SERVING Calories: 363 | Fat: 21.4g | Protein: 35.1g | Sodium: 861mg | Fiber: 1.9g | Carbohydrates: 4.0g | Sugar: 1.1g

Zucchini Chicken Alfredo

This recipe calls for chicken, but the zucchini and Alfredo combination also goes well with shrimp.

INGREDIENTS | SERVES 4

2 large zucchini

½ teaspoon salt

½ teaspoon black pepper

¼ teaspoon paprika

¼ teaspoon garlic powder

1 pound boneless, skinless chicken thighs

2 tablespoons coconut oil

2 tablespoons unsalted butter

2 cups Alfredo Sauce (see recipe in Chapter 5)

Stocking Up on Chicken

Chicken thighs are regularly on sale because they are less popular than chicken breasts. Take advantage of these sales by buying several packages at a time and freezing them for later. You can even cook the chicken before freezing to save time when making recipes down the road.

1. Cut zucchini into long strips using vegetable peeler or spiralizer. Set aside on a paper towel and allow to sweat.

2. Sprinkle salt, black pepper, paprika, and garlic powder over chicken thighs. Heat coconut oil in a medium skillet over medium heat and place chicken in pan. Cook for 5 minutes, flip over, and then cook for another 5 minutes, or until no longer pink.

3. Remove chicken from heat with slotted spoon and chop into large pieces.

4. Add butter to hot pan. Once butter melts, add zucchini and sauté until softened but still firm, about 5 minutes. Add Alfredo sauce and chopped chicken to pan and toss until coated.

PER SERVING Calories: 617 | Fat: 53.7g | Protein: 23.9g | Sodium: 672mg | Fiber: 1.7g | Carbohydrates: 7.3g | Sugar: 5.1g

Pepperoni Meat-Za

Following a ketogenic diet doesn't mean that you have to give up pizza for good. Swap out the carbohydrate-filled crust for a crust made of meat and you're good to go.

INGREDIENTS | SERVES 4

1 pound 85/15 ground beef

1 large egg

½ teaspoon garlic powder

½ teaspoon onion powder

½ teaspoon salt

½ teaspoon black pepper

1 teaspoon dried oregano

¼ cup grated Parmesan cheese

1½ cups Marinara Sauce (see recipe in Chapter 5)

1½ cups shredded mozzarella cheese

15 slices sugar-free pepperoni

1. Preheat oven to 400°F.

2. In a large mixing bowl, mix meat and egg together until combined. Add garlic powder, onion powder, salt, pepper, oregano, and Parmesan cheese and mix. Press meat mixture into a 9" pie plate, forming a pizza crust.

3. Bake for 20 minutes or until meat is no longer pink and thermometer reads 165°F. Remove from oven.

4. Spread marinara sauce evenly over cooked meat. Sprinkle mozzarella over sauce and top with pepperoni slices. Return to oven and bake until cheese is melted and bubbly, about 5 minutes.

PER SERVING Calories: 451 | Fat: 26.6g | Protein: 35.4g | Sodium: 1,185mg | Fiber: 2.1g | Carbohydrates: 9.3g | Sugar: 4.3g

Ground Pork Stir-Fry

You can change the flavor profile of this recipe by simply changing the spices you use. Use rosemary and thyme instead of garlic, onion, and sage.

INGREDIENTS | SERVES 4

2 tablespoons coconut oil

1 medium yellow onion, peeled and sliced

3 cloves garlic, minced

1 large zucchini

1 pound ground pork

1 (10-ounce) bag fresh spinach

1 cup chopped cooked broccoli

1 teaspoon ground sage

1 teaspoon granulated garlic

1 teaspoon granulated onion

1 teaspoon salt

1 teaspoon black pepper

½ teaspoon red pepper flakes (optional)

1 large avocado, diced

1. Heat coconut oil in a medium skillet over medium-high heat. Add sliced onion and minced garlic and sauté until transparent, about 5 minutes.

2. Add zucchini and sauté until soft, another 3–4 minutes. Add ground pork and sauté until no longer pink. When meat is cooked, add spinach and sauté until wilted. Add broccoli, sage, granulated garlic, granulated onion, salt, black pepper, and red pepper flakes (if desired). Toss mixture until evenly covered with spices.

3. Remove from heat and divide into 4 bowls. Top each serving with ¼ avocado.

PER SERVING Calories: 321 | Fat: 15.7g | Protein: 28.8g | Sodium: 727mg | Fiber: 6.7g | Carbohydrates: 15.2g | Sugar: 4.0g

Take It Further

This recipe tastes even better when it sits overnight, as the flavors have more time to develop. Make it for dinner and heat it up in the morning—and put a fried egg on top to increase the fat and protein content.

Bacon-Wrapped Chicken

If you want really crispy bacon, you can partially cook the bacon before wrapping the chicken.
This will help ensure that the bacon is thoroughly cooked by the time the chicken is.

INGREDIENTS | SERVES 4

1 pound (4 individual) boneless, skinless chicken breasts
1 cup cream cheese, softened
½ cup shredded pepper jack cheese
2 tablespoons dried chives
¼ teaspoon salt
¼ teaspoon black pepper
4 slices sugar-free bacon

1. Preheat oven to 400°F.

2. Cut a pocket into each chicken breast with a small paring knife. Set aside.

3. Put cream cheese, pepper jack cheese, chives, salt, and black pepper in a medium bowl and mix until combined.

4. Fill each chicken breast with ¼ of cream cheese mixture and wrap with 1 bacon strip. Secure with a toothpick.

5. Place chicken breasts in a baking pan and bake for 40 minutes or until a meat thermometer reads 165°F.

6. Turn oven to broil and broil on top rack until bacon is crispy, about 5 minutes.

PER SERVING Calories: 442 | Fat: 27.6g | Protein: 36.1g | Sodium: 695mg | Fiber: 0.1g | Carbohydrates: 3.1g | Sugar: 1.9g

Stuffed Green Peppers

You can swap the green peppers in this recipe for red peppers or yellow peppers if you prefer the taste, but keep in mind that this will change the carbohydrate count.

INGREDIENTS | SERVES 4

4 medium green bell peppers

1 tablespoon extra-virgin olive oil

½ cup chopped yellow onion

2 cloves garlic, minced

1 pound 85/15 ground beef

4 slices cooked sugar-free bacon, diced

1 large tomato, diced

2 teaspoons Italian seasoning

¼ cup Marinara Sauce (see recipe in Chapter 5)

½ cup shredded mozzarella cheese

½ cup shredded Cheddar cheese

1. Preheat oven to 375°F.

2. Cut tops off of bell peppers and remove seeds. Set aside.

3. Heat olive oil in a large skillet over medium heat and sauté onion and garlic until transparent, about 5 minutes.

4. Add beef to skillet and cook until browned. Add bacon, tomato, and Italian seasoning and combine. Stir in marinara sauce.

5. Stuff each pepper with ¼ of meat mixture and stand peppers upright in a baking dish. Bake for 50 minutes or until meat reaches an internal temperature of 165°F.

6. Turn oven to broil and sprinkle cheeses on top of meat mixture. Broil for 5 minutes or until cheese is melted and bubbly and peppers start to char. Remove from oven and serve hot.

PER SERVING Calories: 387 | Fat: 9.8g | Protein: 32.0g | Sodium: 489mg | Fiber: 2.5g | Carbohydrates: 9.3g | Sugar: 4.6g

Bunless Bacon Burgers

The combination of avocado and Homemade Mayonnaise in this recipe is so good you won't even miss the bun. For an even more decadent treat, add a fried egg on top.

INGREDIENTS | SERVES 4

1 pound 80/20 ground beef

1/3 cup heavy cream

1/8 teaspoon hot pepper sauce

1 clove garlic, minced

3 tablespoons chopped onion

1/4 teaspoon black pepper

1/4 teaspoon salt

4 slices American cheese

4 slices cooked sugar-free bacon

1 medium avocado, sliced

2 tablespoons Homemade Mayonnaise (see recipe in Chapter 5)

1. Turn oven on to broil.

2. Place beef in a large mixing bowl and add cream, hot sauce, garlic, onion, black pepper, and salt. Mix until combined.

3. Form into 4 patties and place on a broiling rack. Broil for 4 minutes on each side or until beef is no longer pink.

4. Top each burger with a slice of American cheese and leave under broiler for 1 more minute.

5. Remove from oven and top each burger with 1 slice bacon and 1/4 sliced avocado. Drizzle 1/2 tablespoon mayonnaise onto each burger.

PER SERVING Calories: 494 | Fat: 35.5g | Protein: 29.9g | Sodium: 721mg | Fiber: 2.5g | Carbohydrates: 7.2g | Sugar: 2.6g

Shepherd's Pie

This recipe freezes very well, so save yourself some time by doubling the recipe and freezing half. You can use the frozen pie for dinner on a night that you don't feel like cooking.

INGREDIENTS | SERVES 6

2 tablespoons coconut oil

1 medium yellow onion, chopped

3 cloves garlic, minced

2 medium stalks celery, diced

1 medium zucchini, diced

1½ pounds ground lamb

1 teaspoon dried rosemary

1 teaspoon dried thyme

1 teaspoon black pepper

½ teaspoon salt

½ teaspoon garlic powder

4 cups cauliflower florets, boiled

¼ cup heavy cream

3 tablespoons unsalted butter

½ teaspoon garlic salt

¾ cup shredded Cheddar cheese

Some Shepherd's Pie History

Shepherd's pie, which is also called cottage pie, was first developed in an attempt to use up leftover meat. Traditional shepherd's pie uses lamb. When beef is used instead of lamb, the same meal is called cottage pie.

1. Preheat oven to 350°F.

2. Heat coconut oil in a large skillet over medium-high heat. When oil is hot, add onions and garlic and sauté until translucent, about 5 minutes. Add celery and zucchini and sauté until soft, another 5 minutes.

3. Add lamb, herbs, spices, and garlic powder and cook until no longer pink. Pour lamb mixture into a 9" × 13" baking dish.

4. Put boiled cauliflower, cream, butter, and garlic salt in a food processor and process until smooth. Pour cauliflower mixture on top of lamb. Top with cheese.

5. Bake until cheese is melted and pie is bubbly, about 25 minutes. Allow to cool for 10 minutes before serving.

PER SERVING Calories: 357 | Fat: 24.9g | Protein: 20.7g | Sodium: 531mg | Fiber: 4.4g | Carbohydrates: 12.2g | Sugar: 7.1g

Crab Dynamite Baked Avocado

Are you familiar with the dish Dynamite that is popular in some American sushi restaurants? It consists of different kinds of fish and scallops mixed with mayonnaise, and then is cooked under the broiler. This is an easy home version using avocado and crabmeat as a fat bomb!

INGREDIENTS | MAKES 2 FAT BOMBS

1 medium avocado, halved and pitted, skin on

1½ ounces real crabmeat, drained from juices

2 teaspoons Homemade Mayonnaise (see recipe in Chapter 5)

1 teaspoon coconut aminos or tamari

¼ teaspoon freshly ground black pepper

Soy-Free Coconut Aminos

Coconut aminos is a great substitution for soy sauce for people who prefer not using any soy products. Coconut aminos can be purchased through many major retailers online and in stores.

1. Preheat oven to 350°F.

2. Place avocado halves hole-side up in a shallow ramekin or ovenproof dish just large enough to hold them.

3. Mix crabmeat, mayonnaise, coconut aminos, and pepper in a small bowl, then divide and scoop into each avocado cavity.

4. Bake 20 minutes. Serve hot.

PER 1 FAT BOMB Calories: 165 | Fat: 12.8g | Protein: 5.2g | Sodium: 210mg | Fiber: 4.7g | Carbohydrates: 6.6g | Sugar: 0.2g

Baked Avocado with Sriracha and Brie

This baked avocado features melted cheese, hot and creamy, with a bit of spice and garlic to create a complex harmony of flavors.

INGREDIENTS | MAKES 2 FAT BOMBS

1 medium avocado, halved and pitted, skin on

1 ounce coarsely chopped Brie cheese

½ teaspoon sriracha sauce

1. Preheat oven to 350°F.

2. Place avocado halves hole-side up in a shallow ramekin or ovenproof dish just large enough to hold them.

3. Mix Brie with sriracha sauce so it is evenly coated.

4. Divide Brie in half and place into each avocado cavity.

5. Bake 20 minutes. Serve hot.

PER 1 FAT BOMB Calories: 161 | Fat: 13.1g | Protein: 4.3g | Sodium: 114mg | Fiber: 4.6g | Carbohydrates: 6.2g | Sugar: 0.5g

Baked Avocado with Blue Cheese

This is one of the easiest baked avocado recipes, but also one of the most flavorful.

INGREDIENTS | MAKES 2 FAT BOMBS

1 medium avocado, halved and pitted, skin on

2 ounces crumbled blue cheese

1 tablespoon butter, softened

1. Preheat oven to 350°F.

2. Place avocado halves hole-side up in a shallow ramekin or ovenproof dish just large enough to hold them.

3. In a small bowl, mix blue cheese and butter.

4. Place ½ mixture into each avocado cavity.

5. Bake 20 minutes. Serve hot.

PER 1 FAT BOMB Calories: 264 | Fat: 22.4g | Protein: 7.5g | Sodium: 330mg | Fiber: 4.6g | Carbohydrates: 6.5g | Sugar: 0.4g

CHAPTER 5

Soups, Dressings, and Sauces

Bacon Cheddar Soup

If you don't have an immersion blender, you can pour the soup into the pitcher of a regular blender instead. Just make sure that it's not too hot, or you may have an explosive mess on your hands.

INGREDIENTS | SERVES 4

4 slices thick-cut sugar-free bacon

1 small onion, chopped

2 cloves garlic, minced

3 cups cauliflower florets

½ teaspoon dry mustard

½ teaspoon black pepper

3 cups sugar-free chicken broth

2 cups heavy cream

2 cups shredded Cheddar cheese

1 tablespoon grated Parmesan cheese

Homemade Chicken Broth

You can easily make your own chicken broth by covering about 3 pounds of chicken bones with water in a slow cooker and letting it simmer on low for at least 12 hours. Many commercial chicken broths contain unhealthy ingredients and preservatives, and while homemade chicken broth doesn't last as long, it's better for you.

1. Cook bacon over medium-high heat in a medium skillet until crisp, about 10 minutes. Remove bacon from pan, reserving bacon grease. Return pan to heat.

2. Place onions and garlic in bacon grease and sauté until translucent, 3–4 minutes. Chop cauliflower florets into small pieces and add to onions and garlic. Sauté until tender, 7–10 minutes. Add dry mustard and black pepper and stir.

3. Transfer onions, garlic, cauliflower, and bacon grease to a large stock pot. Add chicken broth and heavy cream.

4. Stir all ingredients together and bring to a boil over medium heat. Once mixture begins to boil, reduce heat to a simmer.

5. Insert an immersion blender into the soup and blend until creamy. Add Cheddar cheese and Parmesan cheese and stir until melted.

6. Dice bacon and stir into soup. Serve hot.

PER SERVING Calories: 744 | Fat: 62.7g | Protein: 23.5g | Sodium: 1,342mg | Fiber: 2.2g | Carbohydrates: 12.6g | Sugar: 7.0g

Pumpkin Cream Soup

Instead of using cinnamon, nutmeg, and ginger in this recipe, you can use just over a teaspoon of pumpkin pie spice.

INGREDIENTS | SERVES 6

2 tablespoons coconut oil

2 tablespoons unsalted butter

¼ cup diced onion

2 cloves garlic, minced

3 cups sugar-free chicken broth

1½ cups pumpkin purée

½ teaspoon ground cinnamon

½ teaspoon ground nutmeg

⅛ teaspoon ground ginger

¼ teaspoon salt

¼ teaspoon black pepper

3 cups full-fat canned coconut milk

1. Heat coconut oil and butter in a stockpot over medium high heat. When oil and butter are hot, add onions and garlic and sauté until translucent, 3–4 minutes.

2. Add chicken broth, pumpkin purée, cinnamon, nutmeg, ginger, salt, and pepper and stir until combined.

3. Submerge an immersion blender into soup and blend until smooth and creamy. Allow to simmer for 20 minutes.

4. Stir in coconut milk. Serve hot.

PER SERVING Calories: 317 | Fat: 30.7g | Protein: 3.8g | Sodium: 575mg | Fiber: 1.5g | Carbohydrates: 7.1g | Sugar: 1.8g

Chilled Spicy Avocado Soup

Make this a satisfying vegetarian recipe by using vegetable broth in place of the chicken broth.

INGREDIENTS | SERVES 6

2 tablespoons olive oil

2 cloves garlic, minced

1 small white onion, diced

½ jalapeño, minced

3 large avocados, chopped

3 cups sugar-free chicken broth

¾ teaspoon black pepper

¼ cup fresh lemon juice

2 cups full-fat coconut cream

1. Heat olive oil in a small skillet. When oil is hot, add garlic, onion, and jalapeño and sauté until softened, 3–4 minutes. Remove from heat and allow to cool.

2. Add chopped avocados to a blender with chicken broth, black pepper, lemon juice, coconut cream, and onion and garlic mixture. Blend until smooth.

3. Refrigerate until chilled, about 4 hours. Serve cool.

PER SERVING Calories: 329 | Fat: 29.8g | Protein: 2.4g | Sodium: 481mg | Fiber: 5.0g | Carbohydrates: 11.5g | Sugar: 4.2g

Creamy Broccoli Soup

The creamy nutty flavor of the coconut milk in this recipe complements the broccoli nicely, but if you don't like the coconut flavor, you can use heavy cream instead.

INGREDIENTS | SERVES 6

2 tablespoons unsalted butter

2 stalks celery, diced

1 medium onion, diced

6 cups broccoli florets

½ teaspoon salt

½ teaspoon black pepper

4 cups sugar-free chicken broth

2 cups full-fat canned coconut milk

1. Heat butter over medium-high heat in a large stockpot. Add celery and onion and sauté until translucent, 3–4 minutes.

2. Add broccoli florets, salt, pepper, and chicken broth and bring to a simmer. Allow to simmer until broccoli is fork tender, about 10 minutes.

3. Add coconut milk and blend with an immersion blender until soup is smooth and creamy. Serve hot.

PER SERVING Calories: 221 | Fat: 18.9g | Protein: 5.1g | Sodium: 850mg | Fiber: 0.6g | Carbohydrates: 8.8g | Sugar: 1.7g

Be Choosy with Dairy

Choose grass-fed butter, raw cheese, and organic heavy cream whenever possible.

Chicken Soup

Instead of canned chicken, you can use the meat from a precooked rotisserie chicken or poach a couple of chicken breasts and then shred them.

INGREDIENTS | SERVES 6

2 tablespoons olive oil

3 cloves garlic, minced

1 medium onion, diced

2 stalks celery, diced

4 ounces cream cheese

¾ cup heavy cream

1 (28.5-ounce) can shredded chicken breast

6 cups sugar-free chicken broth

1 teaspoon dried oregano

2 teaspoons Italian seasoning

2 bay leaves

¼ cup fresh chopped parsley

1. Heat olive oil in a large stockpot over medium-high heat. When oil is hot, add garlic and onions and sauté until translucent, 3–4 minutes. Add celery and sauté until soft, about 4 minutes.

2. Add cream cheese and heavy cream to pan and stir until cream cheese is melted.

3. Add remaining ingredients and bring to a boil. Once the soup starts boiling, reduce heat and allow to simmer for 25 minutes. Serve hot.

PER SERVING Calories: 328 | Fat: 23.3g | Protein: 19.0g | Sodium: 1,509mg | Fiber: 0.7g | Carbohydrates: 5.5g | Sugar: 3.5g

Marinara Sauce

Because this recipe freezes well, you can save yourself some time down the road
by making a double batch and freezing what you don't use for later.

INGREDIENTS | MAKES 8 CUPS (SERVES 16)

2 tablespoons unsalted butter

1 small yellow onion, minced

4 cloves garlic, minced

2 (28-ounce) cans crushed tomatoes

1 (14-ounce) can sugar-free tomato sauce

¼ cup extra-virgin olive oil

¼ cup red wine vinegar

2 tablespoons Italian seasoning

¼ cup chopped fresh parsley

¾ teaspoon salt

½ teaspoon black pepper

1. Heat butter in a large stockpot over medium-high heat. Add onions and garlic and sauté until browned, about 5 minutes.

2. Add crushed tomatoes, tomato sauce, olive oil, red wine vinegar, and seasonings. Stir and bring to a simmer.

3. Simmer for 45 minutes, stirring occasionally.

4. Serve immediately or store in the refrigerator in airtight container.

PER SERVING Calories: 82 | Fat: 4.9g | Protein: 1.8g | Sodium: 409mg | Fiber: 2.5g | Carbohydrates: 8.7g | Sugar: 5.0g

Let It Sit for a Bit

Tomato-based meals tend to develop better flavors after they sit for a day or two. For maximum flavor, make this sauce a couple of days before you need to use it and store it in the refrigerator.

Homemade Mayonnaise

You can use olive oil in this recipe in place of avocado oil. If you prefer a milder taste, opt for extra-light olive oil. If you like mayonnaise with a strong olive oil flavor, go for extra-virgin.

INGREDIENTS | SERVES 10

1 large egg, room temperature
Juice from ½ lemon, room temperature
½ teaspoon dry mustard
½ teaspoon salt
¼ teaspoon black pepper
1 cup avocado oil

Creating an Emulsion

Mayonnaise is made by creating an emulsion, or a mixture of oil and water (from the eggs). As you know, oil and water do not mix easily, so it's important to let the eggs and lemon juice reach room temperature before preparing this recipe. If you don't, the emulsion may fail and you'll be left with a runny mess.

1. Combine egg and lemon juice in a narrow container and let sit for 30 minutes.

2. Add dry mustard, salt, pepper, and avocado oil. Insert an immersion blender into mixture until it hits the bottom of the container.

3. Turn the blender on and blend for 30 seconds. As the mixture starts to emulsify, pull the blender out of the mixture slightly to mix in the oil on the top.

4. Transfer to a tightly sealed container and store in the refrigerator.

PER SERVING Calories: 201 | Fat: 21.3g | Protein: 0.7g | Sodium: 123mg | Fiber: 0.0g | Carbohydrates: 0.3g | Sugar: 0.1g

Garlic Aioli

This recipe calls for raw garlic, but if you prefer, you can sauté the garlic in a skillet with a small amount of olive oil before mixing.

INGREDIENTS | MAKES 1 CUP (SERVES 8)

1 cup Homemade Mayonnaise (see recipe in this chapter)
4 cloves garlic, minced
3 tablespoons olive oil
2 tablespoons fresh lemon juice
½ teaspoon salt
¼ teaspoon black pepper

1. Mix all ingredients together in a small bowl until smooth.

2. Cover and refrigerate before serving.

PER SERVING Calories: 204 | Fat: 21.3g | Protein: 0.8g | Sodium: 268mg | Fiber: 0.6g | Carbohydrates: 1.1g | Sugar: 0.2g

Hollandaise Sauce

If you prefer not to use the microwave, you can heat up the butter in a saucepan over low heat and then add it to the blender.

INGREDIENTS | MAKES 1 CUP (SERVES 4)

8 large egg yolks
¼ teaspoon salt
2 tablespoons fresh lemon juice
1 cup unsalted butter

Reduce Waste

Instead of throwing out the egg whites that you don't use in this recipe, scramble them up with some whole eggs and use them in a quiche or make the Bacon-Wrapped Egg Cups found in Chapter 2.

1. Put egg yolks, salt, and lemon juice in a blender and blend until smooth. Put butter in a microwave-safe dish and microwave until melted and hot, about 45–60 seconds.

2. With egg yolk mixture in blender, turn blender on low speed and slowly pour in the butter. The sauce will thicken.

PER SERVING Calories: 517 | Fat: 51.5g | Protein: 5.9g | Sodium: 167mg | Fiber: 0.0g | Carbohydrates: 1.8g | Sugar: 0.4g

Alfredo Sauce

You can replace the heavy cream in this recipe with 1 cup full-fat canned coconut milk, or use half heavy cream and half coconut milk.

INGREDIENTS | MAKES 1½ CUPS (SERVES 5)

½ cup unsalted butter

1 cup heavy cream

3 tablespoons grated Asiago cheese

3 tablespoons grated Parmesan cheese

½ teaspoon granulated garlic

¼ teaspoon ground nutmeg

¼ teaspoon salt

¼ teaspoon black pepper

1. Melt butter in a medium saucepan over medium heat. Add heavy cream and whisk for 2 minutes. Add Asiago cheese and Parmesan cheese and whisk until melted. Continue to cook for about 5 minutes, allowing mixture to simmer.

2. Stir in garlic, nutmeg, salt, and pepper. Remove from heat and serve.

PER SERVING Calories: 354 | Fat: 35.6g | Protein: 3.0g | Sodium: 231mg | Fiber: 0.1g | Carbohydrates: 2.2g | Sugar: 1.4g

Avocado Basil Cream Sauce

Make this recipe only when you plan to use it right away. If you let it sit, the avocado tends to separate from the milk and cream.

INGREDIENTS | MAKES 1½ CUPS (SERVES 12)

1 large avocado

½ cup full-fat canned coconut milk

½ cup heavy cream

1½ tablespoons lemon juice

¼ cup chopped fresh basil

½ teaspoon salt

¼ teaspoon black pepper

Put all ingredients in a food processor or blender and process until smooth.

PER SERVING Calories: 72 | Fat: 6.9g | Protein: 0.6g | Sodium: 199mg | Fiber: 0.8g | Carbohydrates: 1.7g | Sugar: 0.4g

Blue Cheese Dressing

The dressing will thicken as it cools. You can thin it out by adding a little more white wine vinegar when you take it out of the fridge.

INGREDIENTS | MAKES 1½ CUPS (SERVES 12)

⅓ cup Homemade Mayonnaise (see recipe in this chapter)

⅓ cup sour cream

⅓ cup heavy cream

1 tablespoon white wine vinegar

⅛ teaspoon garlic powder

¼ teaspoon salt

¼ teaspoon black pepper

⅓ cup blue cheese crumbles

Put mayonnaise, sour cream, heavy cream, and white wine vinegar in a small bowl and whisk until smooth. Stir in garlic powder, salt, and pepper. Fold in blue cheese crumbles. Refrigerate for at least 30 minutes before serving.

PER SERVING Calories: 93 | Fat: 9.2g | Protein: 1.2g | Sodium: 124mg | Fiber: 0.0g | Carbohydrates: 0.6g | Sugar: 0.4g

Ranch Dressing

You can easily add this dressing to salads, deli rollups, and chicken dishes for a quick boost in fat content.

INGREDIENTS | MAKES 1½ CUPS (SERVES 12)

1 cup Homemade Mayonnaise (see recipe in this chapter)

½ cup sour cream

½ teaspoon white vinegar

¼ cup chopped fresh parsley

2 tablespoons chopped fresh dill

½ teaspoon dried chives

¼ teaspoon garlic powder

¼ teaspoon onion powder

⅛ teaspoon salt

⅛ teaspoon black pepper

Put all ingredients in a mixing bowl and whisk until smooth. Cover and refrigerate for at least 30 minutes before serving.

PER SERVING Calories: 154 | Fat: 15.9g | Protein: 0.8g | Sodium: 112mg | Fiber: 0.1g | Carbohydrates: 1.0g | Sugar: 0.4g

Avocado Italian Dressing

You can make this more of a traditional Italian dressing by using light olive oil in place of avocado. Give it an Asian kick by using toasted sesame oil instead.

INGREDIENTS | MAKES 1½ CUPS (SERVES 12)

1 cup avocado oil
¼ cup white wine vinegar
3 tablespoons water
1 teaspoon garlic salt
1 teaspoon onion powder
2 teaspoons dried oregano
½ teaspoon dried basil
1 teaspoon dried parsley
1 teaspoon salt
1 teaspoon black pepper

1. Whisk all ingredients together in a bowl until combined.

2. Serve immediately, or store at room temperature and shake or mix well before serving.

PER SERVING Calories: 163 | Fat: 17.4g | Protein: 0.1g | Sodium: 357mg | Fiber: 0.2g | Carbohydrates: 0.4g | Sugar: 0.0g

Avocado Butter

This butter works very well on both grilled fish and steak. You can use it whenever you have a lean protein source that you need to add fat to, to achieve your keto requirements. The flavor is very mild and creamy and it will not overpower the flavor of your protein.

INGREDIENTS | SERVES 10

1 large avocado, pitted and peeled
3 tablespoons butter, softened
¼ teaspoon sea salt
¼ teaspoon freshly ground black pepper

1. Combine all ingredients in a food processor and pulse to combine. Place mixture in a container with an airtight lid.

2. Refrigerate up to 5 days until ready to use.

PER SERVING Calories: 53 | Fat: 5.1g | Protein: 0.3g | Sodium: 86mg | Fiber: 0.9g | Carbohydrates: 1.2g | Sugar: 0.0g

Salmon Mousse

This is another recipe you will be proud to serve to your guests—it will make a big impression without a lot of effort on your part. Who said fat bombs can't be shared?

INGREDIENTS | SERVES 6

1½ ounces smoked salmon

4 tablespoons mascarpone cheese

2 tablespoons sour cream

1 large hard-boiled egg yolk, put through a fine-mesh strainer

½ tablespoon fresh lemon juice

1 ounce finely chopped chives

¼ teaspoon sea salt

¼ teaspoon freshly ground black pepper

2 tablespoons cold whipping cream

6 thin slices cucumber

1. Chop salmon finely with a sharp knife.

2. In a small bowl, beat mascarpone and sour cream with an electric mixer until smooth. Place a second small bowl in refrigerator to chill.

3. Add egg yolk and lemon juice to mascarpone mixture.

4. Add salmon, chives, salt, and pepper to mascarpone mixture and stir well.

5. In previously chilled bowl, whip whipping cream with the electric mixer until stiff peaks form.

6. With a spatula gently fold whipped cream into salmon mixture.

7. Fill 6 small glasses with mixture and serve with a spoon and a slice of cucumber.

8. Can be refrigerated up to 1 week.

PER SERVING Calories: 87 | Fat: 7.8g | Protein: 2.8g | Sodium: 154mg | Fiber: 0.2g | Carbohydrates: 1.1g | Sugar: 0.5g

Shrimp Mousse

This recipe makes a great party dish. Just serve with cucumber slices instead of crackers!

INGREDIENTS | SERVES 4

½ tablespoon powdered unflavored gelatin

2 tablespoons hot water

½ cup chopped cooked shrimp

4 ounces coconut cream

½ cup Homemade Mayonnaise (see recipe in this chapter)

1 tablespoon chopped green onion

1 tablespoon finely chopped celery

1. Dissolve gelatin in hot water and let sit 5 minutes.

2. In a small food processor, add shrimp, coconut cream, mayonnaise, and softened gelatin and blend until a very smooth cream is formed.

3. Move cream from food processor to a bowl, add green onion and celery, and mix well.

4. Place shrimp mixture in a cup-sized mold.

5. Refrigerate at least 6 hours or overnight.

6. When ready to eat, dip mold into bowl of hot water to dislodge mousse from container. You can also insert a knife gently between mousse and mold.

7. Invert over a plate and serve.

PER SERVING Calories: 272 | Fat: 25.5g | Protein: 4.4g | Sodium: 155mg | Fiber: 0.1g | Carbohydrates: 1.9g | Sugar: 1.0g

Creamy Crab Mousse

*This recipe will make a great impression on the guests at your
dinner party...and they will never know you are serving them a fat bomb.*

INGREDIENTS | SERVES 4

1 teaspoon powdered unflavored gelatin

2 tablespoons water

1 ounce cream cheese

1 ounce sour cream

2 tablespoons Homemade Mayonnaise
(see recipe in this chapter)

2 ounces canned crabmeat, drained

1 tablespoon minced green onion

1 tablespoon minced celery

⅛ teaspoon garlic salt

½ teaspoon lemon juice

⅛ teaspoon freshly ground black pepper

1. In a cup, sprinkle gelatin over water and let sit 5 minutes.

2. In a small saucepan over medium-low heat, melt cream cheese with sour cream. Once melted, add gelatin and mix with a wire whisk until well incorporated.

3. Remove from heat and let cool about 5 minutes.

4. In a medium bowl, mix cream and gelatin with remaining ingredients, blending well.

5. Place crab and cream mixture into a cup-sized mold.

6. Refrigerate at least 6 hours or overnight.

7. When ready to eat, dip mold into bowl of hot water to dislodge mousse from container. You can also insert a knife gently between mousse and mold.

8. Invert over a plate and serve.

PER SERVING Calories: 104 | Fat: 8.3g | Protein: 4.7g | Sodium: 177mg | Fiber: 0.1g | Carbohydrates: 0.9g | Sugar: 0.5g

Creamy Olive Mousse

A wonderful smooth and salty cream that can pair great with any of the cheese crisps in Chapter 10. This can be refrigerated up to one week.

INGREDIENTS | SERVES 4

1 tablespoon powdered unflavored gelatin

2 tablespoons hot water

12 large kalamata olives, pitted

4 ounces cream cheese

¼ teaspoon dried parsley flakes

⅛ teaspoon red chili flakes

1. In a cup, dissolve gelatin in water and let sit 5 minutes.

2. In a small food processor, add olives, cream cheese, parsley, chili flakes, and softened gelatin and blend until a very smooth cream is formed.

3. Place mixture in a small serving bowl.

4. Refrigerate at least 6 hours or overnight.

PER SERVING Calories: 132 | Fat: 10.3g | Protein: 3.2g | Sodium: 386mg | Fiber: 1.0g | Carbohydrates: 2.2g | Sugar: 0.9g

Cilantro Mousse

A fresh, tangy, creamy flavor that is totally delicious. Great to pair with the Parmesan Vegetable Crisps (see recipe in Chapter 10).

INGREDIENTS | SERVES 6

2 teaspoons powdered unflavored gelatin

2 tablespoons water

1 ounce sour cream

1 ounce goat cheese, softened

2 tablespoons Homemade Mayonnaise (see recipe in this chapter)

3 tablespoons finely chopped fresh cilantro

½ jalapeño pepper, seeded and finely chopped

1 teaspoon lime juice

⅛ teaspoon garlic salt

Get Clean with Cilantro

Cilantro is highly noted for its ability to act as a natural cleansing agent. The chemical compounds in cilantro bind to toxic metals such as mercury and help remove them from the body. Cilantro also acts as a strong antioxidant and may reduce the risk of heart disease.

1. In a cup, sprinkle gelatin over water and let sit 5 minutes.

2. In a small food processor, mix softened gelatin with remaining ingredients and process until a smooth cream is formed, about 30 seconds.

3. Pour mixture into a large enough mold to hold everything.

4. Refrigerate at least 6 hours or overnight.

5. When ready to eat, dip mold into bowl of hot water to dislodge mousse from container. You can also insert a knife gently between mousse and mold.

6. Invert over a plate and serve.

PER SERVING Calories: 62 | Fat: 5.1g | Protein: 3.1g | Sodium: 70mg | Fiber: 0.1g | Carbohydrates: 0.4g | Sugar: 0.2g

Parmesan Mousse

A great mousse to eat by itself or on a cucumber slice. Simple but extremely tasty.

INGREDIENTS | SERVES 6

2 tablespoons olive oil
1 tablespoon chopped green onion
1 medium clove garlic, finely minced
1 cup heavy cream
1 cup grated Parmesan cheese

Hot or Cold?

This recipe can be made into a mousse or a hot dip. To turn into a hot dip, place mixture in a small baking dish. Bake at 350°F for 15 minutes until bubbly and browned. Serve with sliced cucumbers or carrots.

1. In a medium heavy-bottomed saucepan, heat olive oil over medium heat. Add green onion and garlic and cook until brown and crispy, about 3 minutes.

2. Add cream and cheese, lower heat, and simmer another 2 minutes, stirring.

3. Remove pot from heat and strain contents through a wide sieve into a bowl so onion solids get filtered out.

4. Let cream come to room temperature, then refrigerate at least 3 hours.

5. Remove from refrigerator and whip with an electric mixer until light and fluffy.

6. Serve immediately.

PER SERVING Calories: 247 | Fat: 22.3g | Protein: 5.6g | Sodium: 315mg | Fiber: 0.0g | Carbohydrates: 3.7g | Sugar: 1.2g

Mojo de Ajo Aioli

In Mexican and Latin cuisine, mojo de ajo is considered to be the nectar of the gods. Although it is simple to make, mojo de ajo leaves an everlasting impression on those who've been fortunate enough to taste it.

INGREDIENTS | SERVES 16

1 large head garlic
8 ounces extra-virgin olive oil
¼ teaspoon salt
¼ cup lime juice
1 large egg, at room temperature
⅛ teaspoon cayenne pepper

1. Preheat oven to 325°F.

2. Take garlic head apart and peel individual cloves by slightly smashing each clove with the side of a knife, which makes the papery skin easier to peel.

3. Fill an 8" × 8" glass casserole dish with olive oil, salt, and garlic, making sure cloves are fully submerged in the olive oil.

4. Bake 45–50 minutes until garlic is lightly browned. Add lime juice and bake an additional 20 minutes.

5. Remove from oven and let cool.

6. Once at room temperature, smash garlic with fork or potato masher, then pour garlic-oil mixture into large-mouthed, quart-sized mason jar.

7. Add egg and cayenne and blend with immersion blender until mixture starts to firm up and turn white, roughly 30 seconds.

8. Place cap on jar and place in refrigerator to firm up for later use as a spread on lettuce wraps or a dip for vegetables.

PER SERVING Calories: 133 | Fat: 14.1g | Protein: 0.5g | Sodium: 41mg | Fiber: 0.1g | Carbohydrates: 1.0g | Sugar: 0.1g

Holy Jalapeño Mayonnaise

A little bit of heat from the jalapeño gives this mayonnaise just the right amount of kick to a carne asada lettuce wrap or a naked chicken burrito bowl. It also mixes well with salsa to make a delicious dressing for taco salad.

INGREDIENTS | SERVES 16

1 medium jalapeño
8 ounces extra-virgin olive oil
1 large egg, at room temperature
¼ cup lime juice
¼ teaspoon salt

1. Preheat oven to 400°F.

2. Place jalapeño on a baking sheet and roast until slightly browned, roughly 25 minutes.

3. Let jalapeño cool to room temperature. Once cooled, cut off top, remove ribs and seeds, and finely dice.

4. Pour oil into large-mouthed, quart-sized jar.

5. Add egg, lime juice, and salt and blend with immersion blender until mixture starts to firm up and turn white, roughly 30 seconds.

6. Fold diced pepper into mixture with a small spatula.

7. Place cap on jar and place in refrigerator to firm up for later use as a spread or as a binder for baked and crusted chicken or fish.

PER SERVING Calories: 130 | Fat: 14.1g | Protein: 0.4g | Sodium: 41mg | Fiber: 0.0g | Carbohydrates: 0.4g | Sugar: 0.1g

Hail Caesar Dressing

This dairy-free take on the classic dressing is as creamy and delicious as the original version. While a romaine lettuce base is preferred, this dressing also makes an excellent spread inside a grilled chicken lettuce wrap.

INGREDIENTS | SERVES 16

½ medium lemon, juiced

½ tablespoon apple cider vinegar

1 large clove garlic, smashed

1 large egg, at room temperature

½ ounce anchovies

¼ teaspoon salt

¼ teaspoon freshly ground black pepper

1 cup extra-virgin olive oil

1. Place all ingredients except oil into a wide-mouthed, quart-sized jar.

2. Blend ingredients with an immersion blender until well chopped and mixed.

3. Add oil and blend 20–30 seconds more until dressing takes on the consistency of thin mayonnaise.

4. Chill until ready to use. Mix before use.

PER SERVING Calories: 126 | Fat: 13.5g | Protein: 0.7g | Sodium: 73mg | Fiber: 0.0g | Carbohydrates: 0.2g | Sugar: 0.0g

How Did Caesar Salad Get Its Name?

Despite what many may believe, Caesar salad was not named after the Roman emperor. An Italian-born chef, Caesar Cardini, actually invented the dish in the 1920s with remnants in his restaurant kitchen during a dinner rush. The salad was also served with all the ingredients on individual romaine lettuce leaves and eaten as a finger food.

Lemon Greek Dressing

This dressing showcases lemon as the true star of the show. One taste of this on a romaine lettuce salad topped with kalamata olives is truly what dining in the Greek isles tastes like.

INGREDIENTS | SERVES 8

4 large cloves garlic

¼ teaspoon salt

½ cup extra-virgin olive oil

2 lemons, juiced

4 tablespoons red wine vinegar

2 tablespoons minced fresh oregano

⅛ teaspoon freshly ground black pepper

A Note on Herbs

You can substitute dried herbs for their fresh counterparts, but keep in mind that dried herbs are more concentrated so they have a stronger flavor. If you choose to use dried herbs instead of fresh, use only ⅓ of the fresh amount. For example, if the recipe calls for 3 tablespoons of fresh herbs, use only 1 tablespoon of dried herbs.

1. Smash garlic cloves with side of knife to remove papery skins. Sprinkle with salt and rub with side of knife to release garlic oils.

2. Place garlic cloves into a pint-sized jar and cover with olive oil.

3. Add remaining ingredients to jar, tighten lid, and shake to combine.

4. Set in refrigerator overnight in order for flavors to marry. Shake before use. Add more salt to taste if needed.

PER SERVING Calories: 126 | Fat: 13.2g | Protein: 0.2g | Sodium: 73mg | Fiber: 0.4g | Carbohydrates: 1.6g | Sugar: 0.3g

Bacon Olive Spread

Bacon and olive are complementary salty flavors that pair well with cream cheese. This spread is great served on celery sticks or cucumber slices. It can be served immediately or cooled in the refrigerator to enjoy cold.

INGREDIENTS | SERVES 4

4 slices bacon

8 ounces cream cheese, softened to room temperature

2 tablespoons olive oil mayonnaise

1 tablespoon freshly squeezed lemon juice

24 Spanish olives, sliced

1. Cook bacon in a large skillet over medium heat until crisp, 5 minutes per side. Drain on paper towel.

2. In a medium mixing bowl, beat softened cream cheese with a hand mixer until smooth.

3. Add mayonnaise and lemon juice and mix on medium speed until combined.

4. Crumble bacon into bowl followed by sliced olives.

5. Fold bacon and olives into cream cheese mixture by hand with rubber spatula.

PER SERVING Calories: 314 | Fat: 27.2g | Protein: 7.5g | Sodium: 588mg | Fiber: 0.5g | Carbohydrates: 3.5g | Sugar: 2.0g

Crab Rangoon Dip

Here is one of the best ways to enjoy a Chinese takeout favorite without the added carbohydrates. This dip is best enjoyed on celery sticks or Parmesan crisps.

INGREDIENTS | SERVES 4

8 ounces cream cheese, softened to room temperature

2 tablespoons olive oil mayonnaise

1 tablespoon freshly squeezed lemon juice

½ teaspoon sea salt

¼ teaspoon freshly ground black pepper

2 medium cloves garlic, minced

2 green onions, diced

½ cup shredded Parmesan cheese

4 ounces canned white crabmeat

Allicin and Allium

Like shallots, garlic belongs to the genus *Allium*, which also includes onions and leeks. The major compound in garlic, which is called allicin, is responsible for its smell as well as its health benefits, which include boosting the immune system, lowering blood pressure, and reducing the risk of Alzheimer's disease and dementia.

1. Preheat oven to 350°F.

2. In a medium bowl, mix cream cheese, mayonnaise, lemon juice, salt, and pepper with a hand blender until well incorporated.

3. Add garlic, onions, Parmesan, and crabmeat and fold into mixture with a spatula.

4. Transfer mixture to an oven-safe crock and spread out evenly.

5. Bake 30–35 minutes until top of dip is slightly browned. Serve warm.

PER SERVING Calories: 313 | Fat: 24.4g | Protein: 12.5g | Sodium: 829mg | Fiber: 0.2g | Carbohydrates: 4.1g | Sugar: 2.2g

Lemon Thyme Butter

A simple infusion of lemon and fresh herbs into butter makes it a delicious way to season fish, chicken, seafood, and low-glycemic-index vegetables. While the method to make this butter is easy, it makes the food it flavors taste like a gourmet chef prepared them.

INGREDIENTS | SERVES 8

8 tablespoons salted butter, at room temperature
2 tablespoons chopped fresh thyme
2 large cloves garlic, peeled
1 tablespoon fresh lemon juice

1. Combine all ingredients in a food processor and pulse to combine.

2. Place mixture in a log shape on a piece of wax paper and twist ends shut.

3. Refrigerate for about 2 hours before use.

PER SERVING Calories: 104 | Fat: 10.7g | Protein: 0.2g | Sodium: 91mg | Fiber: 0.3g | Carbohydrates: 0.8g | Sugar: 0.1g

CHAPTER 6

Salads

BLT Salad

*The combination of flavors in this bacon, lettuce, and tomato salad
is so delicious that you won't even miss the bread.*

INGREDIENTS | SERVES 4

1 pound sugar-free bacon

1 head romaine lettuce

2 large tomatoes, diced

2 large avocados, diced

½ cup Homemade Mayonnaise (see recipe in Chapter 5)

1 tablespoon white vinegar

Let It Sit

You can eat this salad as soon as it's chilled, or you can let it sit for a few hours or overnight to let the flavors develop. If you choose to let it sit overnight, leave the lettuce out and add it when you're ready to eat so that it stays crunchy.

1. Cook bacon over medium-high heat in a large skillet until crisp, about 10 minutes. Remove from heat, allow to cool, and then roughly chop and put in a medium mixing bowl.

2. Roughly chop romaine lettuce. Add lettuce, tomatoes, and avocado to bacon and toss until combined.

3. In a separate bowl, combine mayonnaise and white vinegar. Pour mayonnaise mixture over bacon mixture and toss to coat. Refrigerate until chilled, about 30 minutes. Serve chilled.

PER SERVING Calories: 621 | Fat: 51.7g | Protein: 21.3g | Sodium: 1,389mg | Fiber: 7.9g | Carbohydrates: 13.7g | Sugar: 3.8g

Taco Salad

Being on a ketogenic diet doesn't mean you have to skip taco night. Ditch the shells for this salad and get the same delicious taco flavor without a great blood sugar spike.

INGREDIENTS | SERVES 4

2 tablespoons butter

1 pound ground beef

1 medium yellow onion, peeled and diced

1 (1-ounce) package sugar-free taco seasoning

1 head romaine lettuce, chopped

1 cup diced tomatoes

1½ cups shredded Cheddar cheese

½ cup Ranch Dressing (see recipe in Chapter 5)

½ cup salsa

½ cup sour cream

½ cup sliced black olives

1. Heat butter in a large skillet over medium-high heat. Add beef and onions and cook together until beef is no longer pink. Add taco seasoning to mixture and stir until evenly combined. Remove from heat and allow to cool.

2. Put chopped lettuce in a large mixing bowl. Add tomatoes, Cheddar cheese, beef mixture, and ranch dressing and toss until combined.

3. Divide up into 4 bowls and top each bowl with ⅛ cup of salsa, ⅛ cup of sour cream, and ⅛ cup of sliced olives.

PER SERVING Calories: 708 | Fat: 51.3g | Protein: 32.7g | Sodium: 1,325mg | Fiber: 5.3g | Carbohydrates: 17.3g | Sugar: 6.9g

Make Your Own Spice

Instead of using a prepared taco seasoning mix, which often contains sugar, artificial ingredients, and preservatives, make your own. Simply combine about 1 tablespoon of chili powder with about 1 teaspoon of cumin and about ¼ teaspoon each of onion powder, garlic powder, oregano, salt, and pepper. You can adjust these proportions to your taste or add some red pepper flakes for a little kick.

Monkey Salad

Traditional monkey salad uses sliced bananas as a base, and that's where the "monkey" name comes from. Because bananas are high in carbohydrates, this version leaves them out, but the flavor is so good you won't miss them.

INGREDIENTS | SERVES 4

2 tablespoons unsalted butter

½ cup unsweetened coconut flakes

½ cup raw unsalted cashews

½ cup raw unsalted almonds

¼ cup 90% dark chocolate shavings

Sweet Treat

Monkey salad is the perfect sweet and satisfying treat. It's loaded with healthy fats that help keep you full between meals, and it's so easy to take on the go.

1. Melt butter in a medium skillet over medium heat. Add coconut flakes and sauté until lightly browned, 3–4 minutes.

2. Add cashews and almonds and sauté for 2 minutes. Remove from heat and sprinkle with dark chocolate shavings. Serve immediately.

PER SERVING Calories: 348 | Fat: 28.8g | Protein: 8.0g | Sodium: 6mg | Fiber: 4.8g | Carbohydrates: 15.0g | Sugar: 4.5g

Salmon and Avocado Salad

Instead of serving this as a salad, you can also spread the cream cheese mixture on each piece of smoked salmon and roll it up.

INGREDIENTS | SERVES 2

¼ cup cream cheese, softened

2 tablespoons extra-virgin olive oil

⅛ teaspoon salt

2 teaspoons lemon juice

8 ounces smoked salmon

2 large avocados, cubed

1. Put cream cheese, olive oil, salt, and lemon juice in a food processor or blender and process until smooth.

2. In a medium bowl, add smoked salmon to avocado and toss in cream cheese dressing. Refrigerate until chilled, 30 minutes to an hour. Serve chilled.

PER SERVING Calories: 578 | Fat: 44.8g | Protein: 25.1g | Sodium: 1,022 mg | Fiber: 9.3g | Carbohydrates: 13.3g | Sugar: 1.5g

Spinach and Prosciutto Salad

The unsalted cashews in this recipe help satisfy that craving for something crunchy when you're eating a salad. As a bonus, they taste great with avocado.

INGREDIENTS | SERVES 4

8 cups baby spinach

12 ounces prosciutto

2 large avocados, diced

½ cup diced red onion

½ cup chopped raw unsalted cashews

½ cup Avocado Italian Dressing (see recipe in Chapter 5)

1. Put spinach in a large mixing bowl. Dice prosciutto and put on top of spinach. Put diced avocado, red onion, and chopped cashews on top of spinach.

2. Add dressing to salad and toss to coat. Serve immediately.

PER SERVING Calories: 430 | Fat: 50.0g | Protein: 29.0g | Sodium: 2,235mg | Fiber: 7.3g | Carbohydrates: 20.6g | Sugar: 2.7g

Be Choosy with Nuts

When buying nuts, opt for raw, unsalted varieties rather than roasted, salted, or sugared versions. Raw nuts generally contain no added ingredients, while roasted, flavored nuts can contain unhealthy oils and sugar.

Chef Salad

Meat and cheese are the basis of a chef salad. Although this recipe calls for ham and turkey and Swiss and Cheddar, you can use any combination you'd like. Try adding roast beef and some pepper jack for a little kick.

INGREDIENTS | SERVES 4

8 cups chopped romaine lettuce

1 cup diced sugar-free ham

1 cup diced turkey

1 cup cubed Swiss cheese

1 cup cubed Cheddar cheese

4 large hard-boiled eggs, sliced

½ cup crumbled sugar-free bacon

½ cup Ranch Dressing (see recipe in Chapter 5)

Combine all ingredients in a large bowl and toss to combine. Serve immediately.

PER SERVING Calories: 700 | Fat: 48.4g | Protein: 48.5g | Sodium: 1,334mg | Fiber: 2.1g | Carbohydrates: 7.3g | Sugar: 2.6g

Gorgonzola Steak Salad

The combination of Gorgonzola crumbles and blue cheese dressing
makes this salad taste like a decadent treat.

INGREDIENTS | SERVES 4

3 tablespoons olive oil

1 pound sirloin steak

1 teaspoon salt

1 teaspoon black pepper

8 cups mixed greens

4 large hard-boiled eggs, chopped

1 cup crumbled Gorgonzola cheese

½ cup Blue Cheese Dressing (see recipe in Chapter 5)

1. Heat olive oil in a large skillet over medium-high heat. While oil is heating, rub steak with salt and pepper. Place steak in hot skillet and cook until desired doneness, about 4 minutes on each side for medium-rare, 7 minutes on each side for medium, and 9 minutes on each side for well-done. Set aside and let rest for 10 minutes.

2. Put mixed greens in a large mixing bowl and top with hard-boiled eggs and crumbled Gorgonzola cheese.

3. Slice steak into thin strips and put on top of greens. Add dressing and toss until coated. Serve immediately.

PER SERVING Calories: 543 | Fat: 39.4g | Protein: 34.2g | Sodium: 1,221mg | Fiber: 1.1g | Carbohydrates: 4.4g | Sugar: 1.7g

Cheeseburger Salad

When you eat this salad, you get all the flavors of a cheeseburger without the insulin- and glucose-spiking bun.

INGREDIENTS | SERVES 4

1 pound 85/15 ground beef

½ teaspoon salt

¼ teaspoon black pepper

⅓ cup sugar-free ketchup

1 tablespoon yellow mustard

1 teaspoon spicy brown mustard

1 head romaine lettuce

1 medium red onion, chopped

2 medium tomatoes, diced

4 dill pickle spears, cubed

1 cup shredded Cheddar cheese

½ cup Homemade Mayonnaise (see recipe in Chapter 5)

1 tablespoon white or apple cider vinegar

1. Brown ground beef in medium skillet over medium heat. Once beef is browned, add salt, pepper, ketchup, yellow mustard, and spicy mustard. Stir until combined. Remove from heat and set aside.

2. Chop romaine lettuce and put into a large mixing bowl. Top with onions, tomatoes, pickles, shredded cheese, and beef.

3. In a separate bowl, combine mayonnaise with vinegar and stir until smooth. Drizzle over salad and toss to coat. Serve immediately.

PER SERVING Calories: 525 | Fat: 38.9g | Protein: 23.4g | Sodium: 1,253mg | Fiber: 3.9g | Carbohydrates: 11.2g | Sugar: 4.4g

Spinach and Tuna Salad

You can swap out the tuna for chicken in this spinach and tuna salad or add hard-boiled eggs for some variations in taste. Make it spicy by adding a pinch of cayenne pepper.

INGREDIENTS | SERVES 2

2 (5-ounce) cans tuna

2 stalks celery, diced

¼ cup Homemade Mayonnaise (see recipe in Chapter 5)

4 cups spinach

4 slices sugar-free bacon, crumbled

1 large avocado, diced

2 tablespoons extra-virgin olive oil

Freshly ground black pepper

1. Combine tuna, celery, and mayonnaise in a small bowl and mix until combined.

2. In a large bowl, mix spinach, bacon crumbles, and avocado. Top with tuna mixture, drizzle with olive oil, and add freshly ground black pepper. Serve immediately.

PER SERVING Calories: 705 | Fat: 54.7g | Protein: 38.6g | Sodium: 1,021mg | Fiber: 6.6g | Carbohydrates: 9.9g | Sugar: 1.1g

Mercury Concerns

If you're concerned about the mercury in tuna, keep in mind that adults can safely eat 18–24 ounces of tuna per month without a significant amount of mercury getting into their systems. If you'd like, swap out the tuna for canned salmon. Canned salmon is higher in omega-3 fatty acids and contains no mercury.

Avocado Egg Salad

Instead of mashing the avocado into the salad along with the mayonnaise, you can cut it up into big chunks and toss it to cover with mayonnaise.

INGREDIENTS | SERVES 4

6 large hard-boiled eggs

¼ cup Homemade Mayonnaise (see recipe in Chapter 5)

½ avocado, chopped

½ teaspoon salt

¼ teaspoon black pepper

⅛ teaspoon crushed red pepper (optional)

1. Peel eggs and put into a medium mixing bowl. Mash eggs with a fork.

2. Add mayonnaise and avocado and continue to mash with a fork until combined. Stir in salt, black pepper, and red pepper, if desired.

PER SERVING Calories: 245 | Fat: 19.5g | Protein: 10.1g | Sodium: 446mg | Fiber: 1.2g | Carbohydrates: 2.6g | Sugar: 0.9g

Spinach, Feta, and Apple Salad

Granny Smith apples tend to be lower in sugar than sweeter varieties such as Pink Lady or Red Delicious. If you have some carbohydrates to spare and want a bit of a sweeter taste, swap the Granny Smith apple for another apple of your choice.

INGREDIENTS | SERVES 2

4 cups baby spinach

8 ounces cooked chicken, cubed

½ cup chopped red onion

½ cup crumbled feta cheese

½ small Granny Smith apple, diced

½ cup toasted pine nuts

¼ cup Ranch Dressing (see recipe in Chapter 5)

Combine all ingredients in a bowl and toss to coat. Serve immediately.

PER SERVING Calories: 714 | Fat: 49.7g | Protein: 41.4g | Sodium: 589mg | Fiber: 3.8g | Carbohydrates: 17.1g | Sugar: 8.4g

An Apple a Day

Apples are rich in quercetin and other flavonoids that slow digestion and help prevent a rapid spike in blood sugar levels.

Kale and Salmon Salad

Baby kale is not as tough as regular kale, and it has a milder taste too. If you're not a big kale lover, try baby kale before knocking it completely.

INGREDIENTS | SERVES 2

6 tablespoons olive oil, divided

2 cloves garlic, minced

8 ounces salmon fillet

½ teaspoon salt

¼ teaspoon black pepper

1 tablespoon lemon juice

4 cups chopped baby kale

1 large avocado, diced

2 tablespoons pine nuts

2 tablespoons apple cider vinegar

1. Heat 2 tablespoons olive oil in a large skillet over medium heat. Add garlic and sauté for 3 minutes.

2. Season salmon with salt and pepper and add to hot pan. Cook for 4 minutes on each side or until fish flakes easily with a fork. Drizzle lemon juice on top. Remove from heat.

3. Divide kale between two plates and top each plate with ½ avocado, 1 tablespoon pine nuts, and 4 ounces salmon.

4. In a separate bowl, combine remaining 4 tablespoons olive oil and apple cider vinegar. Pour half of mixture over each plate.

PER SERVING Calories: 622 | Fat: 50.2g | Protein: 25.0g | Sodium: 676mg | Fiber: 6.3g | Carbohydrates: 11.6g | Sugar: 1.5g

Bacon and Broccoli Salad

The longer this recipe sits, the better it gets, so make it the day
before you plan to eat it for maximum flavor.

INGREDIENTS | SERVES 4

6 cups broccoli florets

8 slices cooked sugar-free bacon, crumbled

8 ounces sharp Cheddar cheese, cubed

1 large avocado, diced

1 cup Homemade Mayonnaise (see recipe in Chapter 5)

2 tablespoons white vinegar

¼ teaspoon salt

¼ teaspoon black pepper

1. Combine raw broccoli, bacon, Cheddar cheese, and avocado in a large bowl.

2. In a separate bowl, combine mayonnaise, vinegar, salt, and pepper and stir until combined. Pour dressing over broccoli mixture and toss to coat. Refrigerate until chilled, about 30 minutes. Serve chilled.

PER SERVING Calories: 827 | Fat: 71.8g | Protein: 26.7g | Sodium: 1,175mg | Fiber: 2.4g | Carbohydrates: 10.4g | Sugar: 0.5g

Go Raw

Broccoli contains a high amount of sulforaphane, a compound that helps stimulate detoxification and may help reduce the risk for certain types of cancers. According to a report in the *Journal of Agricultural and Food Chemistry*, raw broccoli provides more sulforaphane than cooked broccoli, because the cooking process binds the compounds, making it less accessible.

CHAPTER 7

Side Dishes

Mashed Cauliflower

*You can add more butter or cheese to this recipe if you need to increase
the fat content so you can hit your fat goals for the day.*

INGREDIENTS | SERVES 6

1 large head cauliflower

1 cup full-fat canned coconut milk

½ cup cream cheese, softened

¼ cup unsalted butter

½ teaspoon garlic salt

½ teaspoon salt

½ teaspoon black pepper

1. Break cauliflower into florets and steam in a double boiler until fork tender, about 8 minutes.

2. Remove from heat and transfer to a food processor. Add remaining ingredients and process until smooth.

PER SERVING Calories: 227 | Fat: 20.5g | Protein: 3.5g | Sodium: 456mg | Fiber: 1.6g | Carbohydrates: 5.8g | Sugar: 2.1g

Smooth Operator

Using a food processor will make this cauliflower perfectly smooth and creamy. If you prefer a chunkier version, use a handheld mixer instead and stop beating when the cauliflower has reached its desired consistency.

Bacon-Wrapped Asparagus

*Don't let the simplicity of this recipe fool you. These bacon-
wrapped asparagus stalks are always a crowd pleaser.*

INGREDIENTS | SERVES 4

12 asparagus spears, ends trimmed

6 slices sugar-free bacon

1. Cut each strip of bacon in half lengthwise.

2. Wrap a piece of bacon around each asparagus spear and secure in place with a toothpick.

3. Grill over medium heat for 10 minutes, or until bacon is crisp, turning each spear over halfway through cooking time.

Help Insulin with Asparagus

Asparagus is loaded with chromium, a trace mineral that enhances the activity of insulin, helping the hormone deliver glucose more efficiently from the bloodstream into your cells.

PER SERVING Calories: 90 | Fat: 5.8g | Protein: 6.9g | Sodium: 291mg | Fiber: 1.0g | Carbohydrates: 2.2g | Sugar: 0.9g

Creamed Brussels Sprouts

*For a cheesier, gooier side dish, add ½ cup of shredded Cheddar cheese
to these Brussels sprouts before you sprinkle on the pork rinds.*

INGREDIENTS | SERVES 4

5 tablespoons unsalted butter, divided

2 cloves garlic, minced

2 cups sliced Brussels sprouts

¾ cup heavy cream

2 tablespoons grated Parmesan cheese

¼ teaspoon salt

¼ teaspoon black pepper

½ cup crushed pork rinds

1. Preheat oven to 350°F.

2. Heat 2 tablespoons butter in a medium skillet over medium-high heat. Add garlic and sauté for 3 minutes. Add Brussels sprouts and continue to sauté until Brussels sprouts are fork tender, about 5 minutes.

3. Transfer Brussels sprouts, garlic, and melted butter to a 9" × 9" baking dish. Add cream, Parmesan cheese, salt, and pepper. Sprinkle pork rinds evenly over the top of Brussels sprouts and top with remaining butter.

4. Cover and bake for 30 minutes. Serve hot.

PER SERVING Calories: 351 | Fat: 31.9g | Protein: 7.7g | Sodium: 348mg | Fiber: 1.7g | Carbohydrates: 6.1g | Sugar: 2.2g

Fried Cauliflower "Rice"

When shredding the cauliflower, process it just enough to create rice-like pieces, but not so much that it begins to blend together. If you process it too long, it will turn into mashed cauliflower.

INGREDIENTS | SERVES 6

1 large head cauliflower (about 6 cups)
2 tablespoons unsalted butter
2 tablespoons sesame oil
4 cloves garlic, minced
2 green onions, chopped
2 tablespoons coconut aminos
½ teaspoon garlic salt
3 large eggs, beaten
1 large avocado, sliced

Skip the Soy

Coconut aminos sauce is a soy-free seasoning alternative made from the sap of coconut blossoms that you can use in place of soy sauce in any of your recipes. There is absolutely no coconut flavor—it tastes just like soy sauce, but unlike soy sauce, which is highly processed and most likely contains GMOs, coconut aminos is GMO-free and contains 17 amino acids, vitamins, and minerals.

1. Break cauliflower into florets and put through a food processor using the grating attachment.

2. In a large wok or skillet, heat butter and sesame oil. Add minced garlic and sauté on medium for 3 minutes.

3. Add cauliflower and sauté for another 5 minutes, stirring frequently, until cauliflower is softened. Add green onions, coconut aminos, garlic salt, and eggs and toss until eggs are cooked.

4. Top with sliced avocado.

PER SERVING Calories: 182 | Fat: 13.4g | Protein: 5.9g | Sodium: 673mg | Fiber: 3.8g | Carbohydrates: 9.4g | Sugar: 2.3g

Turnip Fries

Turnips are often overlooked at the supermarket, but they make a great alternative to carbohydrate-loaded potatoes when making fries.

INGREDIENTS | SERVES 2

2 large turnips, peeled and cut into 2" sticks
2 tablespoons olive oil
4 tablespoons grated Parmesan cheese
¼ teaspoon salt
¼ teaspoon black pepper
¼ teaspoon chili powder

1. Preheat oven to 425°F.

2. Place turnip sticks on foil-lined baking pan in a single layer. Sprinkle olive oil, Parmesan cheese, salt, pepper, and chili powder over turnips and toss to coat.

3. Bake in the oven for 15 minutes, flip fries over, and then bake for another 15 minutes. Serve warm.

PER SERVING Calories: 173 | Fat: 12.4g | Protein: 4.2g | Sodium: 578mg | Fiber: 2.8g | Carbohydrates: 11.2g | Sugar: 5.6g

Roasted Broccoli with Parmesan

If you like your broccoli slightly charred, broil it for a few minutes before you take it out of the oven.

INGREDIENTS | SERVES 6

1 large head broccoli
2 tablespoons olive oil
2 cloves garlic, minced
¼ teaspoon salt
¼ teaspoon black pepper
¼ cup grated Parmesan cheese

1. Preheat oven to 425°F.

2. Cut broccoli into bite-sized pieces and put onto a foil-lined baking sheet.

3. Drizzle olive oil on top of broccoli, add garlic, salt, and pepper, and toss to coat.

4. Spread out in a single layer and bake for 20 minutes, or until broccoli is tender. Add Parmesan cheese and bake for 5 more minutes, or until cheese is melted.

PER SERVING Calories: 69 | Fat: 4.3g | Protein: 3.0g | Sodium: 192mg | Fiber: 1.7g | Carbohydrates: 5.1g | Sugar: 1.1g

Pre-Digested Protein

Parmesan cheese is aged so long that the proteins in it start to break down before it hits your digestive system. Much of the protein in it has already been broken down into peptides and free amino acids before you eat it—making digestion easier on you.

Bacon-Fried Cabbage

Cabbage comes in several varieties including green, red, and napa. For this recipe, you can use any type of cabbage you want. Cabbage newbies may want to go for green cabbage, which is milder in flavor.

INGREDIENTS | SERVES 4

8 slices sugar-free bacon

4 cups chopped cabbage

¼ cup chopped yellow onion

1 teaspoon garlic powder

1 teaspoon black pepper

½ teaspoon salt

1. Fry bacon in large skillet over medium-high heat until crispy, about 10 minutes. Remove bacon from heat and set aside. Allow to cool, then roughly chop.

2. Add chopped cabbage and chopped onion to hot bacon fat and sauté until cabbage is tender, about 8 minutes. Add garlic powder, black pepper, salt, and chopped bacon to cabbage and toss to combine.

PER SERVING Calories: 263 | Fat: 20.9g | Protein: 8.5g | Sodium: 677mg | Fiber: 2.6g | Carbohydrates: 7.7g | Sugar: 3.9g

Avocado and Cilantro Salad

The cilantro in this recipe imparts a clean flavor that gives this dish a wonderful Mexican quality.

INGREDIENTS | SERVES 4

4 medium avocados, diced

½ cup chopped cilantro

2 tablespoons lemon juice

2 tablespoons avocado oil or extra-virgin olive oil

½ small white onion, sliced thinly

½ cup crumbled feta cheese

½ teaspoon salt

½ teaspoon black pepper

⅛ cup sliced pickled jalapeño peppers

Combine all ingredients in a bowl and toss to coat.

PER SERVING Calories: 344 | Fat: 29.2g | Protein: 5.6g | Sodium: 528mg | Fiber: 9.6g | Carbohydrates: 14.3g | Sugar: 1.8g

Buttery Garlic Spinach

This recipe calls for frozen spinach, but you can use fresh spinach in its place if you prefer. Just thoroughly clean and chop the leaves before starting the recipe.

INGREDIENTS | SERVES 4

3 tablespoons unsalted butter

2 cloves garlic, minced

1 (10-ounce) package frozen spinach, thawed

¼ teaspoon garlic salt

¼ teaspoon black pepper

Heat butter in a skillet over medium-high heat. Add garlic and sauté for 3 minutes. Add spinach and stir until wilted. Toss with garlic salt and black pepper.

PER SERVING Calories: 99 | Fat: 8.1g | Protein: 2.8g | Sodium: 176mg | Fiber: 2.1g | Carbohydrates: 3.6g | Sugar: 0.5g

Cole Slaw

You can add this cole slaw to any meal to quickly increase its fat content. Cole slaw goes especially well with bunless burgers.

INGREDIENTS | SERVES 8

¾ cup Homemade Mayonnaise (see recipe in Chapter 5)

¼ cup sour cream

2 tablespoons white vinegar

1 teaspoon celery salt

¼ teaspoon black pepper

2 tablespoons granulated erythritol

1 large head green cabbage, shredded

2 tablespoons chopped yellow onion

1. Combine mayonnaise, sour cream, vinegar, celery salt, black pepper, and granulated erythritol in a large bowl and whisk until combined and the granulated erythritol is dissolved.

2. Add cabbage and onion to bowl and toss until coated.

3. Refrigerate for 30 minutes. Serve chilled.

PER SERVING Calories: 187 | Fat: 17.3g | Protein: 1.8g | Sodium: 131mg | Fiber: 2.1g | Carbohydrates: 8.6g | Sugar: 0.4g | Sugar alcohol: 3.0g

Cheesy Broccoli

Instead of using only broccoli, you can make this dish with a combination of broccoli and cauliflower for some variety.

INGREDIENTS | SERVES 4

6 cups broccoli florets, fresh or frozen
2 tablespoons extra-virgin olive oil
½ teaspoon salt
¼ teaspoon black pepper
2 tablespoons unsalted butter
1 cup heavy cream
1 cup shredded Cheddar cheese
2 tablespoons grated Asiago cheese
¼ teaspoon dry mustard

1. Preheat oven to 400°F.

2. Put broccoli florets on a foil-lined baking sheet and toss with olive oil, salt, and pepper. Bake for 25 minutes or until broccoli is fork tender.

3. While broccoli is cooking, melt butter in a medium saucepan over medium heat. Add cream and bring to a simmer. Reduce heat to low, add Cheddar cheese and Asiago cheese, and whisk until melted. Stir in dry mustard.

4. Remove from heat and pour over broccoli.

PER SERVING Calories: 470 | Fat: 42.1g | Protein: 12.0g | Sodium: 555mg | Fiber: 0.1g | Carbohydrates: 7.8g | Sugar: 1.8g

Chorizo-Stuffed Jalapeños

There is perhaps no better pairing than chorizo with spicy peppers baked into a delicious creamy mound of cheese. The addition of bacon is truly the icing on the cake.

INGREDIENTS | MAKES 6 FAT BOMBS

1 tablespoon olive oil

¼ medium yellow onion, peeled and minced

6 ounces pork chorizo sausage

4 ounces cream cheese, softened to room temperature

3 medium jalapeño peppers, seeded and sliced in half

3 slices bacon, sliced in half horizontally

Why Do Americans Love Jalapeño Poppers?

Although their origin is a bit fuzzy, poppers were speculated to be an American spinoff of the Mexican classic chili rellenos. Nobody can seem to pinpoint who coined the term "poppers" and decided to batter dip, freeze, and commercialize them in the 1980s, but they have been a popular restaurant staple in California restaurants since at least the 1960s.

1. Preheat oven to 375°F.

2. Add olive oil to a medium skillet over medium heat and sauté onion 2 minutes. Add chorizo to pan and cook another 3–5 minutes. Drain mixture.

3. In mixing bowl, whip softened cream cheese with hand mixer until softened. Fold in sausage and onion mixture with a spatula.

4. Stuff each pepper half with sausage mixture.

5. Wrap 1 bacon slice around each stuffed pepper in a spiral motion, covering the cheese mixture underneath.

6. Bake 10–15 minutes or until bacon becomes crispy and cheese mixture underneath bubbles through and turns slightly brown. Serve warm.

PER 1 FAT BOMB Calories: 233 | Fat: 18.9g | Protein: 10.0g | Sodium: 515mg | Fiber: 0.3g | Carbohydrates: 2.3g | Sugar: 1.1g

Creamed Spinach

*The combination of Parmesan and Asiago cheeses gives this dish
a strong Italian flavor that's sure to please a crowd.*

INGREDIENTS | SERVES 4

4 tablespoons unsalted butter

3 cloves garlic, minced

¼ cup minced shallots

1 (10-ounce) package frozen spinach, thawed

½ cup heavy cream

½ cup grated Parmesan cheese

¼ cup grated Asiago cheese

½ teaspoon salt

¼ teaspoon black pepper

1. Heat butter over medium-high heat and add garlic and shallots. Sauté for 3 minutes. Add thawed and drained spinach and stir in heavy cream.

2. Stir in Parmesan and Asiago cheeses and continue stirring until melted. Season with salt and pepper. Serve hot.

PER SERVING Calories: 308 | Fat: 25.8g | Protein: 8.7g | Sodium: 645mg | Fiber: 2.5g | Carbohydrates: 8.2g | Sugar: 2.1g

Mexican Cauliflower "Rice"

*The fire-roasted tomatoes give this dish a slightly spicy, smoky flavor, but if you
can't find them, you can use regular diced tomatoes in their place.*

INGREDIENTS | SERVES 4

6 cups cauliflower florets

3 tablespoons unsalted butter

½ (14.5-ounce) can fire-roasted diced tomatoes

¼ cup chopped cilantro

1 large avocado, chopped

½ cup sour cream

1. Shred cauliflower with a food processor using the grating attachment.

2. Heat butter in a large skillet over medium-high heat and add shredded cauliflower. Sauté until tender, about 7–8 minutes. Add diced tomatoes and cilantro and stir until combined.

3. Divide into 4 servings and top each serving with ¼ chopped avocado and 2 tablespoons sour cream.

PER SERVING Calories: 241 | Fat: 18.0g | Protein: 4.9g | Sodium: 196mg | Fiber: 6.4g | Carbohydrates: 14.4g | Sugar: 5.3g

Garlicky Green Beans

Save time by buying a bag of green beans that has already been washed, cleaned, and trimmed for you.

INGREDIENTS | SERVES 4

1 pound green beans, trimmed
¼ cup unsalted butter
2 cloves garlic, minced
⅓ cup toasted pine nuts
¼ teaspoon salt
¼ teaspoon black pepper

1. Bring large pot of water to a boil. Add green beans and cook until fork tender, 4–5 minutes.

2. Heat butter in a large skillet over medium heat. Add garlic and pine nuts and sauté for 3 minutes or until pine nuts are lightly browned.

3. Transfer green beans to skillet, add salt and pepper, and toss until coated.

PER SERVING Calories: 210 | Fat: 17.4g | Protein: 3.6g | Sodium: 152mg | Fiber: 3.2g | Carbohydrates: 9.0g | Sugar: 3.7g

Cheesy Bacon Brussels Sprouts

Brussels sprouts may be one of the most hated vegetables in America, but when you try them sautéed in bacon fat, they'll jump to the top of your list of favorites.

INGREDIENTS | SERVES 4

6 slices sugar-free bacon
1 pound Brussels sprouts, trimmed and cut in half lengthwise
1½ cups shredded pepper jack cheese

Benefits of Brussels Sprouts

Serving for serving, Brussels sprouts contain significantly more vitamin C than an orange. They're also rich in vitamin A, beta-carotene, folic acid, iron, magnesium, selenium, and fiber. Chinese medicine practitioners often recommend Brussels sprouts to help with digestive troubles.

1. Cook bacon in a large skillet over medium-high heat until crispy, about 10 minutes.

2. Remove bacon from pan and set aside. Add Brussels sprouts to hot pan and sauté until fork tender, about 8 minutes.

3. Chop bacon into small pieces and add to Brussels sprouts. Sprinkle cheese on top and stir until melted. Serve hot.

PER SERVING Calories: 283 | Fat: 18.9g | Protein: 18 .8g | Sodium: 566mg | Fiber: 3.2g | Carbohydrates: 8.9g | Sugar: 2.1g

Stuffed Baby Bella Mushroom Caps

Mushrooms make an excellent holder for meat-based fat bombs. These bombs use a hearty and earthy-tasting mushroom filled with the proper proportion of tangy cheese and savory sausage.

INGREDIENTS | MAKES 8 FAT BOMBS

1 tablespoon olive oil

8 baby bella mushrooms, cleaned and stems removed

¼ teaspoon salt

4 ounces pork breakfast sausage, at room temperature

4 tablespoons chopped parsley

½ cup shredded Parmesan cheese

1. Preheat oven to 350°F.

2. Rub olive oil on mushroom tops and sprinkle lightly with salt.

3. Mix sausage, parsley, and cheese in a small mixing bowl.

4. Stuff each mushroom cap until mixture forms a nice cap slightly above the mushroom ribbing.

5. Bake on a cookie sheet roughly 20 minutes until sausage becomes browned and cheese browns slightly. Serve warm.

PER 1 FAT BOMB Calories: 90 | Fat: 6.8g | Protein: 5.2g | Sodium: 257mg | Fiber: 0.2g | Carbohydrates: 1.7g | Sugar: 0.5g

Bacon Lovin' Onion Bites

This recipe will be a hit with the boys on game day or as a healthy appetizer for a gathering. But that doesn't mean you can't enjoy them on a daily basis!

INGREDIENTS | MAKES 4 FAT BOMBS

1 large yellow onion
½ pound 80/20 ground chuck
¼ cup diced yellow onion
¼ cup diced mushrooms
2 tablespoons freshly chopped Italian parsley
¼ teaspoon salt
⅛ teaspoon cayenne pepper
1 large egg
½ teaspoon Worcestershire sauce
1 tablespoon coconut oil, melted
12 slices bacon
1 tablespoon butter, melted
1 teaspoon powdered stevia

1. Preheat oven to 350°F.

2. Cut off top and bottom of large onion. Peel skin. Cut in half vertically. Save 4 of the outside layers for a total of 8 halves.

3. In a large mixing bowl, mix meat with diced vegetables, parsley, salt, and cayenne.

4. In a small mixing bowl, whisk together egg, Worcestershire sauce, and coconut oil. Pour over meat mixture and knead together.

5. Form meat into 4 equal-sized balls and surround each ball with 2 onion halves. Wrap each ball with 3 pieces bacon and secure with toothpicks if needed to keep the balls together.

6. Place balls into a shallow baking tray.

7. In a small bowl or cup, mix melted butter and stevia and brush over bacon-wrapped onion balls.

8. Bake 25–30 minutes until bacon is crisped and browned. Serve warm.

PER 1 FAT BOMB Calories: 374 | Fat: 29.9g | Protein: 23.1g | Sodium: 788mg | Fiber: 0.4g | Carbohydrates: 2.4g | Sugar: 0.8g

Meaty Zucchini Balls with Yogurt Sauce

Meatballs take on a refreshing flavor with the omission of bread crumbs and the use of bright and flavorful zucchini and mint. Adding a yogurt sauce gives these meatballs an added Mediterranean flair.

INGREDIENTS | MAKES 12 MEATBALLS

Yogurt Sauce

¼ cup sour cream

⅓ cup plain yogurt

½ tablespoon lemon juice

1 medium clove garlic, minced

1 tablespoon olive oil

¼ teaspoon salt

⅛ teaspoon freshly ground black pepper

Meatballs

1 large egg

½ pound 80/20 ground chuck

½ medium zucchini, grated

2 green onions, thinly sliced

1 tablespoon chopped fresh mint leaves

1 tablespoon chopped fresh basil

1 large clove garlic, minced

½ teaspoon paprika

½ teaspoon salt

¼ teaspoon cayenne pepper

¼ teaspoon freshly ground black pepper

1 tablespoon coconut oil

1. Preheat oven to 350°F.

2. Mix all ingredients for yogurt sauce in a small mixing bowl. Chill at least 1 hour.

3. Whisk egg for meatballs in a small bowl. In a separate medium bowl, mix remaining meatball ingredients thoroughly, adding whisked egg last to bind.

4. Form meat mixture into 12 equal balls and place into a muffin tin to bake. Place tin on top of a cookie sheet and put in oven. Bake meatballs 30 minutes or until meat is browned and internal temperature is at least 165°F.

5. Serve warm with yogurt sauce to dip.

PER 1 MEATBALL WITH SAUCE Calories: 86 | Fat: 7.4g | Protein: 4.2g | Sodium: 169mg | Fiber: 0.2g | Carbohydrates: 1.3g | Sugar: 0.8g

CHAPTER 8

Vegetarian

Peanut Butter Pancakes

If you want to switch it up, swap out the peanut butter in this recipe for cashew butter, almond butter, or sunflower seed butter.

INGREDIENTS | SERVES 4 (2 PANCAKES EACH)

½ cup cream cheese, softened
4 large eggs
⅓ cup unsalted, unsweetened peanut butter
½ teaspoon vanilla extract
¼ teaspoon ground cinnamon
1 tablespoon coconut oil

1. Beat cream cheese, eggs, and peanut butter together in a medium mixing bowl. Stir in vanilla and cinnamon until mixture is smooth.

2. Melt coconut oil in a large skillet and pour ⅛ of the peanut butter mixture into the hot pan. Cook for 3–4 minutes and then flip. Cook for another 2–3 minutes. Repeat until all batter is cooked.

PER SERVING Calories: 328 | Fat: 26.7g | Protein: 13.3g | Sodium: 176mg | Fiber: 2.1g | Carbohydrates: 6.4g | Sugar: 2.5g

Cinnamon Noatmeal

This noatmeal provides the comfort of a hot bowl of oatmeal without all the carbohydrates or sugars found in boxed varieties.

INGREDIENTS | SERVES 4

3½ cups full-fat canned coconut milk
¼ cup cream cheese
⅔ cup flaxseed meal
⅔ cup chia seeds
⅔ cup shredded unsweetened coconut flakes
2 teaspoons ground cinnamon
½ teaspoon ground nutmeg
½ teaspoon vanilla extract
5 tablespoons granulated erythritol

1. Put coconut milk and cream cheese in a large saucepan and heat over medium heat until cream cheese is melted and mixture starts to simmer.

2. Turn heat to medium-low and add flaxseed meal, chia seeds, and coconut flakes to saucepan. Stir until ingredients are mixed together. Add cinnamon, nutmeg, vanilla extract, and erythritol. Serve hot.

PER SERVING Calories: 756 | Fat: 66.7g | Protein: 14.2g | Sodium: 86mg | Fiber: 15.7g | Carbohydrates: 42.6g | Sugar: 1.5g | Sugar alcohol: 15.0g

Coconut Yogurt

A lot of commercial yogurts are full of sugar and artificial ingredients that almost completely negate any health benefits you'd get from them. It's easy to make your own yogurt at home with only two ingredients.

INGREDIENTS | SERVES 4

2 cans (13.5-ounce each) full-fat coconut milk

2 probiotic capsules

Picking a Probiotic

There are so many probiotics available that it can be difficult to know which one to pick. Choose a probiotic that contains at least seven different strains of bacteria and at least 5 billion organisms per dose. Make sure to store the probiotic per the manufacturer's instructions, as exposure to high heat and too much light can kill the bacteria, rending the probiotic useless.

1. Pour coconut milk into a blender. Open probiotic capsules and dump contents into blender. Blend until smooth.

2. Pour mixture into 4 separate sealable oven-safe containers. Seal containers and place on a baking sheet.

3. Put baking sheet with containers in the oven and turn oven light on. Keep the oven door closed and leave containers in the oven for 24 hours.

4. Store in the refrigerator for up to 7 days.

PER SERVING Calories: 376 | Fat: 38.3g | Protein: 3.9g | Sodium: 24mg | Fiber: 0.0g | Carbohydrates: 5.4g | Sugar: 0.0g

Vegetable Omelet

This combination of eggs and vegetables is the perfect pair for a ketogenic dieter. It provides quality fat and a good source of protein, and is loaded with vitamins and minerals.

INGREDIENTS | SERVES 4

2 tablespoons coconut oil

¼ cup chopped white onion

1 small zucchini, diced

¼ cup diced green pepper

2 cups fresh spinach

6 large eggs

¼ cup coconut cream

¼ teaspoon salt

¼ teaspoon black pepper

½ cup shredded Cheddar cheese

1 large avocado, chopped

1. Put coconut oil in a large skillet and heat over medium heat. When skillet is hot, add onions, zucchini, and green pepper. Sauté until soft, about 5 minutes. Add spinach and sauté until wilted.

2. Whisk eggs, coconut cream, salt, and pepper together in a medium bowl. Pour egg mixture over sautéed vegetables and cook for 2–3 minutes, or until eggs begin to set. Lift the edges of the eggs with a spatula and tilt the skillet so that uncooked egg moves to the side of the pan. Continue cooking for about 3 minutes or until egg is almost fully set.

3. Add shredded cheese to half of the egg and flip the other side over with a spatula.

4. Let the omelet cook for 2–3 more minutes or until cheese is melted. Remove from heat and top with chopped avocado.

PER SERVING Calories: 323 | Fat: 24.8g | Protein: 14.5g | Sodium: 361mg | Fiber: 3.3g | Carbohydrates: 7.0g | Sugar: 2.3g

Crustless Quiche

Quiches are a ketogenic diet staple. They're easy to prepare and they store well, so you can make them in bulk and have a piece for breakfast all week.

INGREDIENTS | SERVES 8

12 large eggs
1 cup heavy cream
2 tablespoons olive oil
⅓ cup mushrooms
1 cup fresh spinach
¼ cup chopped white onions
½ cup chopped broccoli
1 teaspoon black pepper
½ teaspoon salt
½ teaspoon garlic powder
2 cups shredded Cheddar cheese
2 cups shredded Colby jack cheese

Make It "Muffins"

If you want to make this quiche more travel-friendly, pour an equal amount of the egg mixture into each well of a regular-sized muffin tin. You'll end up with 12 individual servings that you can just grab and go.

1. Preheat oven to 350°F.

2. Whisk eggs and heavy cream together in a medium bowl and set aside.

3. Heat olive oil in a medium skillet over medium-high heat and add vegetables. Sauté vegetables until soft and spinach is wilted, 3–4 minutes.

4. Add vegetables, black pepper, salt, and garlic powder to egg mixture and whisk together.

5. Butter the bottom of a 9" × 13" baking pan and sprinkle 2 cups of cheese along bottom of pan. Pour egg mixture over cheese and sprinkle remaining cheese on top.

6. Bake for 25 minutes or until egg is set.

PER SERVING Calories: 472 | Fat: 37.1g | Protein: 24.0g | Sodium: 620mg | Fiber: 0.4g | Carbohydrates: 3.9g | Sugar: 1.7g

Tomato Cream Soup

Finish this recipe off with a dollop of sour cream, which, in addition to giving each spoonful a nice creamy texture, also ups the fat content.

INGREDIENTS | SERVES 4

½ cup butter
1 medium yellow onion, diced
2 cloves garlic, minced
1 (28-ounce) can whole peeled tomatoes
3 cups vegetable broth
1 cup full-fat coconut milk
¼ cup chopped fresh basil
¼ cup chopped fresh parsley
½ teaspoon salt
¼ teaspoon black pepper

1. Heat butter in a medium stockpot over medium-high heat. Add onion and garlic and sauté until translucent, 3–4 minutes.

2. Add remaining ingredients and stir until combined.

3. Insert an immersion blender and blend all ingredients together until smooth.

4. Turn heat to high and bring to a boil. Once soup starts boiling, reduce heat and allow to simmer for 30 minutes. Serve hot.

PER SERVING Calories: 367 | Fat: 33.1g | Protein: 3.5g | Sodium: 1,236mg | Fiber: 4.4g | Carbohydrates: 13.8g | Sugar: 7.6g

Stuffed Portobello Mushrooms

You can easily change the flavor of this recipe by using blue cheese, Gorgonzola cheese, or goat cheese in place of feta.

INGREDIENTS | SERVES 4

8 large portobello mushrooms
1 cup crumbled feta cheese
2 cups chopped fresh spinach
¼ cup chopped fresh oregano
2 tablespoons extra-virgin olive oil

The Power of Portobello

Portobello mushrooms are low in carbohydrates and loaded with essential vitamins and minerals, such as thiamine, magnesium, vitamin B_6, and iron, making them the perfect vehicle for getting quality sources of fat and protein.

1. Preheat oven to 350°F.

2. Remove stems from mushrooms and chop stems into small pieces. Put chopped stems, feta, spinach, and oregano in a medium bowl and toss to combine.

3. Brush each mushroom inside and out with olive oil and then stuff with feta mixture. Put on a baking rack and bake for 20 minutes or until mushroom is soft and cheese is melted.

PER SERVING Calories: 99 | Fat: 7.2g | Protein: 4.7g | Sodium: 185mg | Fiber: 1.3g | Carbohydrates: 4.3g | Sugar: 2.9g

Chocolate Chia Pudding

Chia pudding is so simple and versatile, you can make it with just about any combination of ingredients. Try sunflower butter in place of coconut butter and ½ cup brewed coffee in place of ½ cup of the coconut cream.

INGREDIENTS | SERVES 2

1 cup full-fat coconut cream

3 tablespoons unsweetened cocoa powder

2 tablespoons granulated erythritol

¼ cup coconut butter

3 tablespoons chia seeds

1. Put all ingredients except chia seeds in a blender and blend until smooth.

2. Transfer to a sealable container and add chia seeds. Shake to combine.

3. Refrigerate for 8 hours or until chia seeds have absorbed enough liquid to turn mixture into a pudding-like consistency. Serve chilled.

PER SERVING Calories: 553 | Fat: 49.6g | Protein: 6.2g | Sodium: 33mg | Fiber: 12.4g | Carbohydrates: 35.3g | Sugar: 6.1g | Sugar alcohol: 12.0g

Ch-ch-ch-chia

A single ounce of chia seeds contains 9 grams of fat (5 of which are omega-3s) and 4 grams of protein. There are 12 grams of carbohydrates in an ounce, but since 11 of them come from fiber, an ounce of chia seeds clocks in at only 1 net carb, making them a ketogenic diet superfood.

Avocado and Walnut Salad

You can whip up this salad in a flash. Add a few cheese crumbles for a higher fat content.

INGREDIENTS | SERVES 6

2 medium limes

6 large avocados, cubed

2 cups walnut pieces

1 cup cherry tomatoes, halved

½ cup sliced black olives

1 tablespoon extra-virgin olive oil

¼ teaspoon salt

¼ teaspoon black pepper

In a bowl, squeeze juice from limes over avocados. Add remaining ingredients and toss until combined.

PER SERVING Calories: 528 | Fat: 46.9g | Protein: 9.1g | Sodium: 191mg | Fiber: 12.7g | Carbohydrates: 19.8g | Sugar: 2.3g

Coffee Coconut Berry Smoothie

For a different flavor, use blueberries or blackberries (or a combination of all three) in place of the raspberries.

INGREDIENTS | SERVES 2

1 cup full-fat canned coconut milk

1 cup brewed coffee

2 tablespoons unsweetened cocoa powder

¼ cup frozen raspberries

1 tablespoon granulated erythritol

2 tablespoons sugar-free cashew butter

Put all ingredients in a blender and blend until smooth.

PER SERVING Calories: 338 | Fat: 30.9g | Protein: 6.5g | Sodium: 19mg | Fiber: 3.5g | Carbohydrates: 18.8g | Sugar: 0.9g | Sugar alcohol: 6.0g

Frozen Coconut White Chocolate

What this bomb lacks in color it more than makes up for in taste. This treat is a must make for any true lover of coconut.

INGREDIENTS | MAKES 12 FAT BOMBS

¼ cup coconut oil

¼ cup cocoa butter

1 teaspoon vanilla extract

12 drops liquid stevia

1 tablespoon unsweetened shredded coconut

1. Combine coconut oil, cocoa butter, vanilla, and stevia in a small saucepan over medium heat, stirring frequently until ingredients have melted. Turn off heat.

2. Add coconut and stir well to combine.

3. Pour mixture into 12 molds of a silicone-bottomed ice cube tray or silicone candy mold tray until about ¾ full.

4. Freeze until set. Serve from freezer.

PER 1 FAT BOMB Calories: 82 | Fat: 8.9g | Protein: 0.0g | Sodium: 0mg | Fiber: 0.1g | Carbohydrates: 0.2g | Sugar: 0.1g

Creamy Spaghetti Squash

If you want to reduce the carbohydrate count of this dish, replace the spaghetti squash with lightly sautéed zucchini noodles.

INGREDIENTS | SERVES 6

1 small spaghetti squash

3 tablespoons olive oil, divided

½ teaspoon salt

¾ cup cream cheese

¼ cup sour cream

½ cup full-fat canned coconut milk

½ cup heavy cream

⅓ cup grated Parmesan cheese

2 tablespoons grated Asiago cheese

½ teaspoon onion powder

1 teaspoon dried chives

Keep an Eye on It

Be careful not to overcook spaghetti squash. When you do, the flesh turns mushy and loses its spaghetti-like quality. Cook just until fork tender.

1. Preheat oven to 400°F.

2. Carefully cut spaghetti squash in half lengthwise and scoop out the seeds. Brush 2 tablespoons of olive oil over flesh of spaghetti squash and sprinkle salt on top. Place on baking pan, cut side up, and bake for 45 minutes or until squash is fork tender.

3. Scrape squash out of shell with a fork and put in a medium bowl.

4. Add remaining tablespoon of olive oil to a medium saucepan and heat over medium heat. Add cream cheese to saucepan and stir until melted. Add sour cream, coconut milk, heavy cream, cheeses, and onion powder to saucepan, stirring frequently until sauce is bubbling. Remove from heat and pour over spaghetti squash. Toss to coat. Sprinkle chives on top.

PER SERVING Calories: 348 | Fat: 29.7g | Protein: 5.7g | Sodium: 460mg | Fiber: 1.8g | Carbohydrates: 11.9g | Sugar: 5.1g

Cauliflower Casserole

*If you prefer a thicker casserole, you can replace half of the sour cream
in this recipe with equal parts softened cream cheese.*

INGREDIENTS | SERVES 4

6 cups cauliflower florets

¼ cup heavy cream

2 tablespoons butter

¼ teaspoon garlic powder

¼ teaspoon onion powder

⅛ teaspoon paprika

½ teaspoon salt

¼ teaspoon black pepper

1½ cups shredded Cheddar cheese, divided

½ cup fire-roasted diced tomatoes

½ cup sour cream

2 tablespoons diced fresh jalapeños

½ cup sliced black olives

1. Preheat oven to 350°F.

2. Bring a large pot of water to a boil and add cauliflower florets. Boil until fork tender, about 8 minutes. Drain and transfer cauliflower to a food processor or blender. Add heavy cream, butter, garlic powder, onion powder, paprika, salt, and pepper and process until smooth. Add ½ cup of cheese and stir until combined.

3. Pour cauliflower mixture into a 9" × 9" baking pan and spread out evenly. Spread diced tomatoes on top of cauliflower and sour cream on top of tomatoes. Sprinkle with remaining cheese, jalapeños, and olives.

4. Bake for 45 minutes or until cheese is melted and casserole is bubbling. Allow to cool before serving.

PER SERVING Calories: 398 | Fat: 30.0g | Protein: 14.7g | Sodium: 883mg | Fiber: 4.4g | Carbohydrates: 12.9g | Sugar: 5.3g

Zoodles with Avocado Pesto

Traditionally, pesto is made with pine nuts, but for a different flavor you can replace the pine nuts with raw, unsalted walnuts.

INGREDIENTS | SERVES 4

4 large zucchini

2 medium avocados, divided

2 cups chopped fresh basil

1 tablespoon lemon juice

2 cloves garlic

½ cup plus 2 tablespoons extra-virgin olive oil, divided

½ teaspoon salt

¼ teaspoon black pepper

½ cup grated Parmesan cheese

½ cup pine nuts

1 cup kalamata olives

Show Olives Some Love

The monounsaturated fats found in olives have been shown to encourage weight loss by breaking down the fats inside your fat cells and reducing insulin sensitivity. At only 1 gram of carbohydrates for 5 olives, they are a perfect ketogenic diet treat.

1. Cut zucchini into long strips using a vegetable peeler or a spiralizer. Set zucchini "noodles" aside on a paper towel and allow them to sweat.

2. Peel 1 avocado, remove the pit, and scoop out flesh. Add avocado to a blender, along with basil, lemon juice, garlic, ½ cup olive oil, salt, black pepper, and Parmesan cheese and process until smooth.

3. Heat 2 tablespoons olive oil in a large skillet over medium heat. Add zucchini noodles and sauté until softened, but still firm, about 4 minutes. Pour sauce into skillet, along with pine nuts and kalamata olives, and toss to coat zucchini.

4. Remove from heat. Slice remaining avocado and add to zucchini mixture. Toss to combine.

PER SERVING Calories: 714 | Fat: 60.8g | Protein: 11.4g | Sodium: 1,289mg | Fiber: 11.2g | Carbohydrates: 23.2g | Sugar: 8.6g

Baked Zucchini

This baked zucchini dish gives traditional lasagna a run for its money. Increase its nutritional content by adding some mushrooms and sautéed spinach.

INGREDIENTS | SERVES 4

2 tablespoons extra-virgin olive oil
½ cup chopped yellow onion
4 medium zucchini, julienned
1½ cups shredded mozzarella cheese, divided
½ cup full-fat ricotta cheese
2 tablespoons cream cheese, cubed
1¼ cups Marinara Sauce (see recipe in Chapter 5)
2 cloves garlic, minced
¼ cup chopped fresh basil
¼ cup chopped fresh oregano
½ teaspoon salt
½ teaspoon black pepper

1. Preheat oven to 350°F.

2. Heat olive oil in a large skillet over medium heat and add onion. Sauté until translucent, about 3 minutes, then add zucchini. Sauté for another 4 minutes or until zucchini is softened, but still firm.

3. Add ½ cup mozzarella cheese, ricotta cheese, cream cheese, marinara, garlic, basil, oregano, salt, and pepper to the pan. Bring to a simmer and remove from heat once cream cheese is melted.

4. Transfer to an 8" × 8" baking dish. Top with remaining mozzarella and bake for 15 minutes or until cheese is melted and casserole is bubbling.

PER SERVING Calories: 357 | Fat: 24.5g | Protein: 17.0g | Sodium: 1,458mg | Fiber: 3.9g | Carbohydrates: 16.0g | Sugar: 9.4g

Ricotta-Stuffed Eggplant

The best eggplants are those that are firm and shiny without any broken skin. Smaller eggplants also tend to be less bitter than larger ones, so keep that in mind when choosing eggplants for this recipe.

INGREDIENTS | SERVES 4

2 small eggplants
¼ cup extra-virgin olive oil, divided
½ teaspoon salt
¼ teaspoon black pepper
2 cloves garlic, minced
2 tablespoons minced shallots
1 (8-ounce) container full-fat ricotta cheese
½ cup shredded mozzarella cheese

Male versus Female

Did you know that there are male and female eggplants? The male eggplants have fewer seeds than the female eggplants, so they tend to be less bitter. You can determine the sex of an eggplant by looking at the indentation on the bottom. If the indentation is shallow and round, it's a male; if the indentation is deep and more rectangular, it's a female.

1. Preheat oven to 350°F.

2. Cut eggplants in half and scoop out some of the insides to create a bowl. Brush bowls with 2 tablespoons of olive oil and sprinkle with salt and pepper. Dice insides and set aside.

3. Place eggplant halves on a baking sheet, cut side up, and bake for 20 minutes or until eggplant is soft.

4. While eggplant is baking, heat up remaining olive oil in a skillet over medium heat. Add diced eggplant, garlic, and shallots to pan and sauté until soft, about 8 minutes. Remove from heat and allow to cool slightly.

5. Combine cooked eggplant, ricotta, and mozzarella cheese in a bowl. When eggplants are done cooking, fill them with cheese mixture, and return to the oven for 10 minutes or until cheese is melted and bubbly.

PER SERVING Calories: 320 | Fat: 23.2g | Protein: 11.9g | Sodium: 431mg | Fiber: 6.8g | Carbohydrates: 16.4g | Sugar: 8.4g

Avocado Pecan Dressing

This dressing can be used on salads, on shirataki noodles for a pasta salad, or on shirataki rice. The smooth, creamy, and tangy flavor is a nice complement to almost any food.

INGREDIENTS | SERVES 16

½ cup pecans
1 tablespoon green onion, sliced
½ cup olive oil
1 small avocado, pitted and peeled
Juice of 1 lime
¼ teaspoon sea salt
2 tablespoons coconut milk

Helpful Prep Tip

To presoak the pecans, just leave out on the counter overnight in warm water and they will be ready to use in the morning.

1. Soak pecans in a cup of warm water 30 minutes, then drain.

2. In a small food processor, add green onion and process until very fine, about 20 seconds.

3. Add pecans and process until almost a cream, about 30 seconds.

4. Add olive oil and process another 30 seconds until well blended.

5. Add avocado, lime juice, salt, and coconut milk.

6. Process about 30–60 seconds until a smooth cream is formed.

7. Transfer to an airtight container. It will keep in the refrigerator about 3 days.

PER SERVING Calories: 99 | Fat: 10.2g | Protein: 0.5g | Sodium: 37mg | Fiber: 0.9g | Carbohydrates: 1.4g | Sugar: 0.2g

Mixed-Nut Grain-Free Granola Bars

These treats are as tasty as granola bars without any of the grains or sugar. Another excellent addition to consider would be freeze-dried raspberries or blueberries.

INGREDIENTS | MAKES 14 FAT BOMBS

4 ounces pumpkin seeds

4 ounces sunflower seeds

4 ounces coarsely chopped almonds

2 ounces unsweetened shredded coconut

2 ounces coconut oil, melted

4 tablespoons almond butter

1 teaspoon vanilla extract

2 teaspoons cinnamon

⅛ teaspoon salt

3 tablespoons granular Swerve

2 large eggs

1. Preheat oven to 350°F.

2. Place seeds and almonds in food processor and pulse to break them up slightly.

3. Add remaining ingredients and pulse until well combined.

4. Spread mixture into an 8" × 8" silicone baking dish (or a glass dish lightly greased with coconut oil).

5. Bake 20 minutes.

6. Allow bars to cool and cut into 14 equal sections before serving.

PER 1 FAT BOMB Calories: 239 | Fat: 20.7g | Protein: 7.9g | Sodium: 48mg | Fiber: 3.8g | Carbohydrates: 9.9g | Sugar: 1.1g

The Great Granola Debate

While many health-food lovers believe granola to be an excellent nutrient-packed snack, others in the nutrition industry believe otherwise. Traditional granola, though full of fiber and iron from the granola, as well as healthy fats from the seeds and nuts, is also filled with alarming amounts of sugar, making it a less-than-healthy choice.

Cinnamon Roll Bars

With all the flavor of a cinnamon roll and none of the gluten or sugar, this treat is sure to please even the strongest sweet tooth. Enjoy along with Po Cha (Tibetan Butter Tea)—see recipe in Chapter 12—for an added treat.

INGREDIENTS | MAKES 4 FAT BOMBS

1 cup creamed coconut, cut into chunks
1¼ teaspoons cinnamon, divided
2 tablespoons coconut oil
2 tablespoons almond butter

Health Benefits of Cinnamon

Filled with antioxidants, and anti-inflammatory in nature, cinnamon makes an excellent addition to any diet. Cinnamon is known to curb hunger, lower blood pressure, and reduce the risk of heart disease.

1. Line a mini loaf pan with parchment paper or loaf pan liners.

2. Mix creamed coconut and ¼ teaspoon cinnamon with hands thoroughly and press into bottom of loaf pan.

3. Whisk coconut oil, almond butter, and 1 teaspoon cinnamon until combined and spread over creamed coconut layer.

4. Place pan in freezer 10 minutes to set.

5. Cut into 4 equal-sized fat bombs and eat immediately.

PER 1 FAT BOMB Calories: 545 | Fat: 54.4g | Protein: 5.8g | Sodium: 33mg | Fiber: 5.4g | Carbohydrates: 10.4g | Sugar: 0.3g

Frozen Almond Choco-Nut

Although this fat bomb tastes like a familiar candy bar, this knockoff is full of fat and flavor and very low in carbs. This bomb would also be delicious without the added almonds.

INGREDIENTS | MAKES 12 FAT BOMBS

¼ cup coconut oil

¼ cup almond butter

12 drops liquid stevia

2 tablespoons cocoa powder

¼ cup coarsely chopped almonds

1 tablespoon unsweetened shredded coconut

Mounds Sports a Two-Piece

Although not common knowledge to younger generations, Mounds candy bars were originally sold as one piece, not two. Sometime in the 1970s, the creator Peter Paul broke the bar into two pieces, lowered the weight of the candy by an ounce, and raised the price by a nickel.

1. Combine coconut oil, almond butter, and stevia in a small pot over medium heat, stirring frequently until ingredients have melted. Turn off heat.

2. Add cocoa powder and almonds and stir well to combine.

3. Pour mixture into 12 molds of a silicone-bottomed ice cube tray or silicone candy mold tray until about ¾ full.

4. Sprinkle shredded coconut on top of each fat bomb.

5. Freeze until set. Serve from freezer.

PER 1 FAT BOMB Calories: 84 | Fat: 8.1g | Protein: 1.8g | Sodium: 16mg | Fiber: 1.3g | Carbohydrates: 2.2g | Sugar: 0.3g

Frozen Coffee Hazelnut Coconut

Here's another way to enjoy the bold taste of coffee on the go as a delicious cold treat. This bomb is an easy way to replace those expensive sugar-filled iced coffees that are so readily available.

INGREDIENTS | MAKES 12 FAT BOMBS

¼ cup coconut oil
¼ cup almond butter
1 teaspoon instant coffee granules
12 drops liquid stevia
2 tablespoons cocoa powder
12 hazelnuts

1. Combine coconut oil, almond butter, coffee, and stevia in a small saucepan over medium heat, stirring frequently until ingredients have melted. Turn off heat.

2. Add cocoa powder and stir well to combine.

3. Pour mixture into 12 molds of a silicone-bottomed ice cube tray or silicone candy mold tray until about ⅔ full.

4. Place 1 hazelnut into each filled mold.

5. Freeze until set. Serve from freezer.

PER 1 FAT BOMB Calories: 80 | Fat: 7.9g | Protein: 1.6g | Sodium: 16mg | Fiber: 1.1g | Carbohydrates: 2.0g | Sugar: 0.2g

Almond Cookie Popsicles

Sweet and creamy almond flavor, no sugar, and lots of healthy fat. And no dairy, so if you are dairy sensitive you can enjoy this too!

INGREDIENTS | MAKES 8 FAT BOMBS

1½ cups coconut cream, chilled
½ cup almond butter
1 teaspoon vanilla extract
¼ cup erythritol or granular Swerve

1. Place all ingredients in a blender and blend until completely mixed, about 30 seconds.

2. Pour mix into 8 popsicle molds, tapping molds to dislodge air bubbles.

3. Freeze at least 8 hours or overnight.

4. Remove popsicles from molds. If popsicles are hard to remove from containers, run molds under hot water briefly and popsicles will come loose.

PER 1 FAT BOMB Calories: 181 | Fat: 17.0g | Protein: 3.5g | Sodium: 57mg | Fiber: 2.0g | Carbohydrates: 11.1g | Sugar: 2.1g | Sugar alcohol: 6.0g

Coconut Vanilla Popsicles

A simple, clean flavor to please even the most picky eaters. Kids will love this popsicle.

INGREDIENTS | MAKES 8 FAT BOMBS

2 cups unsweetened coconut cream, chilled
¼ cup unsweetened shredded coconut
1 teaspoon vanilla extract
¼ cup erythritol or granular Swerve

1. Place all ingredients in a blender and blend until completely mixed, about 30 seconds.

2. Pour mix into 8 popsicle molds, tapping molds to dislodge air bubbles.

3. Freeze at least 8 hours or overnight.

4. Remove popsicles from molds. If popsicles are hard to remove from containers, run molds under hot water briefly and popsicles will come loose.

PER 1 FAT BOMB Calories: 138 | Fat: 13.7g | Protein: 0.2g | Sodium: 10mg | Fiber: 0.3g | Carbohydrates: 8.7g | Sugar: 2.2g | Sugar alcohol: 6.0g

Dark Chocolate Popsicles

You will be amazed at the smooth, rich, chocolaty flavor of this popsicle. Nobody will ever suspect there is an avocado in there.

INGREDIENTS | MAKES 4 FAT BOMBS

1 medium avocado, pitted and peeled
½ cup coconut cream
⅓ cup cocoa powder
3 tablespoons erythritol or granular Swerve
⅛ teaspoon vanilla extract
⅛ teaspoon salt

1. Place all ingredients in a small food processor or blender and blend until completely mixed, about 30 seconds.

2. Pour mix into 4 popsicle molds, tapping molds to dislodge air bubbles.

3. Freeze at least 8 hours or overnight.

4. Remove popsicles from molds. If popsicles are hard to remove from containers, run molds under hot water briefly and popsicles will come loose.

PER 1 FAT BOMB Calories: 133 | Fat: 11.6g | Protein: 2.1g | Sodium: 81mg | Fiber: 5.0g | Carbohydrates: 17.1g | Sugar: 1.2g | Sugar alcohol: 9.0g

Matcha Popsicles

Creamy, refreshing, and with the energizing qualities of matcha, this is a delicious popsicle for grownups.

INGREDIENTS | MAKES 8 FAT BOMBS

2 cups coconut cream, chilled
2 tablespoons coconut oil
1 teaspoon matcha
¼ cup erythritol or granular Swerve

Green Rocket Fuel

Matcha is a finely ground powder of a specially grown green tea. Matcha is basically a form of whole green tea leaves with extra theanine and chlorophyll. It also contains high levels of catechin antioxidants, and a good amount of caffeine. As matcha contains the whole leaf, you also get fiber and a higher content of nutrients than regular brewed green tea.

1. Place all ingredients in a blender and blend until completely mixed, about 30 seconds.

2. Pour mix into 8 popsicle molds, tapping molds to dislodge air bubbles.

3. Freeze at least 8 hours or overnight.

4. Remove popsicles from molds. If popsicles are hard to remove from containers, run molds under hot water briefly and popsicles will come loose.

PER 1 FAT BOMB Calories: 149 | Fat: 15.2g | Protein: 0.0g | Sodium: 10mg | Fiber: 0.0g | Carbohydrates: 8.0g | Sugar: 2.0g | Sugar alcohol: 6.0g

Salty Almond Butter Cup Fudge

The simple addition of coarse sea salt elevates this fudge to the flavor of a very popular American candy treat. While the cup version of this delicacy is full of sugar and contains dairy, this fudge will satisfy any dairy-free, low-carb, high-fat dieter's sweet tooth.

INGREDIENTS | MAKES 12 FAT BOMBS

½ cup almond butter

½ cup coconut oil

12 drops liquid stevia

3 tablespoons cocoa powder

1 tablespoon vanilla extract

1 teaspoon coarse sea salt

Popularity of the Peanut Butter in Reese's Cups

Many consumers of Reese's Peanut Butter Cups find the taste of the salty filling irreplaceable. Though you can't buy that filling, consumers can buy Reese's branded peanut butter. In the 1990s, Hershey's released their line of Reese's Peanut Butter to compete with the likes of Skippy and Jif. Those following a ketogenic diet should opt to use natural peanut butters instead.

1. Heat a small saucepan over medium heat. Add almond butter and coconut oil and melt.

2. Once melted, add stevia, cocoa powder, and vanilla and stir well to combine.

3. Pour mixture into 12 slots in a silicone candy mold or silicone-bottomed ice cube tray.

4. Sprinkle coarse sea salt on top of each fat bomb.

5. Refrigerate at least 2 hours until set.

PER 1 FAT BOMB Calories: 144 | Fat: 14.1g | Protein: 2.6g | Sodium: 160mg | Fiber: 1.8g | Carbohydrates: 3.3g | Sugar: 0.5g

Toasted Coconut Bark

Although delicious with regular shredded coconut, toasting the shaved coconut meat adds an extra nutty flavor that's hard to beat. The addition of another tropical nut elevates this bark to divine.

INGREDIENTS | SERVES 12

⅓ cup unsweetened coconut flakes
1 cup coconut oil
¼ cup confectioners Swerve
⅔ cup coarsely chopped macadamia nuts

Macadamia Madness

Macadamia nuts have grown so much in popularity that California decided to get in on the growing action in the late 1980s. While the trees take 4–5 years to produce the nuts, they were an excellent investment for the warm climate in the southwestern states. Hawaii, however, is still the largest producer of these tasty nuts.

1. Line an 8" × 8" pan with parchment paper.

2. In a small nonstick pan over medium heat, toast coconut flakes just until they turn light brown. Set aside.

3. Combine coconut oil and sweetener in a small pot over medium heat, stirring frequently until melted. Turn off heat.

4. Add coconut flakes and nuts to pan and stir.

5. Pour mixture into lined pan and spread out with the back of a wooden spoon.

6. Freeze or refrigerate to set bark.

7. Break bark into chunks before serving.

PER SERVING Calories: 220 | Fat: 23.5g | Protein: 0.7g | Sodium: 26mg | Fiber: 0.8g | Carbohydrates: 4.4g | Sugar: 0.4g

CHAPTER 9

Desserts

Pecan-Crusted Cheesecake

The pecan crust in this cheesecake is so good, you'll wonder why you ever made it with graham crackers.

INGREDIENTS | SERVES 12

1 cup pecan halves

½ cup unsalted butter

¾ cup almond meal

½ teaspoon ground cinnamon

1¼ cup erythritol powdered sweetener, divided

16 ounces cream cheese, room temperature

1 cup sour cream, room temperature

4 large eggs, room temperature

2 teaspoons vanilla extract

1 teaspoon lemon juice

½ teaspoon lemon zest

Powerful Pecans

Pecans are one of the most antioxidant-rich tree nuts. They also contain more than 19 vitamins and minerals, including vitamin A, folic acid, magnesium, potassium, and zinc.

1. Preheat oven to 375°F.

2. Place pecans in a food processor and pulse until pecans are crushed.

3. Melt butter in medium saucepan. Add crushed pecans, almond meal, cinnamon, and ¼ cup erythritol to melted butter. Stir until combined.

4. Allow mixture to cool slightly and pour into a 9" pie plate. Press mixture into pie plate so the bottom and sides are adequately covered.

5. Bake in oven until slightly browned, about 10 minutes, then remove.

6. Reduce oven temperature to 325°F.

7. Put cream cheese in a stand mixer and beat until fluffy, about 2 minutes.

8. Add sour cream to cream cheese and beat until incorporated.

9. Add eggs, vanilla, lemon juice, lemon zest, and remaining 1 cup erythritol and beat until smooth.

10. Pour cream cheese mixture on top of pecan crust.

11. Bake for 45 minutes. Cake should still jiggle when you remove it from the oven.

12. Allow to cool, then store in the refrigerator until ready to serve.

PER SERVING Calories: 351 | Fat: 31.4g | Protein: 5.6g | Sodium: 171mg | Fiber: 1.6g | Carbohydrates: 20.1g | Sugar: 2.3g | Sugar alcohol: 15.0g

Chocolate Brownie Cheesecake

Throw a handful or two of nuts into this recipe to increase the unsaturated fat content and make this dessert even more nutritious.

INGREDIENTS | SERVES 12

4 ounces unsweetened chocolate

½ cup unsalted butter

4 large eggs, divided

2¼ cups granulated erythritol, divided

1 teaspoon vanilla extract

½ cup almond flour

½ teaspoon salt

16 ounces cream cheese

¼ cup sour cream

¼ cup full-fat canned coconut milk

½ teaspoon vanilla extract

1. Preheat oven to 325°F.

2. Melt chocolate and butter together in a medium saucepan over low heat.

3. In a large bowl, beat 2 eggs, 1½ cups granulated erythritol, and vanilla extract until combined. Add almond flour and salt. Beat until incorporated. Add chocolate and butter mixture and beat until smooth.

4. Pour brownie mixture into the bottom of a greased 9" springform pan.

5. Bake for 20 minutes, or until a knife inserted in the center of the brownies comes out clean, then remove and reduce oven temperature to 300°F.

6. Beat cream cheese in a stand mixer until fluffy, about 2 minutes.

7. Add sour cream and coconut milk and beat until incorporated. Beat in remaining 2 eggs, remaining ¾ cup granulated erythritol, and vanilla extract.

8. Pour cream cheese mixture over brownie mixture.

9. Bake for 45 minutes. Let cool and store in refrigerator until ready to serve.

PER SERVING Calories: 324 | Fat: 28.0g | Protein: 6.0g | Sodium: 167mg | Fiber: 2.1g | Carbohydrates: 41.7g | Sugar: 1.6g | Sugar alcohol: 36.0g

Lemon Mug Cake with Lemon Icing

Don't skip the zest in this recipe! The small amount of lemon zest really enhances the lemony flavor.

INGREDIENTS | SERVES 2

¾ cup almond flour

3 tablespoons granulated erythritol

½ teaspoon baking powder

⅛ teaspoon salt

Juice and zest of 1 lemon

1 large egg

2 tablespoons butter, melted

2 tablespoons powdered erythritol

½ teaspoon water

½ teaspoon lemon juice

Zest Away

When zesting a lemon, remove only the yellow outer skin. The white part just under the yellow skin has a bitter taste that can be unpleasant. A special kitchen tool called a microplane is available to help make zesting easier.

1. In a medium bowl, mix almond flour, granulated erythritol, baking powder, and salt together. Add lemon juice and zest, egg, and melted butter and whisk until combined.

2. In a small bowl, mix powdered erythritol, water, and lemon juice together.

3. Divide almond flour mixture evenly between 2 microwave-safe mugs.

4. Microwave for 90 seconds each.

5. Drizzle icing mixture on top of each mug cake. Serve warm.

PER SERVING Calories: 247 | Fat: 0.8g | Protein: 3.2g | Sodium: 302mg | Fiber: 4.9g | Carbohydrates: 38.1g | Sugar: 0.6g | Sugar alcohol: 27.0g

Chocolate Mug Cake

This chocolate mug cake is a great way to have a chocolate treat without having to make an entire batch of brownies.

INGREDIENTS | SERVES 2

2 tablespoons unsalted butter, melted

3 tablespoons almond flour

1 tablespoon coconut flour

1 large egg

2 tablespoons granulated erythritol

¼ teaspoon vanilla extract

⅛ teaspoon salt

¾ teaspoon baking powder

1½ tablespoons unsweetened cocoa powder

1. Put all ingredients in a small bowl and whisk until smooth.

2. Split the batter evenly between two microwave-safe mugs.

3. Microwave each mug for 75 seconds or until batter has set.

PER SERVING Calories: 214 | Fat: 18.0g | Protein: 4.6g | Sodium: 372mg | Fiber: 3.9g | Carbohydrates: 19.3g | Sugar: 0.5g | Sugar alcohol: 12.0g

Chocolate Fudge Sauce

This is the perfect chocolate fudge sauce to top off any of your desserts. You can even add it to some full-fat coconut milk and blend for a chocolate milk shake.

INGREDIENTS | SERVES 8

4 ounces cream cheese, softened

4 ounces unsweetened baking chocolate

⅓ cup powdered erythritol

¼ cup heavy cream

½ teaspoon vanilla extract

1. Melt cream cheese and baking chocolate in a double boiler over medium heat, stirring frequently until smooth.

2. Add erythritol and heavy cream and whisk until smooth.

3. Remove from heat and stir in vanilla extract.

4. Serve warm.

PER SERVING Calories: 165 | Fat: 13.8g | Protein: 3.0g | Sodium: 57mg | Fiber: 2.4g | Carbohydrates: 10.9g | Sugar: 0.8g | Sugar alcohol: 6.1g

Chocolate Ice Cream

This recipe calls for the use of an ice-cream maker, but not having one isn't a deal-breaker. Instead of using an ice-cream maker, you can stir the mixture in the bowl every 30–45 minutes while it cools in the refrigerator.

INGREDIENTS | SERVES 4

1 large ripe avocado
1 cup full-fat canned coconut milk
1 cup heavy cream
1 teaspoon vanilla extract
1 cup unsweetened cocoa powder
1 cup granulated erythritol

Make It Your Own

This is a basic chocolate ice cream recipe that you can make your own by adding your own mix-ins. Try unsweetened coconut flakes, dark chocolate shavings, or chopped peanuts.

1. Cut avocado in half and scoop out contents into a medium bowl, excluding the pit. Add coconut milk, heavy cream, and vanilla extract to the bowl. Beat mixture until smooth.

2. Add cocoa powder and granulated erythritol and beat until smooth.

3. Store in a metal bowl in the refrigerator for 6–12 hours, then put mixture into an ice-cream maker, following manufacturer's instructions for use.

4. Serve immediately or store in the freezer until ready to serve.

PER SERVING Calories: 425 | Fat: 39.7g | Protein: 7.2g | Sodium: 36mg | Fiber: 10.3g | Carbohydrates: 66.8g | Sugar: 2.3g | Sugar alcohol: 48.7g

Peanut Butter Cookies

Give these cookies a crunch by using crunchy peanut butter instead of creamy peanut butter or by adding a few handfuls of chopped peanuts.

INGREDIENTS | SERVES 18

1 cup sugar-free peanut butter

¼ cup unsalted butter, softened

1 cup granulated erythritol

1 large egg, lightly beaten

1 teaspoon vanilla extract

½ teaspoon baking soda

¼ teaspoon sea salt

1. Preheat oven to 350°F.

2. In a medium-sized bowl, beat together peanut butter and butter until combined and fluffy.

3. Add granulated erythritol, egg, and vanilla extract and mix until combined.

4. Stir in baking soda and salt.

5. Drop by tablespoonfuls onto an ungreased cookie sheet.

6. Bake for 10 minutes, or until lightly browned.

PER SERVING Calories: 111 | Fat: 9.7g | Protein: 3.9g | Sodium: 71mg | Fiber: 1.3g | Carbohydrates: 13.8g | Sugar: 0.9g | Sugar alcohol: 10.8g

Snickerdoodle Cookies

Change the flavor of these cookies by rolling them in pumpkin pie spice instead of cinnamon before cooking.

INGREDIENTS | SERVES 12

1½ cups almond flour
¼ teaspoon baking soda
⅛ teaspoon salt
½ cup unsalted butter, softened
1 cup plus 2 tablespoons granulated erythritol, divided
1 large egg
1 teaspoon vanilla extract
1 teaspoon ground cinnamon

1. Preheat oven to 350°F.

2. Mix together almond flour, baking soda, and salt in a small mixing bowl.

3. In a separate bowl, beat butter and 1 cup granulated erythritol together until light and fluffy, about 2 minutes. Beat in egg and vanilla.

4. Stir in almond flour mixture.

5. In a separate bowl, mix remaining 2 tablespoons granulated erythritol with cinnamon.

6. Roll dough into 12 balls. Roll balls in cinnamon mixture and place on an ungreased baking sheet.

7. Press down on balls with the palm of your hand or the bottom of a glass to flatten them.

8. Bake for 8 minutes, or until slightly browned.

PER SERVING Calories: 144 | Fat: 13.0g | Protein: 0.6g | Sodium: 57mg | Fiber: 1.6g | Carbohydrates: 21.3g | Sugar: 0.1g | Sugar alcohol: 18.2g

Chocolate Brownies

If you have some calories to spare, top these chocolate brownies with homemade chocolate ice cream and some whipped coconut cream for a decadent sundae.

INGREDIENTS | SERVES 12

1 cup almond flour

4 tablespoons unsweetened cocoa powder

½ teaspoon baking powder

¼ teaspoon salt

¾ cup granulated erythritol

½ cup unsalted butter, melted

3 large eggs

1 teaspoon vanilla extract

1. Preheat oven to 350°F.

2. Mix almond flour, cocoa powder, baking powder, and salt in a small bowl.

3. In a medium bowl, beat granulated erythritol and butter together. Beat in eggs, one at a time, and vanilla.

4. Stir dry ingredients into butter mixture.

5. Pour batter into a greased 8" × 8" baking pan. Bake for 30 minutes, or until a toothpick inserted in the center comes out clean.

PER SERVING Calories: 136 | Fat: 12.1g | Protein: 2.0g | Sodium: 87mg | Fiber: 1.7g | Carbohydrates: 15.2g | Sugar: 0.1g | Sugar alcohol: 12.2g

Mint Chocolate Chip Ice Cream

*When you hear the words "ice cream," avocados may not be the first thing that comes to mind,
but they give this recipe a rich, creamy texture and you won't even be able to taste them.*

INGREDIENTS | SERVES 2

2 large ripe avocados

1 (13.5-ounce) can full-fat coconut milk

½ cup granulated erythritol

1 teaspoon vanilla extract

½ teaspoon peppermint extract

2 squares 90% dark chocolate

No Ice-Cream Maker?
No Worries!

Even if you don't have an ice-cream maker,
you can still enjoy this ice cream. Pour the
mixed ingredients in a stainless steel bowl
and put in the freezer for about 20 minutes. Once the edges of the mixture start
to freeze, whisk the mixture rapidly until
smooth and creamy. Repeat this every
20–30 minutes until ice cream forms.

1. Cut avocados in half and scoop out flesh into a
   medium steel mixing bowl. Add coconut milk and beat
   until smooth. Add granulated erythritol, vanilla extract,
   and peppermint extract. Beat until smooth.

2. Grate chocolate with a handheld grater and fold
   shavings into cream mixture.

3. Pour liquid into an ice-cream maker, following
   manufacturer's instructions.

4. Serve immediately or store in the freezer until ready to
   serve.

PER SERVING Calories: 782 | Fat: 67.9g | Protein: 8.7g | Sodium:
40mg | Fiber: 12.3g | Carbohydrates: 78.5g | Sugar: 7.6g | Sugar
alcohol: 48.7g

Pistachio Pudding

After you try this homemade pistachio pudding, you will never look at the boxed stuff again. It's creamy, delicious, and good for you.

INGREDIENTS | SERVES 4

10 ounces cream cheese, softened
⅓ cup heavy whipping cream
8 drops liquid stevia
1 tablespoon sugar-free pistachio syrup
½ cup crushed pistachios

Pop Some Pistachios

One-half cup of pistachios provides 5 percent of your copper needs for the entire day. Copper is an essential trace mineral that plays an important role in metabolism and the formation of red blood cells.

1. Beat cream cheese in a medium bowl until light and fluffy, about 2 minutes. Add whipping cream and beat until smooth.

2. Beat in stevia and pistachio syrup.

3. Stir in crushed pistachios.

4. Refrigerate until firm, about 45 minutes to 1 hour.

5. Serve chilled.

PER SERVING Calories: 400 | Fat: 34.3g | Protein: 7.6g | Sodium: 273mg | Fiber: 1.5g | Carbohydrates: 8.3g | Sugar: 2.8g | Sugar alcohol: 0.4g

Walnut Blondies

These walnut blondies are divine warm with a scoop of ice cream or a dollop of Coconut Whipped Cream on top (see recipe in this chapter).

INGREDIENTS | SERVES 16

1 cup unsalted butter
1 cup granulated erythritol
1 large egg
1 teaspoon vanilla extract
⅛ teaspoon salt
1¼ cups almond flour
¾ cup crushed walnuts
2 squares 90% dark chocolate, crushed

1. Preheat oven to 350°F. Grease an 8" × 8" baking pan.

2. Melt butter in a medium microwave-safe mixing bowl. Add granulated erythritol and beat until smooth. Beat in egg and vanilla.

3. Stir in salt and almond flour. Fold in walnuts and dark chocolate pieces.

4. Bake for 20 minutes or until a toothpick inserted in the center comes out clean.

PER SERVING Calories: 207 | Fat: 19.2g | Protein: 1.6g | Sodium: 24mg | Fiber: 1.7g | Carbohydrates: 16.3g | Sugar: 1.1g | Sugar alcohol: 12.2g

Chocolate Chip Cookies

Being on a ketogenic diet doesn't mean you have to miss out on classic chocolate chip cookies. This version rivals the real thing, but with none of the unhealthy refined sugar.

INGREDIENTS | SERVES 16

½ cup unsalted butter, softened
¼ cup granulated erythritol
1 teaspoon vanilla extract
2 large eggs
1 cup almond flour
⅓ cup coconut flour
1 teaspoon baking powder
¼ teaspoon salt
4 ounces unsweetened baking chocolate, chopped

1. Preheat oven to 350°F.

2. In a medium bowl, beat butter until light and fluffy, about 2 minutes. Beat in erythritol, vanilla, and eggs until smooth.

3. In a small bowl, combine almond flour, coconut flour, baking powder, and salt.

4. Fold flour mixture into egg mixture. Add chocolate chunks.

5. Drop by the tablespoonful onto a cookie sheet. Bake for 10 minutes.

PER SERVING Calories: 150 | Fat: 12.5g | Protein: 2.2g | Sodium: 83mg | Fiber: 2.8g | Carbohydrates: 8.0g | Sugar: 0.3g | Sugar alcohol: 3.0g

Coconut Whipped Cream

Don't cut corners with this recipe. Making sure the coconut milk is fully chilled before whipping can make the difference between ending up with whipped cream or a sloppy mess.

INGREDIENTS | SERVES 12

1 (13.5-ounce) can full-fat coconut milk
3 teaspoons powdered erythritol
½ teaspoon vanilla extract

Find the Right Milk

Unfortunately, there is a bit of inconsistency when it comes to canned coconut milk. Some brands whip up nicely while others seem to fall flat. If you've followed the directions closely and still can't get a nice whipped cream, try a different brand of coconut milk—and make sure it's full fat.

1. Refrigerate can of coconut milk for 24 hours.

2. Place small mixing bowl and beaters into freezer for 20 minutes.

3. Carefully remove the can of coconut milk from the refrigerator, making sure not to shake or tip it. Open can and use a spoon to scoop out the coconut cream that has risen to the top. Put coconut cream in chilled bowl.

4. Beat the coconut cream with a handheld beater until peaks begin to form, about 3 minutes.

5. Add in powdered erythritol and vanilla and beat until combined.

6. Serve immediately.

PER SERVING Calories: 63 | Fat: 6.4g | Protein: 0.6g | Sodium: 4mg | Fiber: 0.0g | Carbohydrates: 1.7g | Sugar: 0.0g | Sugar alcohol: 0.8g

Pumpkin Donut Holes

These donut holes are the perfect bite-sized treat, especially around the holidays. Just make sure to use pure pumpkin purée instead of premade pumpkin pie filling, which is loaded with sugar.

INGREDIENTS | SERVES 24

2 cups almond flour

¼ cup granulated erythritol

½ teaspoon salt

1 teaspoon baking soda

1 tablespoon pumpkin pie seasoning

2 large eggs

¾ cup canned pumpkin purée

¼ cup unsalted butter, melted

2 tablespoons cream cheese

1 teaspoon vanilla extract

¼ teaspoon maple extract

1. Preheat oven to 325°F.

2. Grease the wells of a 24-cup mini muffin tin.

3. Combine almond flour, erythritol, salt, baking soda, and pumpkin pie seasoning in a medium bowl. Stir until combined.

4. In a small bowl, beat eggs, pumpkin purée, melted butter, cream cheese, vanilla extract, and maple extract until smooth. Fold egg mixture into dry ingredients until just combined.

5. Drop by teaspoonfuls into each well of a mini muffin tin. Bake for 15 minutes or until a toothpick inserted in the center comes out clean.

6. Store at room temperature.

PER SERVING Calories: 75 | Fat: 6.2g | Protein: 0.7g | Sodium: 111mg | Fiber: 1.2g | Carbohydrates: 4.6g | Sugar: 0.2g | Sugar alcohol: 2.1g

Caffè Latte Panna Cotta

Caffè latte is what children have for breakfast in Italy. Isn't this a fun panna cotta?

INGREDIENTS | MAKES 2 FAT BOMBS

½ cup brewed espresso or strong coffee

½ cup heavy whipping cream

1 teaspoon powdered unflavored gelatin

1 tablespoon erythritol or granular Swerve

1. Pour coffee and cream into a small saucepan. Sprinkle gelatin on top and let sit 5 minutes.

2. Add sweetener to saucepan.

3. Place saucepan over low heat and whisk until ingredients are well blended.

4. Simmer on very low heat about 1 minute, stirring constantly.

5. Pour into 2 glasses or molds.

6. Refrigerate until set, at least 6 hours or overnight.

7. Serve in glass or invert over a small plate after dipping glass into hot water a few seconds.

PER 1 FAT BOMB Calories: 217 | Fat: 20.9g | Protein: 4.32g | Sodium: 30mg | Fiber: 0.0g | Carbohydrates: 7.7g | Sugar: 1.7g | Sugar alcohol: 6.0g

Meyer Lemon Panna Cotta

Tangy and creamy, this is the perfect dessert for a hot summer day.

INGREDIENTS | MAKES 2 FAT BOMBS

1 cup coconut milk

1 teaspoon powdered unflavored gelatin

1 tablespoon erythritol or granular Swerve

Zest of 1 Meyer lemon

1 tablespoon coconut oil

1 teaspoon fresh Meyer lemon juice

1. Pour coconut milk into a small saucepan, sprinkle gelatin on top, and let sit 5 minutes.

2. Add remaining ingredients to saucepan.

3. Place saucepan over low heat and whisk until gelatin and zest are completely incorporated, about 3 minutes.

4. Simmer over very low heat about 1 minute, stirring constantly.

5. Pour into 2 glasses or molds.

6. Refrigerate until set, at least 6 hours or overnight.

7. Serve in glass or invert over a small plate after dipping glass into hot water a few seconds.

PER 1 FAT BOMB Calories: 294 | Fat: 29.1g | Protein: 5.3g | Sodium: 21mg | Fiber: 0.3g | Carbohydrates: 9.8g | Sugar: 0.2g | Sugar alcohol: 6.0g

Raspberries and Cream Panna Cotta

A heavenly dream of flavor with real raspberries and cream, sure to uplift anyone's day. Give it a try!

INGREDIENTS | MAKES 2 FAT BOMBS

1 cup heavy whipping cream

1 teaspoon powdered unflavored gelatin

1 tablespoon erythritol or granular Swerve

⅛ teaspoon raspberry flavor

2 tablespoons freeze-dried raspberries

1. Pour cream into a small saucepan, sprinkle gelatin on top, and let sit 5 minutes.

2. Add sweetener and raspberry flavor to saucepan.

3. Place saucepan over low heat and whisk until ingredients are well blended, about 3 minutes.

4. Simmer over very low heat about 1 minute, stirring constantly.

5. Pour into 2 glasses or molds. Sprinkle dried raspberries equally over glasses or molds.

6. Refrigerate until set, at least 6 hours or overnight.

7. Serve in glass or invert over a small plate after dipping glass into hot water a few seconds.

PER 1 FAT BOMB Calories: 426 | Fat: 41.8g | Protein: 5.6g | Sodium: 51mg | Fiber: 0.3g | Carbohydrates: 10.4g | Sugar: 3.9g | Sugar alcohol: 6.0g

Butterscotch Custard

Silky and sweet with a faint hint of bitter from the butterscotch,
this fat bomb could not be more decadent.

INGREDIENTS | MAKES 2 FAT BOMBS

2 tablespoons unsalted butter
½ cup erythritol or granular Swerve
1 cup heavy cream
2 large egg yolks
1 teaspoon vanilla extract
⅛ teaspoon sea salt

1. Preheat oven to 300°F.

2. Place 2 ramekins in a deep baking pan just large enough to hold them.

3. In a small saucepan over medium heat, melt butter and sweetener and cook until butter browns, about 5 minutes.

4. Very slowly add cream, whisking constantly until completely blended with butter, about 5 minutes.

5. In a small bowl, whisk together remaining ingredients until egg yolks are foamy.

6. Slowly pour egg mixture into cream, whisking constantly to combine well.

7. Pour mixture through a fine strainer into ramekins using a spoon to help you.

8. Pour hot water into baking pan halfway up ramekins.

9. Bake until custard is set, about 35 minutes.

10. Remove from oven and let cool in baking pan about 4 hours.

11. Can be stored in refrigerator up to 3 days.

PER 1 FAT BOMB Calories: 572 | Fat: 56.8g | Protein: 5.3g | Sodium: 289mg | Fiber: 0.0g | Carbohydrates: 52.2g | Sugar: 3.7g | Sugar alcohol: 48.0g

Coconut Custard

This is a perfect variation of the famous custard, suitable for people with dairy sensitivities. You will find it so delicious, though, that it will become a well-loved recipe for everyone.

INGREDIENTS | MAKES 2 FAT BOMBS

1 cup coconut cream
1 large egg
1 large egg yolk
½ cup erythritol or granular Swerve
½ teaspoon vanilla extract
½ teaspoon rum extract

1. Preheat oven to 300°F.

2. Place 2 ramekins in a deep baking pan just large enough to hold them.

3. In a small saucepan over low heat, bring coconut cream to a simmer.

4. In a small bowl, whisk together remaining ingredients until eggs are foamy and sweetener is dissolved.

5. Slowly pour egg mixture into coconut cream, whisking constantly to combine well.

6. Pour mixture through a fine strainer into ramekins using a spoon to help you.

7. Pour hot water into baking pan halfway up ramekins.

8. Bake until custard is set, about 35 minutes.

9. Remove from oven and let cool in baking pan about 4 hours.

10. Can be stored in refrigerator up to 3 days.

PER 1 FAT BOMB Calories: 305 | Fat: 28.3g | Protein: 4.5g | Sodium: 59mg | Fiber: 0.0g | Carbohydrates: 52.6g | Sugar: 4.3g | Sugar alcohol: 48.0g

Creamy Chocolate Custard

*Is there such a thing as too much chocolate? Even if you are not a chocolate fan,
this unbelievably rich and smooth recipe will make a convert out of you.*

INGREDIENTS | MAKES 2 FAT BOMBS

2 ounces unsweetened baking chocolate

1 cup heavy cream

1 large egg

1 large egg yolk

½ cup erythritol or granular Swerve

1 teaspoon vanilla extract

4 tablespoons unsweetened whipped cream

1. Preheat oven to 300°F.

2. Place 2 ramekins in a deep baking pan just large enough to hold them.

3. In a small saucepan or a double boiler, over very low heat, melt chocolate while slowly stirring.

4. Once chocolate is fluid, very slowly add cream, whisking constantly until it is completely blended with chocolate, about 5 minutes.

5. In a small bowl, whisk egg, egg yolk, sweetener, and vanilla until eggs are foamy and sweetener is dissolved.

6. Slowly pour egg mixture into cream, whisking constantly to combine well. Pour mixture through a fine strainer into ramekins using a spoon to help you.

7. Pour hot water into baking pan halfway up ramekins.

8. Bake until custard is set, about 35 minutes.

9. Remove from oven and let cool in baking pan about 4 hours.

10. Top with whipped cream before serving.

11. Can be stored in refrigerator up to 3 days.

PER 1 FAT BOMB Calories: 675 | Fat: 61.5g | Protein: 11.2g | Sodium: 91mg | Fiber: 4.7g | Carbohydrates: 60.9g | Sugar: 4.5g | Sugar alcohol: 48.0g

Espresso Custard

With this recipe you can make your Italian mother-in-law proud!

INGREDIENTS | MAKES 2 FAT BOMBS

1 cup heavy cream
¼ cup very strong brewed espresso
1 large egg
1 large egg yolk
½ cup erythritol or granular Swerve
1 teaspoon coffee extract

1. Preheat oven to 300°F.

2. Place 2 ramekins in a deep baking pan just large enough to hold them.

3. In a small saucepan over low heat, bring cream and espresso to a simmer.

4. In a small bowl, whisk together remaining ingredients until eggs are foamy and sweetener is dissolved.

5. Slowly pour egg mixture into cream, whisking constantly to combine well.

6. Pour mixture through a fine strainer into ramekins using a spoon to help you.

7. Pour hot water into baking pan halfway up ramekins.

8. Bake until custard is set, about 35 minutes.

9. Remove from oven and let cool in baking pan about 4 hours.

10. Can be stored in refrigerator up to 3 days.

PER 1 FAT BOMB Calories: 479 | Fat: 46.1g | Protein: 6.9g | Sodium: 85mg | Fiber: 0.0g | Carbohydrates: 52.1g | Sugar: 3.7g | Sugar alcohol: 48.0g

Matcha Berry Fudge

Matcha introduced into this fudge gives it a fresh yet sweet taste. The beautiful color contrasts nicely with fresh or freeze-dried raspberries for a visual treat while you eat.

INGREDIENTS | MAKES 8 FAT BOMBS

¼ cup cocoa butter

½ cup almond butter

2 tablespoons ghee or butter

2 tablespoons coconut oil

⅓ cup canned coconut milk

2 tablespoons matcha (green tea powder)

1 teaspoon vanilla extract

1 tablespoon granular Swerve

2 tablespoons freeze-dried raspberries

What's So Special about Matcha?

Some of the many benefits of this antioxidant-rich powdered tea originating from Japan include enhanced energy, better concentration, and more endurance. In addition, this powder is said to lower cholesterol levels, detoxify the liver, burn calories, and enhance calmness.

1. Grease and line a 9" × 5" loaf pan with parchment paper.

2. Melt cocoa butter, almond butter, ghee, and coconut oil over medium-low heat in a medium saucepan. Remove from heat and cool about 5 minutes.

3. Mix in remaining ingredients except raspberries.

4. Pour mixture into lined loaf pan. Sprinkle with raspberries.

5. Place in refrigerator and allow to set at least 4 hours. Slice into 8 pieces before serving.

PER 1 FAT BOMB Calories: 238 | Fat: 23.5g | Protein: 3.7g | Sodium: 51mg | Fiber: 2.1g | Carbohydrates: 6.2g | Sugar: 0.7g

Almond Pistachio Fudge

This delightful fudge is full of nutty goodness. The addition of firm coconut oil and coconut milk helps give this fudge body and texture.

INGREDIENTS | MAKES 12 FAT BOMBS

¼ cup cocoa butter

½ cup almond butter

½ cup coconut oil

¼ cup canned coconut milk, chilled overnight

2 tablespoons ghee

2 teaspoons vanilla extract

⅛ teaspoon salt

¼ cup chopped pistachios

Pistachios, the Festive Nut

Bright green colored and delicious, this nut is often reserved for holiday parties—probably due to their higher price. Oddly enough, until the 1980s, manufacturers followed the widespread practice of dying the nuts red! Always opt for naturally colored and roasted nuts for the freshest flavor, and to avoid any additives or dyes.

1. Grease and line an 8" × 8" baking pan with parchment paper.

2. Melt cocoa butter in a small saucepan over low heat and set aside.

3. In a large bowl, add all ingredients except nuts and melted cocoa butter. Mix with a hand mixer until texture is fluffy.

4. Pour melted cocoa butter into almond mixture and combine with hand mixer on low speed.

5. Spread mixture evenly into pan and sprinkle with pistachios.

6. Refrigerate at least 4 hours to set. Cut into 12 bars and serve from refrigerator.

PER 1 FAT BOMB Calories: 226 | Fat: 22.8g | Protein: 3.0g | Sodium: 58mg | Fiber: 1.6g | Carbohydrates: 3.3g | Sugar: 0.6g

Brown Butter Rum Pecan Fudge

Browning the butter before making this fudge gives it an extra richness and a gorgeous color. The addition of rum extract makes this fudge's flavor a throwback to vintage butter rum hard candies.

INGREDIENTS | MAKES 6 FAT BOMBS

8 tablespoons butter

2 ounces cream cheese

½ cup peanut butter

1 teaspoon rum extract

16 drops liquid stevia

¼ cup chopped pecans

1. Grease and line an 8" × 8" baking pan with parchment paper.

2. In a small saucepan over medium-low heat, melt butter until it begins to brown slightly, then add cream cheese and stir to combine.

3. Add peanut butter, rum extract, and liquid stevia and stir until melted and well combined.

4. Stir pecans into mixture and spread into baking dish.

5. Allow to cool to room temperature, then place in refrigerator to finish setting, about 2 hours. Slice into 6 pieces to serve.

PER 1 FAT BOMB Calories: 329 | Fat: 30.7g | Protein: 5.9g | Sodium: 159mg | Fiber: 1.5g | Carbohydrates: 5.9g | Sugar: 2.8g

Eggnog Fudge

Nothing says holidays like the creamy, old-fashioned flavor of eggnog. While an excellent fat bomb on its own, eggnog is usually full of too much sugar to make it a worthwhile treat for a low-carb, high-fat dieter. Now you can enjoy the flavor of the holidays without the sugar overload.

INGREDIENTS | MAKES 4 FAT BOMBS

8 tablespoons butter

4 ounces cream cheese, softened

1 tablespoon vanilla extract

1 teaspoon nutmeg

¼ teaspoon cinnamon

⅛ teaspoon ground cloves

2 tablespoons granular Swerve

How Did Eggnog Get Its Name?

While the origin of the drink is still up for debate, the name "eggnog" most likely comes from the small wooden cup it was originally served in, known as a noggin.

1. Grease and line a 9" × 5" loaf pan with parchment paper.

2. In a medium saucepan over medium-low heat, melt butter. Add cream cheese and stir until well melted and combined.

3. Remove from heat, add remaining ingredients, and mix well.

4. Spread mixture into lined loaf pan.

5. Let cool to room temperature, then place in refrigerator to finish setting, at least 2 hours.

6. Slice into 4 pieces before serving.

PER 1 FAT BOMB Calories: 312 | Fat: 29.9g | Protein: 2.0g | Sodium: 286mg | Fiber: 0.2g | Carbohydrates: 8.0g | Sugar: 1.4g | Sugar alcohol: 6.0g

Lemon Lover Cheesecake

Lemon is one of the classic American flavors for drinks, pies, cakes, and treats. Adding it to a basic cheesecake elevates the dessert to a sweet and tart treat without masking the rich and creamy flavor.

INGREDIENTS | MAKES 6 FAT BOMBS

⅓ cup almond meal flour

1 tablespoon butter, melted

2 drops liquid stevia

8 ounces cream cheese, softened to room temperature

2 tablespoons granular Swerve or powdered stevia

1 large egg

½ teaspoon vanilla extract

Zest of ½ small lemon

Juice of 1 small lemon

1. Preheat oven to 325°F.

2. In a small mixing bowl, combine almond meal, butter, and liquid stevia.

3. Line 6 cups of a standard-sized muffin tin with cupcake liners.

4. Equally divide flour mixture between lined cups and press into bottom gently with back of a teaspoon. Bake 10 minutes, then remove.

5. While crust is baking, thoroughly combine cream cheese and Swerve in a medium mixing bowl with a hand mixer.

6. Add remaining ingredients and blend until combined.

7. Divide mixture between cups, return to oven, and bake another 30–35 minutes until cream cheese sets. Edges may be very slightly browned. To test doneness, insert toothpick into center of cake. If it comes out clean, cheesecake is done.

8. Let cool and chill 2–3 hours for best flavor.

PER 1 FAT BOMB Calories: 190 | Fat: 16.1g | Protein: 3.3g | Sodium: 164mg | Fiber: 0.7g | Carbohydrates: 7.4g | Sugar: 1.4g | Sugar alcohol: 4.0g

Vanilla Bean Cheesecake

For those who love cheesecake but are sensitive to dairy, this marriage of coconut and vanilla is the perfect choice. While vanilla pairs well with everything, it is an excellent companion to coconut products, lending both an aroma and flavor of the tropics.

INGREDIENTS | MAKES 6 FAT BOMBS

⅓ cup almond meal flour

1 tablespoon plus ½ cup coconut oil, melted, divided

2 drops liquid stevia

3 cups coconut milk

2 tablespoons granular Swerve or powdered stevia

½ tablespoon lemon juice

⅓ small lemon, zest only

1 teaspoon vanilla extract

1 small vanilla bean, inside scraping only

2 tablespoons powdered unflavored gelatin

⅛ teaspoon sea salt

1. Preheat oven to 350°F.

2. In a small mixing bowl, combine almond meal, 1 tablespoon coconut oil, and liquid stevia.

3. Line 6 cups of a standard-sized muffin tin with cupcake liners.

4. Equally divide flour mixture between 6 cups and press into bottom gently with back of a teaspoon. Bake 10 minutes.

5. Remove crusts from oven and let cool while making filling.

6. Combine remaining ½ cup coconut oil, coconut milk, Swerve, lemon juice and zest, vanilla extract, and vanilla bean scrapings in a medium pot and heat over low heat until warmed slightly.

7. Add gelatin and salt and whisk thoroughly.

8. Remove from heat, pour into bowl, and chill in refrigerator 1 hour. Once cooled, pour into cool baked cups and return to refrigerator to chill overnight.

PER 1 FAT BOMB Calories: 442 | Fat: 44.4g | Protein: 4.3g | Sodium: 67mg | Fiber: 0.9g | Carbohydrates: 9.4g | Sugar: 0.6g | Sugar alcohol: 4.0g

CHAPTER 10

Snacks

Deviled Eggs

Deviled eggs are a staple at any party, and they make the perfect ketogenic diet snack. Whip some up and store them in your refrigerator for when you need some fat and protein in a hurry.

INGREDIENTS | SERVES 6

6 large hard-boiled eggs

¼ cup Homemade Mayonnaise (see recipe in Chapter 5)

1 teaspoon white vinegar

1 teaspoon dry mustard

½ teaspoon salt

¼ teaspoon black pepper

⅛ teaspoon smoked paprika

1. Peel eggs and cut in half lengthwise. Scoop out egg yolks and put in a small mixing bowl.

2. Mash yolks with a fork, then add mayonnaise, vinegar, mustard, salt, and pepper. Continue to mash until combined.

3. Divide mixture into 12 equal portions and fill each egg white half. Sprinkle with paprika.

PER SERVING Calories: 146 | Fat: 11.6g | Protein: 6.6g | Sodium: 296mg | Fiber: 0.1g | Carbohydrates: 0.9g | Sugar: 0.6g

Pepperoni Chips

Make sure to thoroughly blot away the excess grease in this recipe. If you don't you'll end up with soggy chips instead of crispy ones.

INGREDIENTS | SERVES 4

24 sugar-free pepperoni slices

1. Preheat oven to 425°F.

2. Line a baking sheet with parchment paper and lay out pepperoni slices in a single layer.

3. Bake for 10 minutes and then remove from oven and use a paper towel to blot away excess grease. Return to the oven for 5 minutes or until pepperoni is crispy.

PER SERVING Calories: 59 | Fat: 4.3g | Protein: 2.8g | Sodium: 211mg | Fiber: 0.0g | Carbohydrates: 0.0g | Sugar: 0.0g

Pizza Bites

You won't even miss the crust when you try these pizza bites. And the best part? They're ready to go in under 5 minutes.

INGREDIENTS | SERVES 6

24 slices sugar-free pepperoni

½ cup Marinara Sauce (see recipe in Chapter 5)

½ cup shredded mozzarella cheese

1. Turn on oven broiler.

2. Line a baking sheet with parchment paper and put pepperoni slices in a single layer on baking sheet.

3. Put 1 teaspoon of marinara sauce on each pepperoni slice and spread out with a spoon. Add 1 teaspoon of cheese on top of marinara.

4. Put baking sheet in the oven and broil for 3 minutes or until cheese is melted and slightly brown.

5. Remove from baking sheet and transfer to a paper towel–lined baking sheet to absorb excess grease.

PER SERVING Calories: 81 | Fat: 5.6g | Protein: 4.2g | Sodium: 267mg | Fiber: 0.4g | Carbohydrates: 1.7g | Sugar: 0.9g

Prosciutto Chips

These prosciutto chips are so simple and delicious, you'll wonder why you never thought of them before. All you need is some prosciutto and an oven.

INGREDIENTS | SERVES 4

12 ounces (12 slices) of prosciutto

A Little about Prosciutto

Prosciutto is made from the hind leg of a pig, or the ham. It is sliced thinly and rubbed with salt, which draws out the moisture to concentrate the flavor. This process, called curing, can take a few months to several years.

1. Preheat oven to 350°F.

2. Line a baking sheet with parchment paper and lay prosciutto slices out in a single layer. Bake for 12 minutes, or until prosciutto is crispy.

3. Let cool completely before eating.

PER SERVING Calories: 173 | Fat: 10.3g | Protein: 20.7g | Sodium: 1,722mg | Fiber: 0.0g | Carbohydrates: 0.0g | Sugar: 0.0g

Stuffed Olives

You can use any type of olive you want for this recipe, but green olives have a tangy flavor that complements the blue cheese wonderfully.

INGREDIENTS | SERVES 8

¼ cup blue cheese crumbles
¼ cup cream cheese, softened
24 large green olives

1. Beat blue cheese and cream cheese together in a small bowl until light and fluffy.

2. Fill each olive with 1 teaspoon filling. Serve at room temperature.

PER SERVING Calories: 51 | Fat: 4.5g | Protein: 1.4g | Sodium: 200mg | Fiber: 0.3g | Carbohydrates: 0.7g | Sugar: 0.3g

Bacon-Wrapped Chicken Bites

Serve these bacon-wrapped chicken bites with a side of Ranch Dressing (see recipe in Chapter 5) to increase both the flavor and the fat content.

INGREDIENTS | SERVES 6

12 ounces boneless, skinless chicken breast
½ teaspoon salt
½ teaspoon black pepper
5 slices sugar-free bacon

1. Preheat oven to 375°F.

2. Cut chicken into 1" cubes and toss with salt and pepper.

3. Cut each slice of bacon into 3 pieces and wrap each cube of chicken in a piece of bacon. Secure with a toothpick.

4. Put wrapped chicken on a broiler rack and bake for 30 minutes, turning over halfway through cooking. Turn oven to broil and broil for 3–4 minutes or until bacon is crispy.

PER SERVING Calories: 106 | Fat: 4.7g | Protein: 14.8g | Sodium: 453mg | Fiber: 0.1g | Carbohydrates: 0.3g | Sugar: 0.0g

Parmesan Chips

You can make this recipe with any type—or combination of types—of cheeses you want. Try Cheddar, pepper jack, or a combination of Parmesan and Cheddar.

INGREDIENTS | SERVES 4 (MAKES 16 CHIPS)

½ cup grated Parmesan cheese
½ cup shredded Parmesan cheese

1. Preheat oven to 375°F.

2. Mix grated and shredded Parmesan cheese together. Drop by the tablespoon onto parchment paper–lined baking sheets.

3. Bake for 5 minutes or until cheese is crisp and slightly browned.

4. Remove from oven and allow to cool. Peel chips off parchment paper and serve.

PER SERVING Calories: 94 | Fat: 5.7g | Protein: 7.3g | Sodium: 395mg | Fiber: 0.0g | Carbohydrates: 2.1g | Sugar: 0.1g

Pumpkin Pie Coconut Crisps

The possibilities for this recipe are endless. You can experiment with any combination of spices you want. Make them sweet or savory or a combination of both.

INGREDIENTS | SERVES 4

2 tablespoons coconut oil

½ teaspoon vanilla extract

½ teaspoon pumpkin pie spice

1 tablespoon granulated erythritol

2 cups unsweetened coconut flakes

⅛ teaspoon salt

Cuckoo for Coconuts

Coconuts are rich in a specific type of fat called medium-chain triglycerides (MCTs). Instead of circulating through the blood like other fats, MCTs go straight to the liver where they're burned for energy. Because your body doesn't store MCTs, eating them can help boost weight loss.

1. Preheat oven to 350°F.

2. Put coconut oil in a microwave-safe bowl and microwave until melted, about 20 seconds. Add vanilla extract, pumpkin pie spice, and granulated erythritol to coconut oil and stir until combined.

3. Put coconut flakes in coconut oil mixture and toss to coat. Spread out in a single layer on a cookie sheet and sprinkle with salt.

4. Bake for 5 minutes or until coconut is crispy.

PER SERVING Calories: 260 | Fat: 26.4g | Protein: 2.0g | Sodium: 82mg | Fiber: 4.0g | Carbohydrates: 11.2g | Sugar: 2.1g | Sugar alcohol: 3.0g

Jalapeño Poppers

To double the yield of this recipe, cut the jalapeños in half and wrap each half in a half piece of bacon.

INGREDIENTS | SERVES 4

8 jalapeño peppers
½ cup cream cheese, softened
½ cup shredded pepper jack cheese
8 slices sugar-free bacon

Turn Up the Heat

The capsaicin in chili peppers is thermogenic, which means it generates heat by increasing the metabolism of adipose, or fat, tissue. Eating capsaicin-rich foods may help stimulate the body's ability to burn fat.

1. Preheat oven to 425°F.

2. Cut about ⅓ of each pepper off lengthwise to make a little pocket for filling. Scoop out seeds.

3. Mix cream cheese and pepper jack cheese together in a small bowl. Divide filling into 8 equal portions and stuff each pepper with cheese filling.

4. Wrap each pepper in bacon. Lay flat on a cookie sheet lined with aluminum foil and bake for 15–20 minutes, or until bacon is crispy.

PER SERVING Calories: 270 | Fat: 20.6g | Protein: 13.1g | Sodium: 579mg | Fiber: 0.8g | Carbohydrates: 3.8g | Sugar: 2.2g

Green Deviled Eggs

Adding avocado to traditional deviled eggs provides a healthy dose of monounsaturated fats and increases vitamin K, folate, vitamin C, and potassium content.

INGREDIENTS | SERVES 2

4 large hard-boiled eggs
1 large avocado, chopped
¼ cup Homemade Mayonnaise (see recipe in Chapter 5)
1 teaspoon lime juice
1 tablespoon feta cheese
2 teaspoons light olive oil
⅛ teaspoon salt
¼ teaspoon black pepper

1. Peel hard-boiled eggs and cut in half lengthwise. Scoop out yolks and place in a small bowl.

2. Put remaining ingredients, except pepper, in bowl with egg yolks and mash with a fork until combined.

3. Fill each egg white half with an equal amount of the yolk mixture. Sprinkle pepper on top.

PER SERVING Calories: 522 | Fat: 44.7g | Protein: 15.3g | Sodium: 439mg | Fiber: 4.7g | Carbohydrates: 7.9g | Sugar: 1.7g

Guacamole

Guacamole is a ketogenic diet staple. Eat it with some celery stalks, put it on top of your taco bowls, or spoon it right out of the bowl.

INGREDIENTS | SERVES 4

3 large avocados

Juice from 1 lime

2 large Roma tomatoes, diced

2 cloves garlic, minced

¼ cup chopped fresh cilantro

¼ cup chopped red onion

½ teaspoon salt

½ teaspoon black pepper

1. Cut avocados in half lengthwise, remove the pit, and scoop them out of the skin and into a medium bowl. Add lime juice. Use a fork to mash avocado and lime together, leaving some chunks intact.

2. Add tomatoes, garlic, cilantro, onion, salt, and pepper. Mash with a fork until combined.

PER SERVING Calories: 193 | Fat: 14.1g | Protein: 3.0g | Sodium: 303mg | Fiber: 8.3g | Carbohydrates: 14.3g | Sugar: 3.0g

Tuna Salad and Cucumber Bites

These bites are an easy snack that's good on the go. Give yourself a little variety by using canned chicken or canned salmon in place of tuna.

INGREDIENTS | SERVES 4

1 medium cucumber

2 (5-ounce) cans of tuna

2 large hard-boiled eggs, peeled and chopped

½ cup Homemade Mayonnaise (see recipe in Chapter 5)

½ teaspoon salt

½ teaspoon black pepper

2 teaspoons goat cheese

1. Wash and cut cucumber into rounds.

2. Drain tuna and put in a medium bowl with chopped eggs, mayonnaise, salt, and pepper. Mash with a fork until combined.

3. Spread an equal amount of goat cheese on each cucumber slice and top with tuna salad mixture.

PER SERVING Calories: 337 | Fat: 26.4g | Protein: 18.9g | Sodium: 691mg | Fiber: 0.4g | Carbohydrates: 1.9g | Sugar: 1.1g

Bacon-Wrapped Avocado Bites

The combination of bacon and avocado may not sound like a good combination, but don't knock it 'til you try it: the salty, crispy bacon and smooth, creamy avocado make the perfect pair.

INGREDIENTS | SERVES 4

2 large avocados, peeled and pitted
8 slices of sugar-free bacon
½ teaspoon garlic salt

Precook Your Bacon

If you cook avocado too long, the avocado can turn bitter. To avoid this, you can shorten the cooking time of this recipe by slightly precooking the bacon—enough that it's partially cooked but still bendable—and then wrapping it around the avocado and putting it in the oven.

1. Preheat oven to 425°F.

2. Cut each avocado into 8 equal-sized slices, making 16 slices total.

3. Cut each piece of bacon in half. Wrap each half slice of bacon around each piece of avocado.

4. Place avocado on parchment-lined cookie sheet and bake for 15 minutes. Turn oven to broil and continue to cook for another 2–3 minutes until bacon becomes crispy.

PER SERVING Calories: 221 | Fat: 17.1g | Protein: 9.1g | Sodium: 637mg | Fiber: 4.6g | Carbohydrates: 6.3g | Sugar: 0.2g

Pepperoni Cheese Bites

Enjoy this recipe cold or put each pepperoni bite in the oven just until the cheese melts for a warm, tasty treat.

INGREDIENTS | SERVES 2

4 sticks mozzarella string cheese
16 slices sugar-free pepperoni

1. Cut each string cheese into 4 equal pieces.

2. Wrap each piece in a slice of pepperoni and secure with a toothpick.

PER SERVING Calories: 249 | Fat: 15.6g | Protein: 17.6g | Sodium: 668mg | Fiber: 0.0g | Carbohydrates: 3.6g | Sugar: 1.3g

Chocolate Mousse

You'll love this mousse so much you won't even miss the real thing. The avocado adds healthy fats, but the taste is camouflaged by the cocoa powder.

INGREDIENTS | SERVES 4

½ cup cream cheese, softened

½ cup unsalted butter, softened

2 tablespoons granulated erythritol

½ large avocado

2 tablespoons unsweetened cocoa powder

⅔ cup heavy cream

1. Beat cream cheese, butter, and granulated erythritol together in a medium bowl until light and fluffy.

2. Add avocado and cocoa powder and beat until smooth. Stir in heavy cream.

3. Divide into 4 serving dishes and refrigerate until chilled, about 30 minutes. Serve cold.

PER SERVING Calories: 473 | Fat: 46.5g | Protein: 3.6g | Sodium: 125mg | Fiber: 2.2g | Carbohydrates: 11.3g | Sugar: 2.2g | Sugar alcohol: 6.0g

Smoked Salmon and Avocado Rollups

Super-quick and easy dairy-free fat bombs, these rollups make a great party food or an easy appetizer.

INGREDIENTS | MAKES 3 FAT BOMBS

3 ounces (½ medium) avocado pulp

1 teaspoon fresh lemon juice

⅛ teaspoon sea salt

3 (1-ounce) slices smoked salmon

1. In a small bowl, combine avocado, lemon juice, and salt; mash with a fork.

2. Spread ⅓ avocado mixture evenly on top of each salmon slice. Roll slices into individual rolls and secure with a toothpick.

3. Serve immediately.

PER 1 FAT BOMB Calories: 71 | Fat: 4.2g | Protein: 5.6g | Sodium: 665mg | Fiber: 1.6g | Carbohydrates: 2.1g | Sugar: 0.1g

Turmeric-Infused Panna Cotta

Turmeric used to be considered an exotic spice, but it is now widely available in any supermarket, even the fresh root version. Try this pungent condiment, and the earthy but distinct flavor will surely win you over.

INGREDIENTS | MAKES 6 FAT BOMBS

1½ cups coconut milk, refrigerated and cream separated from the water

1½ cups beef stock

1½ tablespoons powdered unflavored gelatin

1 tablespoon turmeric

½ tablespoon sea salt

The Benefits of Turmeric

The main active ingredient in turmeric, called curcumin (not to be confused with the common spice, cumin), is recognized as being a powerful anti-inflammatory. Even a small serving in a dish can assist your body's ability to digest fats and reduce bloating. It's also used medicinally to provide relief to sufferers of joint pain and swelling.

1. In a small saucepan over medium heat, heat coconut cream and beef stock.

2. Whisk in gelatin until completely incorporated.

3. Add turmeric and salt and simmer 5 minutes.

4. Pour mixture evenly into 6 small glasses or ramekins.

5. Refrigerate until set, at least 6 hours or overnight.

6. Serve in glass or invert over a small plate after dipping glass into hot water a few seconds.

PER 1 FAT BOMB Calories: 98 | Fat: 8.1g | Protein: 2.8g | Sodium: 710mg | Fiber: 0.4g | Carbohydrates: 3.1g | Sugar: 1.7g

Hot Mess Prosciutto Cup

*Hot and dripping with melted cheese, how do you like this version
of a hot mess? Couldn't you eat this every day?*

INGREDIENTS | MAKES 1 FAT BOMB

1 slice prosciutto
1 medium egg yolk
½ ounce diced Brie cheese
½ ounce grated Parmesan cheese
½ teaspoon sriracha sauce

1. Preheat oven to 350°F. Use a muffin tin with holes about 2½" wide and 1½" deep.

2. Fold prosciutto slice in half so it becomes almost square.

3. Place it in a muffin tin hole to line it completely.

4. Place egg yolk into prosciutto cup.

5. Add cheeses on top of egg gently without breaking it.

6. Add sriracha sauce on top of everything.

7. Bake about 12 minutes until yolk is cooked and warm but still runny.

8. Let cool 10 minutes before removing from muffin pan.

PER 1 FAT BOMB Calories: 181 | Fat: 12.4g | Protein: 12.6g | Sodium: 677mg | Fiber: 0.0g | Carbohydrates: 3.0g | Sugar: 0.7g

Parmesan Vegetable Crisps

This simple twist on the Parmesan crisp introduces added texture and a mild sweetness while offering additional fiber too. Of course, the added colors of the vegetables make this crisp a beauty for the eyes to feast on before you taste it.

INGREDIENTS | SERVES 4

¾ cup shredded zucchini

¼ cup shredded carrots

2 cups freshly shredded Parmesan cheese

1 tablespoon olive oil

¼ teaspoon freshly ground black pepper

Zucchini: A Kitchen Staple

It's no secret that the right vegetables are an important part of any healthy diet. Zucchini is a fantastic choice for high-fat, low-carbohydrate diets because it has a low carbohydrate content (low glycemic index) and it's full of potassium, a crucial mineral for heart health. Besides that, it also makes a fantastic substitute for pasta lovers looking for low-carbohydrate alternatives.

1. Preheat oven to 375°F. Prepare a cookie sheet with parchment paper or a Silpat mat.

2. Wrap shredded vegetables in a paper towel and wring out excess moisture.

3. Mix all ingredients in a medium bowl until thoroughly combined.

4. Place tablespoon-sized mounds onto prepared cookie sheet.

5. Bake 7–10 minutes until lightly browned.

6. Let cool 2–3 minutes and remove from mat. Enjoy as is or with other fat-bomb dips and spreads.

PER SERVING Calories: 202 | Fat: 14.0g | Protein: 15.5g | Sodium: 684mg | Fiber: 0.5g | Carbohydrates: 2.8g | Sugar: 1.3g

Cheddar Mexi-Melt Crisps

Another versatile cheese for the low-carbohydrate kitchen is Cheddar, the harder the better. Generally the harder Cheddars tend to be the sharpest, so if tart and tangy seems like too much, a mild Cheddar will also work for these crisps.

INGREDIENTS | SERVES 2

1 cup shredded sharp Cheddar cheese
1/8 teaspoon granulated garlic
1/8 teaspoon chili powder
1/8 teaspoon cumin
1/16 teaspoon cayenne pepper
1 tablespoon finely chopped cilantro
1 teaspoon olive oil

1. Preheat oven to 350°F. Prepare a cookie sheet with parchment paper or a Silpat mat.

2. Mix all ingredients in a medium bowl until well combined.

3. Drop by tablespoon-sized portions onto prepared cookie sheet.

4. Cook 5–7 minutes until edges begin to brown.

5. Allow to cool 2–3 minutes before removing from tray with spatula.

6. Enjoy as is or use as a chip for guacamole.

PER SERVING Calories: 133 | Fat: 14.1g | Protein: 0.5g | Sodium: 41mg | Fiber: 0.1g | Carbohydrates: 1.0g | Sugar: 0.1g

Chicken Skin Crisps with Aioli Egg Salad

The rich, garlicky flavor of this fat bomb will transport you straight to the French Riviera.

INGREDIENTS | MAKES 6 FAT BOMBS

Skin from 3 chicken thighs

1 large hard-boiled egg, peeled and chopped

1 large hard-boiled egg yolk, chopped

1 tablespoon Homemade Mayonnaise (see recipe in Chapter 5)

¼ garlic clove, minced

1 tablespoon finely chopped fresh parsley

½ teaspoon sea salt

1. Preheat oven to 350°F. On a cookie sheet, lay out skins as flat as possible.

2. Bake 12–15 minutes until skins turn light brown and crispy being careful not to burn them.

3. Remove skins from cookie sheet and place on a paper towel to cool.

4. In a small bowl, add egg, egg yolk, mayonnaise, garlic, parsley, and sea salt.

5. Mix with a fork until well blended.

6. Cut each crispy chicken skin in 2 pieces.

7. Place 1 tablespoon egg salad mix on each chicken crisp and serve immediately.

PER 1 FAT BOMB Calories: 85 | Fat: 7.1g | Protein: 3.7g | Sodium: 227mg | Fiber: 0.0g | Carbohydrates: 0.3g | Sugar: 0.1g

Chicken Skin Crisps with Spicy Avocado Cream

Sometimes a bit of spice is a great complement to the creaminess of an ingredient. That makes for a well-balanced recipe.

INGREDIENTS | MAKES 6 FAT BOMBS

Skin from 3 chicken thighs
1½ ounces (¼ medium) avocado pulp
1½ ounces sour cream
½ fresh jalapeño pepper, seeded and finely chopped
½ teaspoon sea salt

1. Preheat oven to 350°F. On a cookie sheet, lay out skins as flat as possible.

2. Bake 12–15 minutes until skins turn light brown and crispy being careful not to burn them.

3. Remove skins from cookie sheet and place on a paper towel to cool.

4. In a small bowl, combine avocado pulp, sour cream, jalapeño, and sea salt.

5. Mix with a fork until well blended.

6. Cut each crispy chicken skin in 2 pieces.

7. Place 1 tablespoon avocado mix on each chicken crisp and serve immediately.

PER 1 FAT BOMB Calories: 71 | Fat: 6.0g | Protein: 2.4g | Sodium: 204mg | Fiber: 0.4g | Carbohydrates: 0.8g | Sugar: 0.3g

Kitchen Sink Endive Cups

This recipe has a bit of every good fat and protein you can use in your kitchen on a daily basis.

INGREDIENTS | MAKES 4 FAT BOMBS

1 large hard-boiled egg, peeled

1 ounce canned tuna in olive oil, drained

1 ounce avocado pulp

1 teaspoon fresh lime juice

1 tablespoon Homemade Mayonnaise (see recipe in Chapter 5)

⅛ teaspoon sea salt

⅛ teaspoon freshly ground black pepper

4 Belgian endive leaves, washed and dried

1. In a small food processor, mix all ingredients except endive until well blended.

2. Scoop 1 tablespoon tuna mix onto each endive cup.

3. Serve immediately.

PER 1 FAT BOMB Calories: 69 | Fat: 5.1g | Protein: 3.7g | Sodium: 118mg | Fiber: 0.7g | Carbohydrates: 1.2g | Sugar: 0.2g

Curried Egg Salad Endive Cups

The delicate but complex flavor of the curry blends wonderfully with eggs, giving the egg salad a slightly unusual but successful twist.

INGREDIENTS | MAKES 2 FAT BOMBS

1 large hard-boiled egg, peeled

1 teaspoon curry powder

1 tablespoon coconut oil

⅛ teaspoon sea salt

⅛ teaspoon freshly ground black pepper

2 Belgian endive leaves, washed and dried

1. In a small food processor, mix all ingredients except endive until well blended.

2. Scoop 1 tablespoon egg salad mix onto each endive cup.

3. Serve immediately.

PER 1 FAT BOMB Calories: 101 | Fat: 8.7g | Protein: 3.4g | Sodium: 177mg | Fiber: 0.8g | Carbohydrates: 1.2g | Sugar: 0.3g

Smoky Deviled Eggs with Riga Sprats Mousse

A different take on the usual deviled eggs. This one is chock-full of good fats and quality protein.

INGREDIENTS | SERVES 4

1 teaspoon powdered unflavored gelatin

2 tablespoons hot water

2 ounces smoked Riga Sprats, drained

2 large hard-boiled eggs, peeled, halved, yolks separated from whites

2 tablespoons olive oil

¼ teaspoon Tabasco

¼ teaspoon sweet paprika

Riga Sprats

You may never have heard of Riga Sprats, as they are a delicacy imported from Latvia. They are a kind of small, oily fish *(Sprattus sprattus)* from the same family as the sardine. Riga Sprats are smoked and preserved in oil. They are tender and flavorful and make the perfect base for a fat bomb!

1. Dissolve gelatin in hot water and let sit 5 minutes.

2. In a small food processor, add sprats, egg yolks, gelatin, olive oil, and Tabasco and blend well until a smooth cream forms.

3. With a spoon, fill mousse into holes of egg whites.

4. Sprinkle with paprika.

5. Refrigerate at least 3 hours before serving.

PER SERVING Calories: 146 | Fat: 11.8g | Protein: 6.8g | Sodium: 139mg | Fiber: 0.3g | Carbohydrates: 1.8g | Sugar: 0.3g

Slow Cooker Recipes

Meaty Chili

This recipe calls for a mixture of bacon and pork, but you can use any combination of ground meat that you want.

INGREDIENTS | SERVES 8

8 slices thick-cut sugar-free bacon

1 medium white onion, chopped

1 large green pepper, diced

1 small red pepper, diced

1 pound 85/15 ground beef

1 pound ground pork

1 (14.5-ounce) can fire-roasted diced tomatoes

1 (6-ounce) can tomato paste

3 tablespoons chili powder

1 tablespoon cumin

1 teaspoon garlic powder

2 teaspoons sugar-free hot sauce

1 teaspoon salt

1 cup sugar-free beef broth

1. Cook bacon over medium-high heat in a large skillet until crisp, about 10 minutes.

2. Remove bacon from heat, reserving bacon fat, and chop into small pieces.

3. Put chopped onions and peppers in the same skillet in hot bacon grease and sauté until translucent, 3–4 minutes. Add ground beef and ground pork and cook until no longer pink. Drain liquid.

4. Put beef mixture, chopped bacon, and remaining ingredients in a slow cooker. Stir until ingredients are combined and cook on low for 6 hours.

PER SERVING Calories: 292 | Fat: 17.1g | Protein: 20.8g | Sodium: 1,025mg | Fiber: 3.4g | Carbohydrates: 11.2g | Sugar: 5.5g

Searching for Sugar

Not all hot sauces are the same. Some of them contain sugar, even though it's not necessary. Check your hot sauce labels and choose one that is sugar-free. A lot of popular brands fall into this category.

Classic Sloppy Joes

This traditional sandwich filling makes a great keto recipe to stuff into peppers, spoon over roasted spaghetti squash, or use as a dip for sliced vegetables. It also makes a great party dish. Make ahead at your convenience, then chill or freeze. Reheat in your slow cooker just before your party.

INGREDIENTS | SERVES 8

4 tablespoons olive oil

2 onions, peeled and thinly sliced

1 clove garlic, minced

1 pound 85/15 ground beef

1 pound ground pork

½ cup apple cider vinegar

½ cup tomato paste

¼ teaspoon salt

½ teaspoon black pepper

1. Heat the oil in a large skillet over low heat. Sauté the onions in the skillet over low heat until soft, about 12–15 minutes. For the last 2 minutes of cooking, add the garlic. Stir until cooked and fragrant. Transfer to the slow cooker.

2. Brown the meat in the same pan over medium heat, breaking into chunks; drain. Add the meat, vinegar, tomato paste, salt, and pepper to the slow cooker.

3. Cover and heat on a low setting for 3–4 hours.

PER SERVING Calories: 209 | Fat: 12.6g | Protein: 15.7g | Sodium: 253mg | Fiber: 1.1g | Carbohydrates: 5.9g | Sugar: 3.1g

Beef Stew

This dish is great to come home to on a cold wintry night. It's very simple, and you can set it to cook and leave it alone until it's done.

INGREDIENTS | SERVES 6

1 tablespoon coconut oil

2 pounds stew meat

1 green pepper, coarsely chopped

3 cups pearl onions, peeled

30 cherry tomatoes

1 tablespoon tapioca flour

2 tablespoons granulated erythritol

½ teaspoon salt

¼ teaspoon black pepper

1. Heat the coconut oil in a large skillet over medium heat. Sauté the meat in oil until browned on all sides, then drain and transfer meat to the slow cooker.

2. Place the green pepper, onions, tomatoes, tapioca flour, granulated erythritol, salt, and pepper in the slow cooker.

3. Cover and heat on a low setting for 4–5 hours.

PER SERVING Calories: 285 | Fat: 7.5g | Protein: 35.9g | Sodium: 287mg | Fiber: 2.7g | Carbohydrates: 20.6g | Sugar: 6.9g | Sugar alcohol: 4.0g

Ginger Barbecue Beef

*Fresh ginger has a much more potent flavor than powdered,
dried ginger. Try to use the fresh root if available.*

INGREDIENTS | SERVES 8

3 cloves garlic, peeled and minced

1" fresh gingerroot, peeled and minced

½ cup coconut aminos

½ cup water

2 tablespoons sesame oil

2 tablespoons granulated erythritol

4 teaspoons sesame seeds

3 pounds boneless chuck steak

1 onion

1. Mix garlic and gingerroot in a small bowl with coconut aminos, water, oil, erythritol, and sesame seeds.

2. Cut the beef in slices. Peel and coarsely chop the onion.

3. Arrange the beef and onion in the slow cooker. Pour the sauce mixture over the beef and onions, making sure they are completely coated.

4. Cover and heat on a low setting for 4–5 hours.

PER SERVING Calories: 494 | Fat: 32.0g | Protein: 33.8g | Sodium: 446mg | Fiber: 0.8g | Carbohydrates: 9.0g | Sugar: 0.7g | Sugar alcohol: 3.0g

Venison Roast in Orange

*If you don't have access to venison, substitute beef or pork. Use an inexpensive
cut; the acidic orange juice will tenderize it during cooking.*

INGREDIENTS | SERVES 8

3 pounds venison roast

2 slices sugar-free bacon, cut into small pieces

2 cloves garlic, minced

½ teaspoon salt

½ teaspoon black pepper

1 bay leaf

2 whole cloves

¼ cup orange juice

1. In a large skillet, sauté the venison with the bacon, garlic, salt, and pepper over medium heat until the meat is lightly browned, about 5–8 minutes.

2. Transfer the meat and juices, bay leaf, cloves, and orange juice to the slow cooker.

3. Cover and heat on a low setting for 6–8 hours.

4. Open the slow cooker twice to baste, but no more. Remove the bay leaf before serving.

PER SERVING Calories: 237 | Fat: 6.2g | Protein: 40.1g | Sodium: 278mg | Fiber: 0.1g | Carbohydrates: 1.2g | Sugar: 0.7g

Coconut Soup

This simple dish is deliciously smooth and creamy. You can add cooked beef, chicken, or seafood for other flavors and textures.

INGREDIENTS | SERVES 6

3 tablespoons unsalted butter
1 medium onion, finely chopped
1½ tablespoons tapioca flour
5 cups sugar-free chicken broth, divided
2 cups unsweetened coconut flakes
1¼ cups full-fat canned coconut milk
¼ cup chopped fresh cilantro

1. Melt the butter in a large skillet over medium heat. Sauté the onion in butter until soft, about 10 minutes.

2. Blend the tapioca flour into ½ cup of the chicken broth. Add to the onion and stir over medium heat until thickened.

3. Transfer the mixture to the slow cooker and add the remaining broth.

4. Cover and heat on a low setting for 2–3 hours.

5. Preheat the oven to 350°F. Place the coconut flakes in a single layer on a baking sheet. Toast in the oven for 10 minutes, stirring occasionally, until the coconut is slightly browned.

6. An hour before serving, add the coconut milk to the slow cooker. Stir to combine.

7. To serve, ladle the soup into bowls and sprinkle with toasted coconut. Sprinkle with freshly chopped cilantro.

PER SERVING Calories: 301 | Fat: 28.2g | Protein: 3.9g | Sodium: 783mg | Fiber: 3.0g | Carbohydrates: 10.8g | Sugar: 2.9g

Country Chicken Stew

This recipe takes some advance planning, but it's a sure way to impress dinner guests. Serve this with sliced avocado and plenty of sour cream.

INGREDIENTS | SERVES 6

2 pounds chicken thighs, cut into pieces

1 large carrot, peeled and chopped

1 large onion, peeled and chopped

1 cup sugar-free chicken stock

2 cups water, divided

1 bouquet garni

1 teaspoon whole black peppercorns

2 tablespoons unsalted butter, divided

1 tablespoon tapioca flour

¼ pound salt pork

10 pearl onions

½ pound mushrooms

1 tablespoon fresh chopped parsley

Too Salty?

If your soup is too salty, put a piece of raw potato in the soup or add a spoonful each of cider vinegar and erythritol. If soup is too greasy, drop in a lettuce leaf, then take it back out after 2 minutes. The leaf will take some grease along with it.

1. Place the chicken thighs, carrot, onion, stock, 1 cup water, bouquet garni, and peppercorns in a large zip-top plastic bag. Make sure the chicken is completely submerged in the marinade with the vegetables. Place in the refrigerator to marinate overnight.

2. After marinating overnight, remove the chicken; strain the marinade and save the juice, discarding the vegetables and spices.

3. Melt 1 tablespoon butter in a large skillet over medium heat and mix in the tapioca flour until blended. Add the marinated chicken, stir for a few minutes, then slowly stir in the strained marinade and the remaining 1 cup of water. Mix to make sure there are no lumps.

4. Transfer to the slow cooker. Cover and heat on a low setting for 4–6 hours.

5. Cube the salt pork and peel the pearl onions. Place the pork with the onions in a medium pot, and cover with water. Heat over high heat until boiling; drain and discard the liquid.

6. Clean the mushrooms by wiping with a damp cloth, then halve them. Sauté the boiled pork, boiled onions, and mushrooms in remaining butter in a large skillet over medium heat until the pork is browned. Drain, then transfer to the slow cooker with the meat.

7. Cover the slow cooker and heat on a low setting for another 2 hours. Before serving, stir in the parsley.

PER SERVING Calories: 487 | Fat: 30.3g | Protein: 40.9g | Sodium: 845mg | Fiber: 1.8g | Carbohydrates: 12.5g | Sugar: 4.8g

Pull-Apart Pork

*This is excellent on keto "sandwiches," or served by itself. It also freezes well
and can be stored in single-serving containers for quick meals.*

INGREDIENTS | SERVES 6

1 tablespoon coconut oil

2 pounds pork stew meat, cubed

2 yellow onions, peeled and chopped

4 medium tomatoes, chopped

4 cloves garlic, minced

2 teaspoons hot chili powder

¼ teaspoon ground cinnamon

¼ teaspoon cayenne pepper

2 teaspoons dried oregano

2 teaspoons ground cumin

½ teaspoon salt

¼ cup apple cider vinegar

1. Melt the coconut oil in a large skillet over medium heat. Sauté the pork and onions in the oil until the meat is lightly browned, about 5–8 minutes.

2. Mix the tomatoes and garlic together in a large bowl.

3. Mix the spices, salt, and vinegar in a small bowl.

4. Place half of the tomato mixture in the bottom of the slow cooker. Sprinkle with ¼ of the spice mixture.

5. Place the meat mixture over the tomato layer, and sprinkle with ½ of the spice mixture.

6. Place the remaining tomato mixture on top of the meat, and sprinkle with the remaining spice mixture.

7. Cover and heat on a low setting for 6–8 hours.

PER SERVING Calories: 414 | Fat: 27.0g | Protein: 27.4g | Sodium: 324mg | Fiber: 2.1g | Carbohydrates: 8.0g | Sugar: 3.6g

Hamburger Vegetable Soup

It's easy to adapt this soup to suit your taste buds. Try adding some fresh herbs such as parsley, or use ground pork or turkey instead of beef. A topping of freshly grated Parmesan adds flavor and makes a great presentation too.

INGREDIENTS | SERVES 6

½ pound ground beef

6 cups sugar-free beef broth

3 medium fresh tomatoes, diced

1 large yellow onion, peeled and chopped

½ cup chopped celery

½ teaspoon salt

½ teaspoon black pepper

1 cup chopped fresh asparagus

1 cup fresh green beans

1. Brown the ground beef in a medium skillet over medium-high heat, breaking and crumbling into smaller pieces, about 7–10 minutes. Drain off grease.

2. Place the ground beef, beef broth, tomatoes, onion, celery, salt, and pepper in slow cooker. Cover and cook on a low setting for 6 hours.

3. Add the asparagus and green beans. Cover and cook on low 1–2 more hours before serving.

PER SERVING Calories: 97 | Fat: 3.6g | Protein: 8.7g | Sodium: 1,113mg | Fiber: 2.2g | Carbohydrates: 6.9g | Sugar: 3.6g

Thicken It Up

To create a thicker soup, remove some of the cooked vegetables from the broth and purée them in a blender, then stir them back into the soup. Or add full-fat coconut milk for an even richer soup.

East Indian Green Curried Chicken

This incredible dish has complex flavors and a fiery heat. Serve over steamed cauliflower, Fried Cauliflower "Rice" (see recipe in Chapter 7), or Garlicky Green Beans (see recipe in Chapter 7).

INGREDIENTS | SERVES 6

1½ cups unsweetened full-fat canned coconut milk, divided

1½ tablespoons green curry paste

6 (4-ounce) boneless, skinless chicken breasts

½ cup sliced canned bamboo shoots

¼ cup fish sauce

1 tablespoon granulated erythritol

¼ cup chopped fresh mint leaves

2 fresh green chili peppers, minced

Stocking Up on Ethnic Staples

If your local grocery store doesn't carry certain ethnic spices or ingredients, you may be able to find them on the Internet or at specialty shops. Just make sure to stock up on shelf-stable necessities so you can make these dishes whenever you like.

1. Heat ½ cup of the coconut milk and the green curry paste in a medium skillet over medium heat; stir until well blended. Add the chicken and sauté for 10 minutes.

2. Place the chicken breasts into the slow cooker. Stir in the remaining coconut milk, bamboo shoots, fish sauce, and erythritol.

3. Cover and cook on a low setting for 6–7 hours.

4. Stir in the mint and chili peppers. Cover and cook an additional 30 minutes.

PER SERVING Calories: 259 | Fat: 14.3g | Protein: 26.0g | Sodium: 747mg | Fiber: 0.7g | Carbohydrates: 8.2g | Sugar: 1.5g | Sugar alcohol: 2.0g

Chicken Peanut Stew

Sprinkle with chopped peanuts and flaked coconut before serving over freshly cooked cauliflower "rice."

INGREDIENTS | SERVES 4

4 (4-ounce) boneless, skinless chicken breasts

1 large green bell pepper

2 medium yellow onions

1 (6-ounce) can tomato paste

¾ cup unsalted sugar-free crunchy peanut butter

3 cups sugar-free chicken broth

1 teaspoon salt

1 teaspoon chili powder

1 teaspoon granulated erythritol

½ teaspoon ground nutmeg

1. Cut the meat into 1" cubes.

2. Remove the stem and seeds from the pepper and cut into ¼" rings. Peel the onions and cut into ¼" rings.

3. Combine all the ingredients in the slow cooker; stir until all ingredients are well mingled.

4. Cover and cook on a low setting for 4–6 hours.

PER SERVING Calories: 472 | Fat: 27.3g | Protein: 38.1g | Sodium: 1,307mg | Fiber: 7.8g | Carbohydrates: 26.1g | Sugar: 11.2g | Sugar alcohol: 1.0g

Cauliflower and Ham Chowder

Serve with an array of pickled vegetables to offset the creamy sweet flavor of this soup.

INGREDIENTS | SERVES 6

1 cup canned full-fat coconut milk

1 tablespoon tapioca flour

2 cups diced sugar-free ham

3 cups chopped fresh cauliflower

1 small white onion, peeled and finely chopped

1 cup grated Swiss cheese

2 cups water

1 cup heavy cream

1. Mix the coconut milk and tapioca flour in the slow cooker.

2. Add the ham, cauliflower, onion, Swiss cheese, and water to the slow cooker.

3. Cover and cook on a low setting for 8–9 hours.

4. Ten minutes before serving, stir in the cream.

PER SERVING Calories: 374 | Fat: 28.6g | Protein: 19.3g | Sodium: 670mg | Fiber: 1.3g | Carbohydrates: 7.8g | Sugar: 2.8g

French Countryside Chicken and Pork Stew

Top with chopped parsley and a dollop of sour cream right before serving.

INGREDIENTS | SERVES 4

3 pounds boneless pork chops

4 (4-ounce) boneless, skinless chicken breasts

2 tablespoons olive oil

10 pearl onions, peeled

4 cloves garlic, minced

2 cups sugar-free beef broth

¼ cup sugar-free chicken stock

2 tablespoons Dijon mustard

4 ounces (½ cup) fresh mushrooms, quartered

1 teaspoon warm water

1 teaspoon tapioca flour

Preparing Pearl Onions

When using pearl onions, cook them first in boiling water for 3 minutes. Plunge them into cold water. Remove them from the water and cut off the ends before easily removing the skin.

1. Cut pork and chicken into ½" cubes.

2. Heat olive oil in a large skillet over medium-high heat. Sauté the pork, chicken, onions, and garlic until the meat is browned, about 7 minutes.

3. Drain off grease and add mixture to the slow cooker.

4. Combine beef broth, chicken stock, and mustard in a medium bowl and pour mixture into the slow cooker. Add mushrooms on top.

5. Cover and cook on a low setting for 8–9 hours.

6. About 30 minutes before serving, make a paste of the warm water and tapioca flour; add to the slow cooker, stirring well. Cook uncovered, stirring occasionally, until a gravy develops.

PER SERVING Calories: 579 | Fat: 17.5g | Protein: 86.7g | Sodium: 1,498mg | Fiber: 1.4g | Carbohydrates: 12.3g | Sugar: 4.1g

Chili Coconut Chicken

The coconut milk provides a nice balance to the red chilies. Serve this over Fried Cauliflower "Rice" or Mashed Cauliflower (see recipes in Chapter 7).

INGREDIENTS | SERVES 4

½ teaspoon black mustard seeds

½ teaspoon cumin seeds

½ teaspoon coriander seeds

3 tablespoons coconut oil

8 curry leaves

1 medium red onion, peeled and finely chopped

1 tablespoon Ginger-Garlic Paste (see sidebar recipe)

3 dried red chilies, roughly pounded

½ teaspoon turmeric powder

½ teaspoon salt

1½ pounds boneless, skinless chicken, cubed

Water, as needed

1 cup full-fat canned coconut milk

Ginger-Garlic Paste

Combine 4 ounces chopped garlic and 4 ounces of fresh peeled and chopped gingerroot in a food processor. While pulsing, slowly drizzle in one tablespoon of olive oil. Continue pulsing until a smooth paste forms. Store the paste in an airtight jar in the refrigerator. The paste will keep for up to 2 weeks in the refrigerator.

1. In a small skillet over medium heat, dry-roast the mustard seeds, cumin seeds, and coriander seeds. When the spices release their aroma, about 3 minutes, remove from heat and let cool. In a spice grinder, grind to a coarse powder. Set aside.

2. In a large skillet, heat the coconut oil over medium heat. Add the curry leaves and the onions; sauté for about 1 minute.

3. Add the Ginger-Garlic Paste and dried red chilies. Sauté over medium heat until the onions are well browned and the oil begins to separate from the sides of the onion mixture, about 8 minutes.

4. Add the ground seeds, turmeric powder, and salt; sauté for 1 minute.

5. Add the chicken pieces; mix well and transfer into a 3–4-quart slow cooker. You can add up to ¼ cup of water if the ground spices don't incorporate as well as you'd like, although not necessary.

6. Cover and cook on high for 2–3 hours, or on low for 4–6 hours, or until the chicken is cooked through.

7. During the last 30 minutes, add the coconut milk and simmer. Serve hot.

PER SERVING Calories: 415 | Fat: 25.8g | Protein: 36.9g | Sodium: 596mg | Fiber: 1.2g | Carbohydrates: 8.3g | Sugar: 2.9g

Mixed Vegetables in Coconut Sauce

Use your choice of seasonal vegetables to make this dish. Serve with Turnip Fries or Mashed Cauliflower (see recipes in Chapter 7), or over roasted spaghetti squash and your choice of any hot pickle.

INGREDIENTS | SERVES 4

1 cup unsweetened desiccated coconut

1 tablespoon toasted cumin seeds

2 green serrano chilies, seeded

Water, as needed

2 small carrots, peeled and chopped

½ pound frozen cut green beans, thawed

¼ cup Coconut Yogurt (see recipe in Chapter 8)

¼ cup sour cream

½ teaspoon turmeric powder

½ teaspoon salt

1 tablespoon coconut oil

1 teaspoon black mustard seeds

8 curry leaves

1. In a food processor, grind the coconut, cumin seeds, and green chilies along with a few tablespoons of water to make a thick paste. Set aside.

2. In a slow cooker, combine the carrots, green beans, and 1½ cups of water. Cover and cook on high for 1½ hours, or on low for 3 hours, or until the vegetables are soft. Drain off any remaining water.

3. Add the yogurt, sour cream, coconut paste, turmeric, and salt to the vegetables. Simmer until the vegetables are completely cooked through, another 45 minutes on high or 1½ hours on low. When cooked through, turn off the heat and set aside.

4. In a small skillet, heat the coconut oil over medium heat. Add the mustard seeds and curry leaves. When the seeds begin to crackle, remove from heat and pour over the cooked vegetables. Serve hot.

PER SERVING Calories: 259 | Fat: 22.5g | Protein: 3.7g | Sodium: 327mg | Fiber: 5.3g | Carbohydrates: 14.1g | Sugar: 4.4g

Lamb Vindaloo

You can also prepare this with pork or beef; adjust seasonings to taste. The cooking times will stay the same.

INGREDIENTS | SERVES 4

¾ cup rice vinegar

¼ cup water

1 teaspoon black peppercorns, roughly pounded

1 tablespoon minced garlic

2 teaspoons red chili powder

2 green serrano chilies, minced

1½ pounds boneless lean lamb, cubed

3 tablespoons light olive oil

1 tablespoon grated gingerroot

1 large red onion, peeled and finely chopped

6 whole dried red chilies, roughly pounded

1 (1") cinnamon stick

½ teaspoon turmeric powder

½ teaspoon salt

Selecting Lamb

Color can be a great help when buying lamb. Younger lamb is pinkish red with a velvety texture. It should have a thin layer of white fat surrounding it. If the meat is much darker in color, it means that the lamb is older and flavored more strongly.

1. In the slow cooker insert, combine the rice vinegar, water, black peppercorns, garlic, red chili powder, and green chilies. Add the lamb and coat evenly with the marinade. Refrigerate, covered, for 1 hour.

2. In a deep pan, heat the oil over medium heat. Add the gingerroot and sauté for about 10 seconds. Add the onion and sauté for about 7–8 minutes or until golden brown.

3. Add the dried red chilies, cinnamon stick, and turmeric powder; sauté for 20 seconds.

4. Remove the lamb pieces from the marinade. Add the lamb to the pan with onions and sauté on high heat for about 10 minutes or until the lamb is browned and the oil starts to separate from the mixture.

5. Transfer the browned lamb back to the slow cooker. Mix with the marinade and salt. Cover and cook on high for 4–5 hours, or on low for 8–10 hours, or until the lamb is cooked through and tender. Serve hot.

PER SERVING Calories: 426 | Fat: 31.6g | Protein: 22.8g | Sodium: 406mg | Fiber: 1.5g | Carbohydrates: 6.1g | Sugar: 1.9g

Spicy Shrimp and Cheese Dip

Cooking tip: If the dip is too thick, add coconut milk or heavy cream in half-cup increments until it's the consistency you like. This dip is heavenly with the addition of 1 cup chopped cooked scallops.

INGREDIENTS | SERVES 12

2 slices sugar-free bacon

2 medium yellow onions, diced

2 cloves garlic, minced

1 cup popcorn shrimp (not the breaded kind), cooked

1 medium tomato, diced

3 cups shredded Monterey jack cheese

¼ teaspoon sugar-free hot sauce

¼ teaspoon cayenne pepper

¼ teaspoon black pepper

Cleaning

Use a rough sponge to remove any dried-on food from the slow cooker when cleaning it. A scouring pad could scratch the surface, creating a place for bacteria to grow.

1. Cook the bacon in a medium skillet over medium heat until crisp, about 5–10 minutes. Keep grease in pan. Lay the bacon on a paper towel to cool.

2. When cool, crumble the bacon with your fingers.

3. Add the onions and garlic to the bacon drippings in the skillet and sauté over medium-low heat until they are soft and fragrant, about 10 minutes.

4. Combine all the ingredients in the slow cooker; stir well. Cook covered on a low setting for 1–2 hours, or until the cheese is fully melted.

PER SERVING Calories: 144 | Fat: 10.0g | Protein: 10.0g | Sodium: 294mg | Fiber: 0.5g | Carbohydrates: 2.5g | Sugar: 1.2g

Creamy Pecan Beef Dip

Try this unique dip at your next gathering. Serve with bell pepper wedges and cucumber rounds. Provide plenty of veggies—this dip goes quickly!

INGREDIENTS | SERVES 6

3 ounces sliced smoked beef
2 tablespoons finely chopped onion
½ cup finely chopped pecans
2 tablespoons minced green pepper
8 ounces cream cheese
½ cup sour cream
2 tablespoons heavy cream
⅛ teaspoon white pepper

1. Finely shred the smoked beef.

2. Combine all ingredients in the slow cooker.

3. Cover and heat on a low setting for 2–3 hours or until dip bubbles at edges. Do not overheat.

PER SERVING Calories: 283 | Fat: 24.7g | Protein: 6.2g | Sodium: 286mg | Fiber: 1.0g | Carbohydrates: 4.0g | Sugar: 2.5g

Artichoke Dip

For a truly unique appetizer, dollop this dip on top of Parmesan Chips (see recipe in Chapter 10). Alternatively, use bell pepper strips and celery sticks to scoop and add crunch.

INGREDIENTS | SERVES 6 AS AN APPETIZER

⅓ cup Homemade Mayonnaise (see recipe in Chapter 5)
½ cup grated Parmesan cheese
⅓ cup full-fat sour cream
1 clove garlic, finely minced
6 ounces (1½ cups) marinated artichoke hearts, chopped into penny-sized pieces

1. Combine the mayonnaise, Parmesan, sour cream, and garlic. Mix in the chopped artichoke hearts.

2. Place the mixture in the slow cooker, cover, and cook on a low setting for 1 hour. Mix periodically while it is cooking to ensure that all ingredients combine and meld together.

PER SERVING Calories: 163 | Fat: 13.5g | Protein: 4.4g | Sodium: 297mg | Fiber: 3.6g | Carbohydrates: 5.7g | Sugar: 0.9g

Storage Tip

Store the slow cooker with the lid alongside instead of on top to prevent the chance that mold will grow if you don't use it for several weeks.

Smoothies and Drinks

Coconut Chia Smoothie

You can turn this into a chocolate coconut chia smoothie by adding a couple of tablespoons of unsweetened cocoa powder before blending.

INGREDIENTS | SERVES 1

1 cup full-fat canned coconut milk

2 tablespoons chia seeds

2 tablespoons coconut oil, melted

¼ cup frozen blueberries

1. Place all ingredients in a blender and blend until smooth.

2. Serve cold.

PER SERVING Calories: 835 | Fat: 79.4g | Protein: 9.4g | Sodium: 33mg | Fiber: 10.8g | Carbohydrates: 23.0g | Sugar: 3.3g

Choosing Coconut Milk

The coconut milk that comes in a box is full of preservatives and low in fat. Some sweetened varieties contain sugar or other sweeteners that increase carbohydrate content. Look for full-fat coconut milk in a can that contains only coconut milk or a combination of coconut milk and guar gum.

Chocolate Almond Smoothie

Turn this into a chocolate coconut smoothie by using coconut milk and coconut butter instead of almond milk and almond butter.

INGREDIENTS | SERVES 2

1 cup unsweetened almond milk

¼ cup sugar-free almond butter

2 tablespoons unsweetened cocoa powder

¼ cup heavy cream

1½ cups ice

5 drops liquid stevia

1. Put all ingredients in a blender and blend until smooth.

2. Serve cold.

PER SERVING Calories: 309 | Fat: 28.4g | Protein: 9.2g | Sodium: 192mg | Fiber: 6.0g | Carbohydrates: 11.0g | Sugar: 1.9g

Pumpkin Pie Smoothie

Don't confuse pumpkin purée with canned pumpkin pie filling. Pure pumpkin purée contains only the flesh of a pumpkin, while pumpkin pie filling contains sweeteners that increase sugar and carbohydrate content.

INGREDIENTS | SERVES 2

½ cup pumpkin purée

1 cup full-fat canned coconut milk

½ teaspoon pumpkin pie spice

¼ large avocado

2 tablespoons coconut oil, melted

¼ teaspoon maple extract

¼ cup unsweetened whey protein powder

1. Put all ingredients in a blender and blend until smooth.

2. Serve cold.

PER SERVING Calories: 422 | Fat: 38.1g | Protein: 12.6g | Sodium: 35mg | Fiber: 2.8g | Carbohydrates: 8.1g | Sugar: 1.2g

Green Smoothie

The type of whey protein powder you choose for this recipe will make a big difference in the taste. Switch it up by alternating between chocolate and vanilla.

INGREDIENTS | SERVES 2

1 cup full-fat canned coconut milk

½ avocado

¼ cup whey protein powder

½ teaspoon vanilla extract

½ cup baby spinach

2 drops liquid stevia

1. Put all ingredients in a blender and blend until smooth.

2. Serve immediately.

PER SERVING Calories: 326 | Fat: 27.5g | Protein: 12.6g | Sodium: 41mg | Fiber: 2.9g | Carbohydrates: 7.3g | Sugar: 0.3g

Watch Your Whey

Although protein is the major nutrient in protein powders, a lot of them contain sweeteners that add a significant amount of carbohydrates. When choosing a protein powder, look for one that is low in net carbohydrates and doesn't contain artificial ingredients.

Honeydew and Avocado Smoothie

This creamy, sweet smoothie packs plenty of protein and healthy fats to keep you full and going strong throughout the day. Try substituting cantaloupe or your favorite melon for a slightly different flavor.

INGREDIENTS | SERVES 1

¼ medium avocado, peeled and pit removed

¼ cup chunks honeydew melon

½ cup full-fat canned coconut milk

¼ cup water

1 tablespoon chia seeds

2 tablespoons unsweetened whey protein powder

Ice, to thicken (optional)

1. Place avocado, melon, coconut milk, water, chia seeds, and protein powder in a blender and blend until smooth.

2. Add ice to thicken, if desired.

3. Serve cold.

PER SERVING Calories: 407 | Fat: 31.9g | Protein: 15.1g | Sodium: 43mg | Fiber: 8.2g | Carbohydrates: 17.1g | Sugar: 3.6g

Honeydew and Cantaloupe: Sweet Treats

Honeydew melon is related to the cantaloupe, but it has a smooth green flesh and a slightly milder flavor. Both fruits are often served for dessert. You can consume more than half of the recommended daily amount of vitamin C with just one wedge of honeydew melon; one wedge of cantaloupe will provide over 100 percent of the recommended daily amount of vitamin C, and 120 percent of vitamin A.

Carrot Asparagus Green Smoothie

The addition of flaxseed to this smoothie lends a delicious hint of nutty flavor, and boosts the vitamin and mineral content as well.

INGREDIENTS | SERVES 4

1 cup watercress
1 cup chopped asparagus
2 small carrots, peeled and chopped
2 tablespoons whole flaxseed
2 cups full-fat canned coconut milk
1 cup water

1. Combine watercress, asparagus, carrots, flaxseed, and coconut milk in a blender and blend until thoroughly combined.

2. Add water while blending until desired texture is reached.

PER SERVING Calories: 266 | Fat: 24.8g | Protein: 4.4g | Sodium: 35mg | Fiber: 2.8g | Carbohydrates: 8.2g | Sugar: 1.8g

Flaxseed

Organic, nonorganic, ground, and whole, flaxseed can be found in grocery aisles with nuts or near produce. You can purchase the whole seed product and use them in sandwiches, salads, and main dishes by using a coffee grinder to grind them until thoroughly powdered.

Avocado Raspberry Smoothie

Sweet and satisfying, this smoothie makes a great breakfast—or a decadent dessert. Try swapping out the raspberries with blueberries, blackberries, or even cloudberries for a more exotic touch.

INGREDIENTS | SERVES 1

¼ medium avocado, peeled and pit removed
¼ cup raspberries
½ cup chopped fresh mint
1 cup heavy cream
2 tablespoons coconut oil, melted
½ cup water

1. Place avocado, raspberries, mint, cream, and coconut oil in a blender and blend until smooth.

2. Add water while blending until desired consistency is reached.

PER SERVING Calories: 1134 | Fat: 114.0g | Protein: 6.4g | Sodium: 95mg | Fiber: 5.3g | Carbohydrates: 15.2g | Sugar: 8.1g

Lime and Coconut Smoothie

The tart taste of lime in this green smoothie is balanced with the sweet and creamy coconut milk. This recipe will bring the tastes of tropical locales into your kitchen, and is great to share with friends.

INGREDIENTS | SERVES 4

1 cup fresh spinach
2 tablespoons chia seeds
2 large limes, peeled and seeded
2 cups full-fat canned coconut milk
½ cup water, divided

1. Combine spinach, chia seeds, limes, and coconut milk in a blender with half of the water and blend until thoroughly combined.

2. Add remaining water while blending until desired consistency is reached.

PER SERVING Calories: 265 | Fat: 24.8g | Protein: 3.9g | Sodium: 21mg | Fiber: 3.3g | Carbohydrates: 9.1g | Sugar: 0.5g

Limes and Joints

Although many patients suffering from arthritis decide to exercise and eat differently, few know the powerful effects limes can have on joints! These vitamin C–filled fruits can pack a punch in reducing arthritis symptoms to a minimum and making everyday life seem less achy!

Ginger Strawberry Smoothie

The soothing effects of ginger make this recipe perfect for optimizing digestion. If you prefer a thicker, colder shake, add crushed ice ½ cup at a time until suitably thick and creamy.

INGREDIENTS | SERVES 4

1 cup watercress
¾ cup frozen strawberries
½" piece gingerroot, peeled
1 cup full-fat canned coconut milk
1 cup heavy cream, divided

1. Combine watercress, strawberries, ginger, coconut milk, and ½ cup heavy cream in a blender and blend until thoroughly combined.

2. Add remaining heavy cream as needed while blending until desired consistency is reached.

PER SERVING Calories: 327 | Fat: 32.2g | Protein: 2.7g | Sodium: 33mg | Fiber: 0.6g | Carbohydrates: 6.0g | Sugar: 3.0g

Almond Berry Smoothie

Almonds are the star of this flavorful smoothie—almond butter and whole almonds combine for a mix of crunchy and smooth textures. The omega-3 content of this smoothie is boosted with the addition of flaxseed, which adds even nuttier flavor.

INGREDIENTS | SERVES 4

2 cups unsweetened homemade almond milk, divided (see sidebar in Banana Nut Smoothie recipe in this chapter)

2 tablespoons unsweetened almond butter

¼ cup raw almonds

1 tablespoon whole flaxseed

1 cup fresh spinach

1 cup strawberries

½ cup heavy cream

1. Combine 1 cup almond milk with the almond butter, almonds, and flaxseed in a blender and emulsify. For a smoother texture, emulsify completely until no nut pieces remain. For a chunky texture, be sure to leave some pieces of almond intact.

2. Add spinach, strawberries, and heavy cream and blend until thoroughly combined.

3. Add remaining 1 cup of almond milk as needed while blending until desired consistency is reached.

PER SERVING Calories: 240 | Fat: 21.3g | Protein: 5.7g | Sodium: 123mg | Fiber: 3.6g | Carbohydrates: 8.1g | Sugar: 3.3g

Kale and Brazil Nut Smoothie

This unusual blend of ingredients delivers sound nutrition and unique flavor. Kale is a nutritional powerhouse that provides an abundance of vitamins A and K. Ninety-one percent of Brazil nuts' calories come from fat, making them a perfect addition to the ketogenic diet.

INGREDIENTS | SERVES 2

2 cups chopped kale

¼ cup Brazil nuts, frozen

2 tablespoons coconut oil, melted

2 cups full-fat canned coconut milk

½ teaspoon ground cinnamon

½ teaspoon ground allspice

Ice, to thicken

1. Place kale, nuts, coconut oil, coconut milk, cinnamon, and allspice in a blender and blend until thoroughly combined.

2. With the blender running, add ice in small batches until desired consistency is reached. If smoothie is too thick, add splashes of water to thin out the consistency.

PER SERVING Calories: 681 | Fat: 68.9g | Protein: 7.7g | Sodium: 35mg | Fiber: 2.3g | Carbohydrates: 10.6g | Sugar: 0.8g

Triple Green Smoothie

This smoothie features spinach, avocado, and lime for a boost of vitamins, whole nutrition, and a balance of flavors. If the taste of spinach is too strong for your palate, try substituting romaine lettuce or watercress.

INGREDIENTS | SERVES 4

1 cup fresh spinach

2 avocados, peeled and pits removed

1 large lime, peeled and seeded

1 cup full-fat coconut milk, divided

¾ cup full-fat plain Greek yogurt, divided

1. Combine spinach, avocados, lime, ½ cup coconut milk, and ½ cup yogurt in a blender and blend until thoroughly combined.

2. Add remaining ½ cup coconut milk and ¼ cup yogurt while blending until desired texture is reached.

PER SERVING Calories: 270 | Fat: 22.8g | Protein: 6.6g | Sodium: 33mg | Fiber: 5.1g | Carbohydrates: 10.8g | Sugar: 2.2g

Fiber Benefits

Leafy greens, vegetables, and fruits all contain some amount of this miracle substance. Because the human body is almost completely unable to digest fiber, we benefit from its tendency to make our stomachs feel full and clear our intestinal tracts by remaining nearly intact throughout digestion. Although fiber is available in pill and powder forms, those are a far cry from a healthy bowl of spinach or broccoli.

Calming Cucumber Smoothie

The light taste of cucumber and the refreshing fragrance of mint combine with romaine lettuce in this delightful smoothie. Toasted almonds make a great addition to this smoothie; try adding a tablespoon of sliced toasted almonds in addition to the coconut flakes.

INGREDIENTS | SERVES 4

1 cup chopped romaine lettuce
2 cucumbers, peeled
¼ cup chopped mint
1 cup full-fat canned coconut milk, divided
¼ cup unsweetened coconut flakes

Cucumbers Aren't Just Water

Even though a cucumber is mostly water (and fiber), these green veggies have detoxifying and rehydrating properties. By consuming one serving of cucumbers per day, you'll not only fulfill a full serving of vegetables and stave off hunger, you'll have clear, hydrated skin!

1. Combine romaine, cucumbers, mint, and ½ cup coconut milk in a blender and combine thoroughly.

2. Add remaining coconut milk while blending.

3. Divide smoothie mixture into 4 glasses. Top each glass with 1 tablespoon coconut flakes to garnish.

PER SERVING Calories: 151 | Fat: 13.9g | Protein: 2.2g | Sodium: 11mg | Fiber: 1.6g | Carbohydrates: 5.4g | Sugar: 1.8g

Coconut Cream Dream Smoothie

Coconut cream pie is a delicious dessert, but it packs empty calories and very few vitamins and minerals. This recipe blends the star ingredients of coconut cream pie in a healthy green smoothie.

INGREDIENTS | SERVES 4

1 cup chopped romaine lettuce
Flesh of 2 mature coconuts
1 tablespoon lemon juice
1 medium avocado, peeled and pit removed
¼" piece gingerroot, peeled
½ cup full-fat canned coconut milk
½ cup full-fat plain Greek-style yogurt
Ice, to thicken

1. Combine romaine, coconut flesh, lemon juice, avocado, ginger, and coconut milk in a blender until thoroughly combined.

2. Add the yogurt while blending until just combined.

3. Slowly add ice while blending until desired texture is reached.

PER SERVING Calories: 844 | Fat: 74.3g | Protein: 10.6g | Sodium: 56mg | Fiber: 20.5g | Carbohydrates: 35.9g | Sugar: 13.9g

Spiced Cashew Butter Smoothie

Mix up the usual peanut butter—and almond butter—filled smoothies by swapping in cashew butter instead! Cashew butter is slightly sweet and very creamy. Raw cashew butter is best, as it contains higher levels of nutrients than its roasted counterparts.

INGREDIENTS | SERVES 1

½ avocado, peeled and pit removed

1 tablespoon unsalted, unsweetened cashew butter

½ cup heavy cream

½ cup full-fat canned coconut milk

½ teaspoon ground cinnamon

½ teaspoon ground allspice

½ teaspoon sugar-free vanilla extract

½ cup ice

1. Combine avocado, cashew butter, heavy cream, coconut milk, cinnamon, allspice, and vanilla extract in a blender and combine thoroughly.

2. Slowly add ice while blending until desired texture is reached.

3. Pour smoothie mixture into a glass.

PER SERVING Calories: 961 | Fat: 90.7g | Protein: 10.3g | Sodium: 71mg | Fiber: 10.5g | Carbohydrates: 24.4g | Sugar: 3.8g

Cashew Benefits

Cashews have a lower fat content than most nuts, but that does not mean they're not a great addition to the ketogenic diet. Cashews are high in heart-healthy monounsaturated fats, such as those found in olive oil, and have been found to reduce high triglycerides in the blood. In general, nuts promote heart health and lower the risk of weight gain, so add more servings to your diet to live your best!

Spiced Chocolate Smoothie

The flavors in this smoothie are reminiscent of Mexican hot chocolate—without all the added sugar and carbohydrates the traditional version contains. If cayenne powder is too spicy for your taste buds, simply omit it from this smoothie. Try adding a pinch of nutmeg instead.

INGREDIENTS | SERVES 1

½ cup full-fat canned coconut milk

1 tablespoon coconut oil, melted

1 tablespoon ground flaxseed or chia seeds

¼ teaspoon cayenne powder

½ teaspoon ground cinnamon

2½ tablespoons unsweetened cocoa powder

¼ teaspoon unsweetened vanilla extract

½ cup water

½ cup ice

1 cinnamon stick, to garnish

1. Combine coconut milk, coconut oil, ground seeds, cayenne, cinnamon, cocoa powder, vanilla extract, and water in a blender and combine thoroughly.

2. Slowly add ice while blending until desired texture is reached.

3. Pour smoothie mixture into a glass and garnish with cinnamon stick, if desired.

PER SERVING Calories: 412 | Fat: 40.3g | Protein: 6.0g | Sodium: 18mg | Fiber: 7.8g | Carbohydrates: 14.3g | Sugar: 0.3g

Cayenne for Digestive Health

You would think that such a spicy addition would cause stomach discomfort, but this pepper has amazing benefits. Cayenne has the ability to promote a digestive enzyme that works to kill bad bacteria ingested from foods while promoting the good bacteria that optimizes the digestive process. Cayenne also fights off the bad bacteria that cause stomach ulcers!

Orange Coconut Smoothie

Packed with brain-stimulating and immune-system-boosting vitamin C, this smoothie is a great option when everyone around you seems to be sick. Its power is intensified with the antioxidant-rich coconut milk.

INGREDIENTS | SERVES 4

1 cup chopped iceberg lettuce

2 medium oranges, peeled

2 cups full-fat canned coconut milk

2 tablespoons coconut oil, melted

1. Blend lettuce and oranges until just combined.

2. Add coconut milk and coconut oil slowly while blending until desired consistency is reached.

PER SERVING Calories: 301 | Fat: 29.1g | Protein: 2.8g | Sodium: 15mg | Fiber: 1.1g | Carbohydrates: 8.2g | Sugar: 4.0g

Vitamin C

Oranges are well known for their immunity-building power, and rightfully so! Consuming oranges every day can help the human body fight off illnesses from the common cold to serious cancers and heart disease. You can thank the rich beta-carotenes and the vitamin C. An orange is a definite must for health and longevity.

Peanut Butter Cup Smoothie

Love the candy treat but not the sugar? This smoothie is truly the drinkable version, ready in minutes for breakfast on the go.

INGREDIENTS | MAKES 1 FAT BOMB

½ (13.5-ounce) can coconut milk

1 tablespoon powdered unflavored gelatin

2 tablespoons peanut butter

2 tablespoons cocoa powder

1 teaspoon vanilla extract

6 drops liquid stevia

4 ice cubes

1. Pour milk and gelatin into a blender and blend to combine.

2. Add remaining ingredients except ice cubes and blend another minute until well mixed.

3. Place ice cubes into blender and process until smoothie thickens. Serve immediately.

PER 1 FAT BOMB Calories: 626 | Fat: 55.4g | Protein: 19.1g | Sodium: 44mg | Fiber: 5.6g | Carbohydrates: 19.3g | Sugar: 4.1g

Banana Nut Smoothie

This smoothie combines ample protein and the healthy fats you need. In addition to the vitamins, minerals, and nutrients from the lettuce and banana, the healthy fats from the coconut milk make this smoothie a powerful start to any day.

INGREDIENTS | SERVES 4

1 cup full-fat canned coconut milk

1 cup chopped iceberg lettuce

1 cup heavy cream

½ teaspoon vanilla extract

1 cup unsweetened vanilla almond milk, divided

1 medium banana, sliced

1. Combine coconut milk, lettuce, heavy cream, and vanilla extract in a blender with ½ cup almond milk and blend thoroughly.

2. Continue adding remaining almond milk while blending until desired consistency is reached.

3. To serve, divide smoothie into 4 glasses. Top each glass with an equal amount of sliced banana.

PER SERVING Calories: 353 | Fat: 32.9g | Protein: 3.1g | Sodium: 71mg | Fiber: 0.9g | Carbohydrates: 10.5g | Sugar: 5.6g

Make Your Own Almond Milk

Although there are a number of almond milks on the market, they are often full of sugar or unhealthy additives. Some people choose to create their own lower-cost, lower-sugar version at home. If you'd like to create your own almond milk, combine ½ cup water and 1 cup almonds and blend thoroughly. Add a touch of vanilla extract to make a vanilla version. Strain before using.

Gingerbread Gem Smoothie

Ginger is an often forgotten spice in American cuisine unless it's Christmastime. This delicious, dairy-free smoothie will taste and smell like a Christmas cookie bake-off.

INGREDIENTS | MAKES 1 FAT BOMB

6 ounces unsweetened almond milk

1 tablespoon powdered unflavored gelatin

1 tablespoon almond butter

½ teaspoon vanilla extract

½ teaspoon ground ginger

½ teaspoon cinnamon

6 drops liquid stevia

6 ice cubes

1. Pour milk and gelatin into a blender and blend to combine.

2. Add remaining ingredients except ice cubes and blend another minute until well mixed.

3. Place ice cubes into blender and process until smoothie thickens. Serve immediately.

PER 1 FAT BOMB Calories: 146 | Fat: 9.8g | Protein: 10.3g | Sodium: 176mg | Fiber: 2.8g | Carbohydrates: 5.5g | Sugar: 0.8g

Strawberry Vanilla Smoothie

Strawberries are a great fruit to up the flavor of any smoothie without adding too much sugar.

INGREDIENTS | MAKES 1 FAT BOMB

½ (13.5-ounce) can coconut milk

1 tablespoon powdered unflavored gelatin

1 tablespoon coconut oil, softened but not melted

1 teaspoon vanilla extract

¼ cup chopped fresh strawberries

6 drops liquid stevia

6 ice cubes

1. Pour milk and gelatin into a blender and blend to combine.

2. Add remaining ingredients except ice cubes and blend another minute until well mixed.

3. Place ice cubes into blender and process until smoothie thickens. Serve immediately.

PER 1 FAT BOMB Calories: 541 | Fat: 51.2g | Protein: 10.1g | Sodium: 37mg | Fiber: 0.8g | Carbohydrates: 9.1g | Sugar: 2.6g

Vanilla Avocado Smoothie

Avocado not only adds body to this smoothie, it makes this smoothie a beautiful green color too. Of course, the healthy omega-3 fats make this shake an even more filling fat bomb.

INGREDIENTS | MAKES 1 FAT BOMB

½ (13.5-ounce) can coconut milk

1 tablespoon powdered unflavored gelatin

1 tablespoon ground flaxseed

½ medium avocado, pitted and peeled

1 teaspoon vanilla extract

6 drops liquid stevia

4 ice cubes

1. Pour milk, gelatin, and flaxseed into a blender and blend to combine.

2. Add remaining ingredients except ice cubes and blend another minute until well mixed.

3. Place ice cubes into blender and process until smoothie thickens. Serve immediately.

PER 1 FAT BOMB Calories: 561 | Fat: 50.5g | Protein: 12.5g | Sodium: 44mg | Fiber: 6.5g | Carbohydrates: 13.8g | Sugar: 0.8g

Matcha Madness Smoothie

Matcha not only adds antioxidants to this smoothie, but also a beautiful green hue. The best quality matcha powders add a bit of earthy flavor and a subtle sweetness too.

INGREDIENTS | MAKES 1 FAT BOMB

½ (13.5-ounce) can coconut milk

1 tablespoon powdered unflavored gelatin

2 tablespoons almond butter

1 teaspoon vanilla extract

1 tablespoon matcha

6 drops liquid stevia

4 ice cubes

1. Pour milk and gelatin into a blender and blend to combine.

2. Add remaining ingredients except ice cubes and blend another minute until well mixed.

3. Place ice cubes into blender and process until smoothie thickens. Serve immediately.

PER 1 FAT BOMB Calories: 609 | Fat: 55.0g | Protein: 16.9g | Sodium: 137mg | Fiber: 4.0g | Carbohydrates: 15.3g | Sugar: 1.5g

Eggnog Smoothie

Traditional eggnog would make an excellent choice for a fat bomb, if it wasn't for all the sugar included. This smoothie has all the fat and flavor without the added carbs.

INGREDIENTS | MAKES 2 FAT BOMBS

2 large eggs, yolk and white separated
8 ounces heavy cream
½ teaspoon vanilla extract
1 teaspoon nutmeg
⅛ teaspoon ground cloves
⅜ teaspoon cinnamon, divided
8 drops liquid stevia
2 tablespoons granular Swerve
8 ice cubes

1. In a medium bowl, beat egg whites with a hand mixer until stiff peaks form. Set aside.

2. In a separate large bowl, beat yolks with mixer until color changes to pale yellow. Add cream, vanilla, nutmeg, cloves, ⅛ teaspoon cinnamon, stevia, and Swerve and stir to combine.

3. Fold whites into yolk mixture.

4. Pour mix into blender with ice cubes and blend until mixture thickens.

5. Sprinkle remaining cinnamon on top of each glass and serve immediately.

PER 1 FAT BOMB Calories: 472 | Fat: 44.5g | Protein: 8.7g | Sodium: 114mg | Fiber: 0.5g | Carbohydrates: 16.7g | Sugar: 3.5g

Key Lime Pie Smoothie

Using full-fat dairy lends richness to this tropical-tasting treat.

INGREDIENTS | MAKES 1 FAT BOMB

6 ounces half-and-half

1 tablespoon powdered unflavored gelatin

1 teaspoon vanilla extract

2 tablespoons freshly squeezed key lime juice

1 teaspoon lime zest

6 drops liquid stevia

6 ice cubes

1. Pour half-and-half and gelatin into a blender and blend to combine.

2. Add remaining ingredients except ice cubes and blend another minute until well mixed.

3. Place ice cubes into blender and process until smoothie thickens. Serve immediately.

PER 1 FAT BOMB Calories: 263 | Fat: 18.6g | Protein: 11.2g | Sodium: 82mg | Fiber: 0.3g | Carbohydrates: 10.7g | Sugar: 8.4g

Cinnamon Roll Smoothie

The only difference between the sugar- and gluten-filled version of the roll and this smoothie is the time it takes to make it, and of course the fact that it fits into a low-carb, high-fat diet.

INGREDIENTS | MAKES 1 FAT BOMB

6 ounces half-and-half

1 tablespoon softened cream cheese

1 teaspoon vanilla extract

½ teaspoon plus ⅛ teaspoon cinnamon, divided

6 drops liquid stevia

6 ice cubes

1. Pour half-and-half and cream cheese into a blender and blend to combine.

2. Add vanilla, ½ teaspoon cinnamon, and stevia and blend another minute until well mixed.

3. Place ice cubes into blender and process until smoothie thickens. Sprinkle ⅛ teaspoon cinnamon on top and serve.

PER 1 FAT BOMB Calories: 285 | Fat: 22.8g | Protein: 6.0g | Sodium: 121mg | Fiber: 0.9g | Carbohydrates: 9.7g | Sugar: 8.4g

More Popular Than IKEA

While it may be enormously popular in America, the cinnamon roll was actually created in Sweden. Next to these delicious fried cinnamon treats, furniture would be Sweden's second most popular export.

Blueberry Chocolate Smoothie

Blueberries covered in dark chocolate, while delicious, are full of sugar. The darker the chocolate, the sweeter blueberries taste. While this smoothie has no sugar, it certainly is not short on taste.

INGREDIENTS | MAKES 1 FAT BOMB

½ (13.5-ounce) can coconut milk

1 tablespoon powdered unflavored gelatin

1 tablespoon coconut oil, softened but not melted

2 tablespoons cocoa powder

¼ cup frozen blueberries

6 drops liquid stevia

6 ice cubes

1. Pour milk and gelatin into a blender and blend to combine.

2. Add remaining ingredients except ice cubes and blend another minute until well mixed.

3. Place ice cubes into blender and process until smoothie thickens. Serve immediately.

PER 1 FAT BOMB Calories: 559 | Fat: 52.7g | Protein: 12.1g | Sodium: 39mg | Fiber: 5.0g | Carbohydrates: 16.4g | Sugar: 3.5g

Creamy Coconut Smoothie

Feel free to add a splash of rum extract and a pineapple wedge.

INGREDIENTS | MAKES 1 FAT BOMB

½ (13.5-ounce) can coconut milk

1 tablespoon powdered unflavored gelatin

1 tablespoon coconut oil, softened but not melted

1 teaspoon vanilla extract

1 tablespoon unsweetened shredded coconut

6 drops liquid stevia

6 ice cubes

1. Pour milk and gelatin into a blender and blend to combine.

2. Add remaining ingredients except ice cubes and blend another minute until well mixed.

3. Place ice cubes into blender and process until smoothie thickens. Serve immediately.

PER 1 FAT BOMB Calories: 561 | Fat: 54.6g | Protein: 10.2g | Sodium: 38mg | Fiber: 0.7g | Carbohydrates: 7.2g | Sugar: 0.9g

Amaretto Chilled Coffee

What a delightful treat for a summer evening. Instead of a cocktail, enjoy this cool and satisfying fat bomb.

INGREDIENTS | MAKES 2 FAT BOMBS

2 cups cooled brewed coffee

4 teaspoons erythritol, divided

4 drops amaretto flavor, divided

½ cup heavy cream, chilled

1 teaspoon crumbled roasted almonds

1. Pour coffee into a medium bowl and mix with half the erythritol and half the amaretto flavor.

2. In a blender, add chilled cream, remaining amaretto flavor, and remaining erythritol. Blend on high until cream is whipped.

3. When ready to serve, pour coffee mix over ice in 2 glasses.

4. Spoon whipped cream on top of coffee mix. Decorate with chopped almonds.

5. Serve immediately with a spoon and a straw.

PER 1 FAT BOMB Calories: 213 | Fat: 21.4g | Protein: 1.7g | Sodium: 27mg | Fiber: 0.1g | Carbohydrates: 9.9g | Sugar: 1.7g | Sugar alcohol: 8.0g

Coconut Coffee

This coffee recipe is a great way to introduce healthy fat early in your day.

INGREDIENTS | MAKES 1 FAT BOMB

1½ cups hot brewed coffee

2 teaspoons erythritol or granular Swerve, or 2 drops stevia glycerite

1 tablespoon coconut oil

1 tablespoon butter

⅛ teaspoon sea salt

1. Place all ingredients in a blender.

2. Blend on high about 15 seconds.

3. Serve immediately.

PER 1 FAT BOMB Calories: 221 | Fat: 23.6g | Protein: 0.6g | Sodium: 388mg | Fiber: 0.0g | Carbohydrates: 8.0g | Sugar: 0.0g | Sugar alcohol: 8.0g

Caffeine-Free Coconut Vanilla Tea

A hot drink that is a breakfast in itself, this recipe does not have caffeine or dairy, so it is suitable for the strictest of diets.

INGREDIENTS | MAKES 1 FAT BOMB

1 teabag rooibos tea

1½ cups hot water

2 teaspoons erythritol or granular Swerve

1 tablespoon coconut oil

⅛ teaspoon vanilla extract

1. Place teabag in water and brew about 8 minutes.

2. Place brewed tea in a blender with remaining ingredients.

3. Blend on high 15 seconds.

4. Serve immediately.

PER 1 FAT BOMB Calories: 120 | Fat: 12.8g | Protein: 0.0g | Sodium: 2mg | Fiber: 0.0g | Carbohydrates: 8.5g | Sugar: 0.1g | Sugar alcohol: 8.0g

Creamy Mexican Hot Chocolate

Mexican chocolate is a true indulgence: rich and thick with a touch of cinnamon flavor. You can serve this sugar-free version to your family and they will love it any time of year. Try it this fall next to a blazing campfire.

INGREDIENTS | MAKES 2 FAT BOMBS

1 cup water

1 cup heavy cream

2 teaspoons erythritol or granular Swerve

⅓ cup cocoa powder

1 teaspoon cinnamon

⅛ teaspoon vanilla extract

4 tablespoons unsweetened whipped cream

1. In a small saucepan over very low heat, combine all ingredients except whipped cream.

2. Heat while stirring constantly until cocoa powder is completely dissolved, about 5 minutes. Do not boil.

3. When ready to serve, pour chocolate into 2 cups and top with whipped cream.

PER 1 FAT BOMB Calories: 538 | Fat: 48.9g | Protein: 5.6g | Sodium: 53mg | Fiber: 6.0g | Carbohydrates: 17.1g | Sugar: 4.1g | Sugar alcohol: 4.0g

Po Cha (Tibetan Butter Tea)

Tibetan butter tea is originally made with yak butter and a potent brew of smoky tea leaves. You do not have to look for yak butter to recreate this flavorful drink at home; you'll still reap all the benefits of starting your day off right with a high-fat treat.

INGREDIENTS | MAKES 2 FAT BOMBS

4 cups water

2 tablespoons black tea leaves

2 tablespoons butter

2 tablespoons heavy cream

⅛ teaspoon sea salt

1 drop smoke flavor

1. In a small saucepan over high heat, bring water to a boil, then lower heat to low.

2. Add tea leaves to water and simmer about 3 minutes. Strain.

3. Combine brewed tea with remaining ingredients in a blender and mix on high about 3 minutes.

4. Serve immediately.

PER 1 FAT BOMB Calories: 157 | Fat: 16.0g | Protein: 0.4g | Sodium: 241mg | Fiber: 0.0g | Carbohydrates: 1.9g | Sugar: 0.4g

The Original Recipe

This Tibetan recipe is a staple of their culture. Po cha is consumed every day, multiple times a day. The drink has many benefits, including giving warmth to the drinker and providing a stable, long-lasting energy source, which is much needed at high altitudes.

Thai Iced Tea

A great variation of Thai iced coffee. It's great during the heat of summer, but should be enjoyed year-round.

INGREDIENTS | MAKES 2 FAT BOMBS

4 cups water

2 tablespoons Ceylon variety black tea leaves

2 cardamom pods, crushed

1 teaspoon star anise seeds

2 teaspoons erythritol or granular Swerve

4 tablespoons heavy cream

2 tablespoons coconut milk

⅛ teaspoon vanilla extract

1. In a small saucepan over high heat, bring water to a boil, then lower heat to low.

2. Add tea leaves, cardamom, and anise seeds and simmer about 3 minutes. Strain.

3. Let brewed tea cool, then pour over ice in 2 tall glasses.

4. In a small bowl, combine sweetener, cream, coconut milk, and vanilla and stir well until sweetener has dissolved.

5. Pour cream mix on top of tea without stirring so layers remain separate.

6. Serve immediately with a tall spoon and a straw.

PER 1 FAT BOMB Calories: 150 | Fat: 13.8g | Protein: 1.4g | Sodium: 13mg | Fiber: 1.0g | Carbohydrates: 9.2g | Sugar: 0.9g | Sugar alcohol: 4.0g

Thai Iced Coffee

Every Thai restaurant serves some version of this drink. Now you can enjoy this version, which is full of beneficial fat.

INGREDIENTS | MAKES 2 FAT BOMBS

4 cups strong brewed coffee, cooled

4 teaspoons erythritol or granular Swerve

2 tablespoons coconut milk

⅛ teaspoon vanilla extract

4 tablespoons heavy cream

1. Pour coffee into a large bowl and mix with sweetener, coconut milk, and vanilla.

2. Pour coffee mixture over ice in 2 tall glasses. Pour cream on top of coffee without stirring so layers remain separate.

3. Serve immediately with a tall spoon and a straw.

PER 1 FAT BOMB Calories: 138 | Fat: 13.6g | Protein: 1.5g | Sodium: 21mg | Fiber: 0.0g | Carbohydrates: 9.3g | Sugar: 0.9g | Sugar alcohol: 8.0g

CHAPTER 13

Savory Fat Bombs

Avocado, Macadamia, and Prosciutto Balls

*The subtle, smooth flavors of avocado and macadamia nuts make a
perfect counterpoint for salty prosciutto and spicy pepper.*

INGREDIENTS | MAKES 6 FAT BOMBS

4 ounces macadamia nuts

4 ounces (½ large) avocado pulp

1 ounce cooked prosciutto, crumbled
(see sidebar in Prosciutto and Egg Balls
recipe in this chapter)

¼ teaspoon freshly ground black pepper

1. In a small food processor, pulse macadamia nuts until evenly crumbled. Divide in half.

2. In a small bowl, combine avocado, half the macadamia nuts, prosciutto crumbles, and pepper and mix well with a fork.

3. Form mixture into 6 balls.

4. Place remaining crumbled macadamia nuts on a medium plate and roll individual balls through to coat evenly.

5. Serve immediately.

PER 1 FAT BOMB Calories: 164 | Fat: 16g | Protein: 2.9g | Sodium: 97mg | Fiber: 2.3g | Carbohydrates: 3.6g | Sugar: 0.8g

Bacon Jalapeño Balls

Enjoy a little kick of fire in these Mexican-flavored fat bombs.

INGREDIENTS | MAKES 6 FAT BOMBS

3 ounces cooked bacon

3 ounces cream cheese

2 tablespoons reserved bacon fat

1 teaspoon seeded and finely chopped
jalapeño pepper

1 tablespoon finely chopped cilantro

1. On a cutting board, chop bacon into small crumbs.

2. In a small bowl, combine cream cheese, bacon fat, jalapeño, and cilantro; mix well with a fork.

3. Form mixture into 6 balls.

4. Place bacon crumbles on a medium plate and roll individual balls through to coat evenly.

5. Serve immediately or refrigerate up to 3 days.

PER 1 FAT BOMB Calories: 153 | Fat: 13.0g | Protein: 5.7g | Sodium: 296mg | Fiber: 0g | Carbohydrates: 0.8g | Sugar: 0.5g

Barbecue Balls

An easy way to get your barbecue fix—and your fat too. You will be surprised how much these fat bombs taste like barbecue sauce.

INGREDIENTS | MAKES 6 FAT BOMBS

4 ounces cream cheese
4 tablespoons bacon fat
½ teaspoon smoke flavor
2 drops stevia glycerite
⅛ teaspoon apple cider vinegar
1 tablespoon sweet smoked chili powder

1. In a small food processor, process all ingredients except chili powder until they form a smooth cream, about 30 seconds.

2. Scrape mixture and transfer into a small bowl, then refrigerate 2 hours.

3. Form into 6 balls with the aid of a spoon.

4. Sprinkle balls with chili powder, rolling around to coat all sides.

5. Serve immediately or refrigerate up to 3 days.

PER 1 FAT BOMB Calories: 145 | Fat: 13.9g | Protein: 1.3g | Sodium: 119mg | Fiber: 0.5g | Carbohydrates: 1.4g | Sugar: 0.7g

Carbonara Balls

Do you like Italian food and have a craving for spaghetti carbonara?
This is the fat-bomb version of that fantastic recipe.

INGREDIENTS | MAKES 6 FAT BOMBS

3 ounces cooked bacon

3 ounces mascarpone cheese

2 large hard-boiled egg yolks

¼ teaspoon freshly ground black pepper

1. On a cutting board, chop bacon into small crumbs.

2. In a small bowl, combine mascarpone, egg yolks, and pepper; mix well with a fork.

3. Form mascarpone mixture into 6 balls.

4. Place bacon crumbles on a medium plate and roll individual balls through to coat evenly.

5. Serve immediately or refrigerate up to 3 days.

PER 1 FAT BOMB Calories: 148 | Fat: 12.6g | Protein: 6.7g | Sodium: 249mg | Fiber: 0.0g | Carbohydrates: 0.8g | Sugar: 0.0g

Two Different Ways to Cook Bacon

There are two different ways you can get your bacon ready for this recipe or any other recipe in this book. For the pan-frying method: Place the bacon slices closely together in a cold frying pan. Cook over medium heat without moving the slices for about 5 minutes. The bacon should by then move easily and not be stuck to the bottom of the pan. Flip the bacon and cook for about 5 more minutes. Remove from the pan and drain on a paper towel. For the oven method: Preheat oven to 400°F. Place a rack on a baking sheet. Lay the bacon slices on the rack and bake for 10–15 minutes depending on desired doneness level.

Brie Hazelnut Balls

This is another super-easy fat-bomb recipe, bursting with delicious flavor. The warm notes of toasted hazelnuts and fresh flavor of thyme really brighten the soft flavor of Brie.

INGREDIENTS | MAKES 6 FAT BOMBS

4 ounces Brie cheese

2 ounces toasted hazelnuts

⅛ teaspoon finely chopped fresh thyme

1. In a small food processor, process all ingredients until they form a coarse dough, about 30 seconds.

2. Scrape mixture and transfer to a small bowl and refrigerate 2 hours.

3. Form into 6 balls with the aid of a spoon.

4. Serve immediately or refrigerate up to 3 days.

PER 1 FAT BOMB Calories: 122 | Fat: 10.4g | Protein: 5.3g | Sodium: 118mg | Fiber: 0.9g | Carbohydrates: 1.7g | Sugar: 0.5g

Pizza Balls

This recipe takes the ultimate Italian dish and magically transforms it into a fat bomb. Whenever the urge for pizza hits you, reach for this instead.

INGREDIENTS | MAKES 6 FAT BOMBS

2 ounces fresh mozzarella

2 ounces cream cheese

1 tablespoon olive oil

1 teaspoon tomato paste

6 large kalamata olives, pitted

12 fresh basil leaves

1. In a small food processor, process all ingredients except basil until they form a smooth cream, about 30 seconds.

2. Form mixture into 6 balls with the aid of a spoon.

3. Place 1 basil leaf on top and bottom of each ball and secure with a toothpick.

4. Serve immediately or refrigerate up to 3 days.

PER 1 FAT BOMB Calories: 91 | Fat: 7.6g | Protein: 2.7g | Sodium: 193mg | Fiber: 0.4g | Carbohydrates: 1.1g | Sugar: 0.5g

Creamy and Crunchy Egg Balls

These fat bombs are a delightful combination of soft, creamy, and crunchy textures, and savory, salty flavors.

INGREDIENTS | MAKES 6 FAT BOMBS

2 medium eggs, hard-boiled and peeled

2 tablespoons cream cheese

1 tablespoon coconut oil, melted

2 slices prosciutto, cooked and crumbled (see sidebar in Prosciutto and Egg Balls recipe in this chapter)

1. Place eggs, cream cheese, and coconut oil in a food processor and pulse until well mixed.

2. Place food processor bowl in refrigerator a minimum 30 minutes or until mixture solidifies.

3. Once egg mixture is solid, remove from refrigerator and shape into 6 balls with the aid of a spoon.

4. Place prosciutto crumbles on a medium plate and roll individual balls through to coat.

5. Serve immediately or refrigerate in an airtight container up to 4 days.

PER 1 FAT BOMB Calories: 68 | Fat: 5.4g | Protein: 3.3g | Sodium: 131mg | Fiber: 0.0g | Carbohydrates: 0.4g | Sugar: 0.3g

Creamy Olive Balls

*The sharp and tangy flavor of kalamata olives combines beautifully
with the creaminess of cheese in this recipe.*

INGREDIENTS | MAKES 6 FAT BOMBS

6 large kalamata olives, pitted

2 tablespoons cream cheese

1 tablespoon coconut oil, melted

2 tablespoons hemp hearts

Hemp Hearts

Hemp hearts are the shelled seeds of the hemp plant. They do not contain any psychoactive compounds, but they do contain a lot of great omega-3s. They are becoming more and more popular because of their great nutrient content and sustainable origin. They have great macros for a fat bomb: Per 30-gram serving, hemp hearts contain 10 grams of plant-based protein and 10 grams of omega-3s.

1. Place olives, cream cheese, and coconut oil in a food processor and pulse until very well mixed.

2. Place food processor bowl in refrigerator a minimum 30 minutes or until mixture solidifies.

3. Once mixture is solid, remove from refrigerator and shape into 6 balls with the aid of a spoon.

4. Place hemp hearts on a medium plate and roll individual balls through to coat.

5. Serve immediately or refrigerate in an airtight container up to 4 days.

PER 1 FAT BOMB Calories: 65 | Fat: 5.7g | Protein: 1.5g | Sodium: 110mg | Fiber: 0.4g | Carbohydrates: 0.8g | Sugar: 0.2g

Curried Tuna Balls

*Just a touch of spice gives this recipe a different twist on the usual fat bomb.
It's enough to keep your taste buds entertained and satisfied.*

INGREDIENTS | MAKES 6 FAT BOMBS

3 ounces tuna in oil, drained
2 ounces cream cheese
¼ teaspoon curry powder, divided
1 ounce crumbled macadamia nuts

1. In a small food processor, process tuna, cream cheese, and half the curry powder until they form a smooth cream, about 30 seconds.

2. Form mixture into 6 balls.

3. Place crumbled macadamia nuts and remaining curry powder on a medium plate and roll individual balls through to coat evenly.

4. Serve immediately or refrigerate up to 3 days.

PER 1 FAT BOMB Calories: 92 | Fat: 7.3g | Protein: 4.7g | Sodium: 90mg | Fiber: 0.4g | Carbohydrates: 1.1g | Sugar: 0.5g

Salted Caramel and Brie Balls

*You will love this super-easy and fast recipe. It features three
ingredients and takes under 5 minutes to make.*

INGREDIENTS | MAKES 6 FAT BOMBS

4 ounces roughly chopped Brie cheese
2 ounces salted macadamia nuts
½ teaspoon caramel flavor

1. In a small food processor, process all ingredients until they form a coarse dough, about 30 seconds.

2. Form mixture into 6 balls with the aid of a spoon.

3. Serve immediately or refrigerate up to 3 days.

PER 1 FAT BOMB Calories: 131 | Fat: 11.8g | Protein: 4.7g | Sodium: 152mg | Fiber: 0.8g | Carbohydrates: 1.3g | Sugar: 0.5g

Prosciutto and Egg Balls

*This is another dairy-free fat bomb. The coconut oil provides a great source of good
fats and is casein- and lactose-free, suitable for people with dairy intolerances.
It also helps the fat bomb stick together without changing the flavor.*

INGREDIENTS | MAKES 6 FAT BOMBS

2 medium hard-boiled eggs, peeled

2 tablespoons Homemade Mayonnaise
(see recipe in Chapter 5)

⅛ teaspoon freshly ground black pepper

⅛ teaspoon sea salt

1 tablespoon coconut oil, melted

2 slices prosciutto, cooked and crumbled
(see sidebar)

Prosciutto Crumbles

To make easy prosciutto crumbles, simply
bake them in the oven. Preheat oven to
350°F. Place the thin prosciutto slices on a
cookie sheet and bake them for about 12
minutes. Remove from the oven and let
cool. Once cold and crispy, chop finely with
a sharp kitchen knife until reduced to
crumbles.

1. Place eggs, mayonnaise, pepper, and salt in a small bowl. Mash with a fork to mix and combine while still retaining some texture.

2. Pour melted coconut oil into mixture and blend in well.

3. Place bowl in refrigerator a minimum 30 minutes or until mixture solidifies.

4. Once egg mixture is solid, remove from refrigerator and shape into 6 balls with the aid of a spoon.

5. Place prosciutto crumbles on a medium plate and roll individual balls through to coat.

6. Serve immediately or refrigerate in an airtight container up to 4 days.

PER 1 FAT BOMB Calories: 83 | Fat: 7.4g | Protein: 3.1g | Sodium:
191mg | Fiber: 0.0g | Carbohydrates: 0.3g | Sugar: 0.2g

Spicy Bacon and Avocado Balls

These fat bombs carry some of the flavors of guacamole. They are slightly spicy, but if you want to increase the fire, just leave some of the jalapeño seeds in.

INGREDIENTS | MAKES 6 FAT BOMBS

4 slices bacon

1 medium avocado, pitted and peeled

2 tablespoons coconut oil

1 tablespoon bacon fat

1 tablespoon finely chopped green onions

2 tablespoons finely chopped cilantro

1 small jalapeño pepper, seeded and finely chopped

¼ teaspoon sea salt

Hot Jalapeños

Jalapeño peppers can vary greatly in their degree of heat. In the same batch you can find quite mild ones and some very spicy ones. Even if you like it hot, start your recipes without the seeds...you can always add heat, but you can't remove it!

1. In a medium nonstick skillet over medium heat, cook bacon until golden, about 4 minutes each side.

2. Drain bacon on a paper towel. Save bacon fat for later in a glass cup.

3. Once bacon is cool, chop 2 slices into crumbles.

4. Cut remaining 2 slices into 3 pieces each; these will be the bases for your fat bombs.

5. Smash avocado with a fork in a small bowl.

6. Add coconut oil and cooled bacon fat to avocado.

7. Add onion, cilantro, jalapeño, salt, and bacon crumbles. Blend well with a fork.

8. Refrigerate a minimum 30 minutes.

9. Form mixture into 6 balls with the aid of a spoon.

10. Place remaining 6 bacon pieces on a plate, then top each with an avocado ball.

11. Serve immediately or refrigerate up to 3 days.

PER 1 FAT BOMB Calories: 132 | Fat: 12.0g | Protein: 3.1g | Sodium: 230mg | Fiber: 1.6g | Carbohydrates: 2.3g | Sugar: 0.2g

Kalamata Olive and Feta Balls

This recipe brings you the flavors of Greece on a warm sunny day by the Mediterranean Sea.

INGREDIENTS | MAKES 6 FAT BOMBS

2 ounces cream cheese

2 ounces feta

12 large kalamata olives, pitted

⅛ teaspoon finely chopped fresh thyme

⅛ teaspoon fresh lemon zest

1. In a small food processor, process all ingredients until they form a coarse dough, about 30 seconds.

2. Scrape mixture and transfer to a small bowl, then refrigerate 2 hours.

3. Form into 6 balls with the aid of a spoon.

4. Serve immediately or refrigerate up to 3 days.

PER 1 FAT BOMB Calories: 77 | Fat: 6.0g | Protein: 1.9g | Sodium: 307mg | Fiber: 0.7g | Carbohydrates: 1.5g | Sugar: 0.7g

Salmon Mascarpone Balls

Omega-3s are essential fatty acids, which means your body cannot manufacture them and must get them from your diet. This recipe is not only rich in beneficial omega-3s, but it also has a creamy, smooth mouthfeel.

INGREDIENTS | MAKES 6 FAT BOMBS

3 ounces smoked salmon, chopped

3 ounces mascarpone cheese

½ teaspoon maple flavor

½ teaspoon chopped chives

3 tablespoons hemp hearts

Smoked Salmon

When buying smoked salmon, please make sure you get either wild or sustainably farmed. Often, conventionally farmed salmon contains high levels of antibiotics. Antibiotics from industrially farmed animals contribute to the creation of antibiotic-resistant superbugs.

1. In a small food processor, combine salmon, mascarpone, maple flavor, and chives. Pulse a few times until blended together.

2. Form mixture into 6 balls.

3. Put hemp hearts on a medium plate and roll individual balls through to coat evenly.

4. Serve immediately or refrigerate up to 3 days.

PER 1 FAT BOMB Calories: 110 | Fat: 9.2g | Protein: 5.4g | Sodium: 103mg | Fiber: 0.2g | Carbohydrates: 0.7g | Sugar: 0.1g

For the Love of Pork Bombs

Any day with bacon is a great day. Add Braunschweiger, pistachios, and cream cheese, and the flavors become a symphony of perfect pork cuisine for any true bacon lover!

INGREDIENTS | MAKES 12 FAT BOMBS

8 slices bacon

8 ounces Braunschweiger, at room temperature

¼ cup chopped pistachios

6 ounces cream cheese, at room temperature

1 teaspoon Dijon mustard

Is Braunschweiger the Same as Liverwurst?

While the ingredients in both sausages are similar (pork and pork liver), many times Braunschweiger also contains bacon. Braunschweiger is generally soft and spreadable, whereas liverwurst is firmer and better for slicing.

1. Cook bacon in a medium skillet over medium heat until crisp, 5 minutes per side. Drain on paper towels and let cool. Once cooled, crumble into bacon-bit-sized pieces.

2. Place Braunschweiger with pistachios in a small food processor and pulse until just combined.

3. In a small mixing bowl, use a hand blender to whip cream cheese and Dijon mustard until combined and fluffy.

4. Divide Braunschweiger mixture into 12 equal servings. Roll into balls and cover in a thin layer of cream cheese mixture.

5. Chill at least 1 hour. When ready to serve, place bacon bits on a medium plate, roll balls through to coat evenly, and enjoy.

6. Fat bombs can be refrigerated in an airtight container up to 4 days.

PER 1 FAT BOMB Calories: 161 | Fat: 13.2g | Protein: 6.7g | Sodium: 336mg | Fiber: 0.3g | Carbohydrates: 2.1g | Sugar: 0.7g

Bacon and Scallion Bites

Not all cheesecakes are sweet. With bacon and scallions in the mix, this version makes an excellent savory appetizer or midday snack.

INGREDIENTS | MAKES 6 FAT BOMBS

⅓ cup almond meal flour

1 tablespoon butter, melted

8 ounces cream cheese, softened to room temperature

1 tablespoon bacon grease

1 large egg

4 slices bacon, cooked, cooled, and crumbled into bits

1 large green onion, tops only, thinly sliced

1 medium clove garlic, minced

⅛ teaspoon freshly ground black pepper

Savor the Savory Flavor

Perhaps not as popular, but certainly as delicious, the savory cheesecake makes for an excellent treat. Most savory cakes served in restaurants include flavor combinations such as garlic and Parmesan, bacon and chive, and prosciutto and olive.

1. Preheat oven to 325°F.

2. In a small mixing bowl, combine almond meal and butter.

3. Line 6 cups of a standard-sized muffin tin with cupcake liners. Equally divide flour mixture between cups and press into the bottom gently with the back of a teaspoon. Bake in oven 10 minutes, then remove.

4. While the crust is baking, thoroughly combine cream cheese and bacon grease in a medium mixing bowl with a hand mixer. Add egg and blend until combined.

5. Fold bacon, onion, garlic, and pepper into cheese mixture with a spatula.

6. Divide mixture between cups, return to oven, and bake another 30–35 minutes until cheese sets. Edges may be slightly browned. To test doneness, insert toothpick into center of cake. If it comes out clean, cheesecake is done.

7. Let cool 5 minutes and serve warm.

PER 1 FAT BOMB Calories: 208 | Fat: 18.1g | Protein: 3.4g | Sodium: 153mg | Fiber: 0.7g | Carbohydrates: 3.2g | Sugar: 1.3g

Egg Tapenade Balls

You may have used chia seeds before, but they were probably soaked in some liquid! You will be surprised at how well they work as a coating element. They're a little crunchy with mild flavor and have a perfect nutritional profile!

INGREDIENTS | MAKES 6 FAT BOMBS

2 medium hard-boiled eggs, peeled

6 large kalamata olives, pitted

1 anchovy fillet

1 tablespoon coconut oil, melted

2 tablespoons chia seeds

A Fancy French Word

Tapenade is a fancy French word for a basic olive spread usually consisting of olives, capers, and anchovies. Anchovies provide great flavor and healthy omega-3s. You can always skip them if you do not enjoy the flavor.

1. Place eggs, olives, anchovy fillet, and coconut oil in a food processor and pulse until mixed but not overblended.

2. Place food processor bowl in refrigerator a minimum 30 minutes or until mixture solidifies.

3. Once egg mixture is solid, remove from refrigerator and shape into 6 balls with the aid of a spoon.

4. Place chia seeds on a medium plate and roll individual balls through to coat.

5. Serve immediately or refrigerate in an airtight container up to 4 days.

PER 1 FAT BOMB Calories: 69 | Fat: 5.2g | Protein: 2.6g | Sodium: 136mg | Fiber: 1.5g | Carbohydrates: 1.9g | Sugar: 0.2g

Chicken Skin Crisps Alfredo

Alfredo sauce must be one of the most well-loved sauces for both chicken and noodles. Here you can get all the flavor of Alfredo sauce without any of the carbs usually involved!

INGREDIENTS | MAKES 6 FAT BOMBS

Skin from 3 chicken thighs
2 tablespoons ricotta cheese
2 tablespoons cream cheese
1 tablespoon grated Parmesan cheese
¼ garlic clove, minced
¼ teaspoon ground white pepper

Chicken Skin Crisps

You can either buy chicken thighs and remove the skin to make your chicken skin crisps, or you can ask your local butcher or farmer from the farmers' market to sell you just chicken skin. You will be surprised; chicken skin is not so hard to find, and it will make superb crisps to use instead of crackers.

1. Preheat oven to 350°F. On a cookie sheet, lay out skins as flat as possible.

2. Bake 12–15 minutes until skins turn light brown and crispy being careful not to burn them.

3. Remove skins from cookie sheet and place on a paper towel to cool.

4. In a small bowl, add cheeses, garlic, and pepper. Mix with a fork until well blended.

5. Cut each crispy chicken skin in 2 pieces.

6. Place 1 tablespoon Alfredo cheese mix on each chicken crisp and serve immediately.

PER 1 FAT BOMB Calories: 75 | Fat: 5.9g | Protein: 3.3g | Sodium: 44mg | Fiber: 0.0g | Carbohydrates: 0.7g | Sugar: 0.2g

Chicken Skin Crisps Satay

If you like Thai food, this fat-bomb recipe will absolutely delight you!

INGREDIENTS | MAKES 6 FAT BOMBS

Skin from 3 chicken thighs
2 tablespoons chunky peanut butter
1 tablespoon coconut cream
1 teaspoon coconut oil
1 teaspoon seeded and minced fresh jalapeño pepper
¼ garlic clove, minced
1 teaspoon coconut aminos

Precious Liquid Fat

When you cook the chicken skins you will end up with a pan full of chicken fat. You can drain that into a glass jar and save it for later. This fat can be stored in the refrigerator for a couple of months and it can be used in any recipe as a 100 percent dairy-free substitute for butter.

1. Preheat oven to 350°F. On a cookie sheet, lay out skins as flat as possible.

2. Bake 12–15 minutes until skins turn light brown and crispy being careful not to burn them.

3. Remove skins from cookie sheet and place on a paper towel to cool.

4. In a small food processor, add peanut butter, coconut cream, coconut oil, jalapeño, garlic, and coconut aminos.

5. Mix about 30 seconds until well blended.

6. Cut each crispy chicken skin in 2 pieces.

7. Place 1 tablespoon peanut sauce on each chicken crisp and serve immediately. If sauce is too runny, refrigerate 2 hours before using.

PER 1 FAT BOMB Calories: 91 | Fat: 7.5g | Protein: 3.5g | Sodium: 51mg | Fiber: 0.4g | Carbohydrates: 1.5g | Sugar: 0.6g

Goat Cheese and Herbs Panna Cotta

Herbed goat cheese is a very popular item in fancy cheese stores. Now you can replicate that fancy flavor with the right amount of good fat for your keto diet.

INGREDIENTS | MAKES 6 FAT BOMBS

1½ cups heavy whipping cream

¾ cup sour cream

6 ounces soft goat cheese

1 teaspoon Herbes de Provence

2 teaspoons powdered unflavored gelatin

1 teaspoon sea salt

1. In a small saucepan over medium heat, combine heavy cream, sour cream, goat cheese, and Herbes de Provence, stirring until cheese melts.

2. Whisk in gelatin and salt until completely incorporated.

3. Simmer on very low heat about 5 minutes, stirring constantly.

4. Pour mixture evenly into 6 small glasses or ramekins.

5. Refrigerate until set, at least 6 hours or overnight.

6. Serve in glass or invert over a small plate after dipping glass into hot water a few seconds.

PER 1 FAT BOMB Calories: 343 | Fat: 31.5g | Protein: 9.1g | Sodium: 558mg | Fiber: 0g | Carbohydrates: 2.5g | Sugar: 2.5g

Gorgonzola Panna Cotta

This is the kind of recipe you would eat at a dinner party or in a fancy restaurant. Isn't it wonderful that even the fanciest recipes can sometimes be as easy as they are delicious?

INGREDIENTS | MAKES 6 FAT BOMBS

12 ounces crumbled Gorgonzola cheese

1½ cups heavy whipping cream

2 teaspoons powdered unflavored gelatin

12 pecan halves

How to Serve Panna Cotta

You can serve panna cotta in a small pretty glass or cup, so it can be eaten with a spoon as a mousse might be served. The other option is to use a mold or ramekin, so it can be inverted onto a plate. If you choose this option, right before serving, dip each ramekin three-quarters of the way in warm water to loosen the panna cotta, then invert onto a plate.

1. In a small saucepan over medium heat, melt Gorgonzola in heavy cream using a whisk to break clots, about 2 minutes.

2. Whisk in gelatin until completely incorporated.

3. Pour mixture evenly into 6 small glasses or ramekins.

4. Refrigerate until set, at least 6 hours or overnight.

5. Decorate each glass with 2 pecan halves and serve.

PER 1 FAT BOMB Calories: 433 | Fat: 38.3g | Protein: 15.6g | Sodium: 676mg | Fiber: 0.3g | Carbohydrates: 3.4g | Sugar: 2.1g

Porcini Mushroom Panna Cotta

*The porcini mushrooms add an earthy flavor
that is sure to be a hit at your next dinner party!*

INGREDIENTS | MAKES 6 FAT BOMBS

2 ounces dried porcini mushrooms
1 cup hot water
1 teaspoon powdered unflavored gelatin
1 tablespoon butter
1 cup heavy cream
1 tablespoon coconut aminos
3 tablespoons grated Parmesan cheese

1. Soak porcini mushrooms in hot water about 30 minutes to rehydrate.

2. Drain mushrooms, reserving the soaking water. Squeeze out excess water from mushrooms, then chop finely.

3. Place 3 tablespoons soaking water in a glass. Sprinkle gelatin in soaking water and let stand about 5 minutes.

4. In a small nonstick skillet over high heat, melt butter, then add mushrooms and sauté about 3 minutes, stirring.

5. Add soaking water with gelatin, cream, coconut aminos, and Parmesan; stir and bring to a boil, about 1 minute.

6. Remove from heat.

7. Pour mixture evenly into 6 small glasses or ramekins.

8. Refrigerate until set, at least 6 hours or overnight.

9. Serve in glass or invert over a small plate after dipping glass into hot water a few seconds.

PER 1 FAT BOMB Calories: 205 | Fat: 16.3g | Protein: 4.9g | Sodium: 118mg | Fiber: 2.4g | Carbohydrates: 6.7g | Sugar: 1.1g

Cheesy Muffin Prosciutto Cup

Salty prosciutto, creamy melted cheeses, and a nourishing egg—sounds like a perfect combination.

INGREDIENTS | MAKES 1 FAT BOMB

1 (0.5-ounce) slice prosciutto
1 medium egg yolk
½ ounce diced Brie cheese
⅓ ounce diced mozzarella cheese
½ ounce grated Parmesan cheese

1. Preheat oven to 350°F. Use a muffin tin with holes about 2½" wide and 1½" deep.

2. Fold prosciutto slice in half so it becomes almost square.

3. Place it in muffin tin hole to line it completely.

4. Place egg yolk into prosciutto cup.

5. Add cheeses on top of egg yolk gently without breaking it.

6. Bake about 12 minutes until yolk is cooked and warm but still runny.

7. Let cool 10 minutes before removing from muffin pan.

PER 1 FAT BOMB Calories: 221 | Fat: 15.3g | Protein: 15.8g | Sodium: 725mg | Fiber: 0.0g | Carbohydrates: 2.9g | Sugar: 0.3g

Egg and Mascarpone Prosciutto Cup

This fat bomb can become a whole breakfast! Great taste, nutrition, and the right macronutrient ratios to start your day.

INGREDIENTS | MAKES 1 FAT BOMB

1 (0.5-ounce) slice prosciutto
1 medium egg
1 tablespoon mascarpone cheese

1. Preheat oven to 350°F. Use a muffin tin with holes about 2½" wide and 1½" deep.

2. Fold prosciutto slice in half so it becomes almost square.

3. Place it in a muffin tin hole to line it completely.

4. Break egg into prosciutto cup.

5. Gently place mascarpone on top of egg.

6. Bake about 12 minutes until egg white is cooked and yolk is still runny but warm.

7. Let cool 10 minutes before removing from muffin pan.

PER 1 FAT BOMB Calories: 158 | Fat: 12.3g | Protein: 10.0g | Sodium: 357mg | Fiber: 0.0g | Carbohydrates: 0.6g | Sugar: 0.2g

CHAPTER 14

Sweet Fat Bombs

Cocoa Coconut Butter Fat Bombs

In addition to coconut oil, this recipe uses coconut butter, which differs from the oil. Coconut butter is the puréed meat of mature coconuts, while coconut oil has been separated from the coconut meat. One cannot be substituted for the other.

INGREDIENTS | SERVES 12

1 cup coconut oil

½ cup unsalted butter

6 tablespoons unsweetened cocoa powder

15 drops liquid stevia

¾ cup coconut butter

Make Your Own

Coconut butter isn't always easy to find. It's simple, and more cost effective, to make your own. To make 2 cups of coconut butter, put 6 cups of unsweetened coconut flakes into a blender with a pinch of salt and blend until completely smooth. This usually takes 5–6 minutes.

1. Put coconut oil, butter, unsweetened cocoa powder, and stevia in a small saucepan, stirring frequently until all ingredients are melted.

2. Melt coconut butter in a separate small pan.

3. Pour 2 tablespoons of cocoa mixture into each well of a 12-cup silicone mold.

4. Add 1 tablespoon of melted coconut butter to each well.

5. Place in the freezer until hardened, about 30 minutes.

6. Store in the refrigerator.

PER SERVING Calories: 303 | Fat: 31.3g | Protein: 1.3g | Sodium: 4mg | Fiber: 2.3g | Carbohydrates: 4.2g | Sugar: 0.7g

Almond Butter Fat Bombs

You can replace the almond butter in this recipe with any nut butter of your choice. Cashew butter and peanut butter work really well too. Just make sure that your nut butter doesn't contain any added sugar.

INGREDIENTS | SERVES 12

⅓ cup coconut oil

⅓ cup unsalted butter

⅓ cup unsweetened almond butter

2 tablespoons cream cheese

15 drops liquid stevia

Do It Yourself!

Making your own almond butter is simple and a great way to ensure that it doesn't contain any hidden sugar. Simply put almonds in a food processor and process until the oils break down and a nut butter forms. To up the fat content and make the almond butter smoother, add a couple of teaspoons of almond oil (or another oil of your choice).

1. Place all ingredients in a small saucepan and stir over medium-low heat until all ingredients are melted and mixed together.

2. Pour an equal amount of mixture into each well of a 12-cup silicone mold.

3. Place in the freezer until hardened, about 30 minutes.

4. Store in the refrigerator.

PER SERVING Calories: 145 | Fat: 14.7g | Protein: 1.8g | Sodium: 31mg | Fiber: 0.9g | Carbohydrates: 1.7g | Sugar: 0.3g

Raspberry Cheesecake Fat Bombs

You can replace the raspberries in this recipe with blackberries, blueberries, or strawberries. Combine them all for a delicious mixed berry cheesecake bomb.

INGREDIENTS | SERVES 12

½ cup frozen raspberries

10 drops liquid stevia

1 teaspoon vanilla extract

¾ cup cream cheese, room temperature

¼ cup coconut oil, room temperature

Be Careful with Berries

Berries are full of fiber so their net carbohydrate count is not as high as some other fruits. In fact, 1 cup contains 7 net carbohydrates. You still need to be careful when eating berries on a ketogenic diet. Don't overdo it and always make sure to count your macronutrients to make sure that berries fit into your plan that day.

1. Place raspberries in a food processer and process until smooth. Add stevia and vanilla extract and process until incorporated.

2. Add cream cheese and coconut oil and process until all ingredients are well combined.

3. Place an equal amount of mixture in each well of a 12-cup silicone mold.

4. Place in freezer until hardened, about 30 minutes.

5. Store in the refrigerator.

PER SERVING Calories: 92 | Fat: 8.5g | Protein: 0.9g | Sodium: 52mg | Fiber: 0.4g | Carbohydrates: 1.3g | Sugar: 0.8g

Cashew Butter Cup Fat Bombs

Many commercially available cashew butters contain an added sweetener, so be careful when choosing one. If you can't find one at the store, you can always make your own.

INGREDIENTS | SERVES 12

1 cup coconut oil

¾ cup unsalted butter, divided

6 tablespoons unsweetened cocoa powder

15 drops liquid stevia

¼ cup unsalted sugar-free cashew butter

2 tablespoons heavy whipping cream

Nut Butters at Home

Making cashew butter is the same basic process as making coconut butter. To make about 1½ cups of cashew butter, put 2 cups of unroasted, unsalted cashews in a food processor with a pinch of salt and 1 tablespoon of coconut oil. Process for about 30 seconds and then scrape down the sides of the food processor. Continue processing until smooth, scraping the sides when necessary. Be patient, as the process can take several minutes.

1. Put coconut oil, ½ cup of the butter, cocoa powder, and stevia in a small saucepan and stir over medium heat until melted and well combined.

2. Pour an equal amount of the mixture into each well of a mini muffin tin lined with cupcake wrappers. Place muffin tin in the freezer and allow to harden, about 30 minutes.

3. Place remaining ¼ cup butter, cashew butter, and whipping cream in a small bowl and beat with a handheld mixer until combined and fluffy.

4. Once the chocolate mixture in the freezer has hardened, spoon an equal amount of the cashew butter mixture on top of each well and place in the freezer. Allow to harden, at least 30 minutes.

5. Store in refrigerator.

PER SERVING Calories: 304 | Fat: 31.5g | Protein: 1.6g | Sodium: 3mg | Fiber: 1.1g | Carbohydrates: 3.1g | Sugar: 0.3g

Coconut Peppermint Fat Bombs

You can replace the peppermint extract in this recipe with any other pure extract. Try lemon, orange, almond, or maple.

INGREDIENTS | SERVES 12

1 cup coconut butter

¼ cup unsweetened shredded coconut

1 tablespoon coconut oil

½ teaspoon peppermint extract

1. Put all ingredients in a small saucepan and heat over low heat until melted and well combined.

2. Pour an equal amount of mixture into each well of a 12-cup muffin tin lined with cupcake wrappers.

3. Place in the freezer and allow to harden, about 30 minutes.

4. Store in the refrigerator.

PER SERVING Calories: 169 | Fat: 15.5g | Protein: 1.4g | Sodium: 7mg | Fiber: 2.9g | Carbohydrates: 5.6g | Sugar: 1.5g

Lemon Cheesecake Fat Bombs

Fresh lemon juice straight from the lemon is best for this recipe, but if you're out of lemons, you can use bottled versions too.

INGREDIENTS | SERVES 12

¼ cup cream cheese, softened

⅔ cup unsalted butter

2 tablespoons heavy whipping cream

1 tablespoon lemon juice

¼ teaspoon lemon extract

10 drops liquid stevia

1. Beat cream cheese, butter, and whipping cream together in a small bowl until smooth. Add lemon juice, lemon extract, and stevia until combined.

2. Drop by tablespoons onto a cookie sheet lined with wax paper and place in the freezer until hardened, about 30 minutes.

3. Store in the refrigerator.

PER SERVING Calories: 116 | Fat: 11.8g | Protein: 0.5g | Sodium: 19mg | Fiber: 0.0g | Carbohydrates: 0.4g | Sugar: 0.3g

Cinnamon Bun Fat Bombs

These cinnamon bun fat bombs have the same flavor as a cinnamon roll fresh from the oven but without the sugar and carbohydrates.

INGREDIENTS | SERVES 12

1 cup coconut butter, softened

¼ teaspoon plus ⅛ teaspoon ground cinnamon, divided

¼ teaspoon ground nutmeg

¼ teaspoon vanilla extract

¼ cup crushed walnuts

Smooth It Out

The crushed walnuts finish off these fat bombs with a nice crunch, but you could also grind the walnuts instead for a smooth, but still decadent, finish.

1. Combine coconut butter, ¼ teaspoon cinnamon, nutmeg, and vanilla extract in a small bowl and mix until well combined.

2. Separate the mixture into 12 equal parts and roll into ball shapes. Place on a cookie sheet lined with wax paper.

3. Mix crushed walnuts with remaining cinnamon in a small bowl. Roll balls in nut mixture until coated.

4. Place finished balls on a cookie sheet lined with wax paper and refrigerate until ready to eat.

5. Store in the refrigerator.

PER SERVING Calories: 163 | Fat: 14.9g | Protein: 1.7g | Sodium: 6mg | Fiber: 2.9g | Carbohydrates: 5.8g | Sugar: 1.4g

Mixed Nut Butter Bombs

*The combination of cashew butter, peanut flour, and almond extract
is enough to satisfy every nut lover's craving.*

INGREDIENTS | SERVES 12

½ cup unsalted, unsweetened cashew butter

1 cup defatted unsweetened peanut flour

¼ cup unsalted butter, melted

¼ teaspoon almond extract

Defatting Peanuts

Defatted peanut flour is a peanut flour that has had a large percentage of its fat removed through a mechanical process. The fat content of defatted peanut flour still falls around 25 percent of calories, but the shelf life is significantly increased.

1. Mix cashew butter and peanut flour together in a small bowl until well combined.

2. Stir in melted butter until smooth. Add almond extract and stir until combined.

3. Scoop out tablespoons of mixture onto a cookie sheet covered in wax paper.

4. Place in the freezer until hardened, about 30 minutes.

5. Store in the refrigerator.

PER SERVING Calories: 113 | Fat: 8.6g | Protein: 4.5g | Sodium: 11mg | Fiber: 1.0g | Carbohydrates: 4.7g | Sugar: 0.4g

Peanut Butter Fat Bombs

The crunchy peanut butter and crushed peanuts in this recipe give these peanut butter fat bombs an unbeatable texture. If you prefer less crunch, use smooth peanut butter instead.

INGREDIENTS | SERVES 12

1 cup coconut oil

½ cup unsalted butter

½ cup unsalted, unsweetened crunchy peanut butter

2 tablespoons cream cheese

10 drops liquid stevia

¼ cup crushed unsalted peanuts

1. Place coconut oil, butter, peanut butter, cream cheese, and stevia in a small saucepan and stir over medium heat until melted.

2. Sprinkle crushed peanuts evenly in each well of a 12-cup mini muffin pan. Pour peanut butter mixture over the peanuts.

3. Place in the freezer until hardened, about 30 minutes.

4. Store in the refrigerator.

PER SERVING Calories: 313 | Fat: 31.6g | Protein: 3.6g | Sodium: 9mg | Fiber: 1.3g | Carbohydrates: 3.1g | Sugar: 0.9g

Maple Fat Bombs

These Maple Fat Bombs provide comforting maple flavor without all of the carbohydrates contained in regular maple syrup.

INGREDIENTS | SERVES 12

¼ cup unsalted butter

½ cup coconut butter

10 drops liquid stevia

½ teaspoon maple extract

¼ teaspoon ground cinnamon

½ cup crushed walnuts

Choosing Your Maple

There are four different types of maple extract: pure, natural, imitation, and artificial. Imitation and artificial extracts are made in a lab and often contain no real maple product at all. Stick to pure or natural extracts.

1. Place butter, coconut butter, stevia, maple extract, and cinnamon in a small saucepan and stir over medium heat until melted. Mix thoroughly.

2. Remove mixture from heat and stir in crushed walnuts.

3. Fill each well of a 12-cup mini muffin pan lined with cupcake wrappers or a silicone mold with an equal amount of the mixture.

4. Place pan or mold in the freezer until mixture hardens, about 30 minutes.

5. Store in the refrigerator.

PER SERVING Calories: 139 | Fat: 13.3g | Protein: 1.5g | Sodium: 3mg | Fiber: 1.7g | Carbohydrates: 3.4g | Sugar: 0.8g

Blueberry Fat Bombs

Blueberries and cream cheese are a winning combination, but if you want a different flavor, make this a triple berry fat bomb by using a combination of blueberries, blackberries, and strawberries.

INGREDIENTS | SERVES 12

¾ cup blueberries, divided

¼ cup coconut cream

⅓ cup cream cheese, softened

½ cup coconut butter, melted

½ cup coconut oil, melted

8 drops liquid stevia

Use What You've Got

Silicone molds are extremely helpful when you're on a ketogenic diet, especially if you're planning to make fat bombs a regular part of your diet. If you don't want to purchase silicone molds, you can use ice cube trays, but it will be harder to remove the bombs from the tray.

1. Place ½ cup of the berries, coconut cream, and cream cheese in a food processor and process until smooth. Add melted coconut butter, melted coconut oil, and liquid stevia and process again until smooth.

2. Fill up each well of a 12-cup silicone mold or mini muffin tin lined with cupcake wrappers with an equal amount of the blueberry mixture and drop the remaining blueberries on top.

3. Place in the freezer until hardened, about 30 minutes. Store in the refrigerator.

PER SERVING Calories: 188 | Fat: 18.1g | Protein: 1.1g | Sodium: 27mg | Fiber: 1.6g | Carbohydrates: 4.4g | Sugar: 2.0g

Avocado Fat Bomb Smoothie

The avocado in this recipe will make your smoothie nice and creamy without changing the flavor.

INGREDIENTS | SERVES 2

1 cup full-fat coconut milk

½ large avocado

¼ cup ice

1 teaspoon vanilla extract

1 tablespoon granulated erythritol

2 tablespoons coconut butter

Combine all ingredients in blender and blend until smooth. Serve immediately.

PER SERVING Calories: 434 | Fat: 40.5g | Protein: 4.4g | Sodium: 24mg | Fiber: 5.9g | Carbohydrates: 18.4g | Sugar: 1.4g | Sugar alcohol: 6.0g

Chocolate Orange Fat Bombs

The citrus notes in the orange extract in this recipe bring out the flavor of the unsweetened cocoa powder. You can make this a double-chocolate fat bomb instead by swapping out the orange extract for chocolate extract.

INGREDIENTS | SERVES 12

½ cup unsalted butter

½ cup coconut oil

5 tablespoons unsweetened cocoa powder

1 teaspoon orange extract

1. Mix all ingredients together in a small saucepan over medium-low heat until melted and smooth.

2. Pour into each well of a 12-cup silicone mold and place into the freezer until hardened, about 30 minutes.

3. Store in the refrigerator.

PER SERVING Calories: 152 | Fat: 16.0g | Protein: 0.5g | Sodium: 1mg | Fiber: 0.8g | Carbohydrates: 1.4g | Sugar: 0.1g

Bacon Maple Pancake Balls

These fat bombs have the flavor of breakfast pancakes with maple syrup and bacon. They're a great way to start the day off right!

INGREDIENTS | MAKES 6 FAT BOMBS

3 ounces cooked bacon

3 ounces cream cheese

½ teaspoon maple flavor

¼ teaspoon salt

3 tablespoons crushed pecans

Food Flavoring versus Sugar-Free Syrup

A lot of recipes on the ketogenic diet call for sugar-free syrup. Such syrups contain ingredients like acesulfame potassium, sodium hexametaphosphate, or phosphoric acid. Those artificial flavors, preservatives, and fillers are not health-building ingredients; on the contrary, they load the body with toxins, which make it much harder to lose unwanted pounds. A good organic maple flavor will only contain a maple distillate and pure grain alcohol in minimal quantities.

1. On a cutting board, chop bacon into small crumbs.

2. In a small bowl, combine cream cheese and bacon crumbles with maple flavor and salt; mix well with a fork.

3. Form mixture into 6 balls.

4. Place crushed pecans on a medium plate and roll individual balls through to coat evenly.

5. Serve immediately or refrigerate up to 3 days.

PER 1 FAT BOMB Calories: 138 | Fat: 11.3g | Protein: 6.0g | Sodium: 387mg | Fiber: 0.3g | Carbohydrates: 1.3g | Sugar: 0.6g

Vanilla Macadamia Fat Bombs

You can skip the first step in this recipe by purchasing macadamia nut flour instead of grinding whole macadamia nuts, but it can be more expensive that way.

INGREDIENTS | SERVES 12

½ cup macadamia nuts

1 cup cream cheese, softened

½ cup heavy whipping cream

1 teaspoon vanilla extract

⅛ teaspoon salt

10 drops liquid stevia

1. Place macadamia nuts in a food processor and process until you achieve a fine meal consistency. Add remaining ingredients and process until smooth.

2. Pour mixture into each well of a 12-cup silicone mold and freeze until hardened, about 30 minutes.

3. Store in the refrigerator.

PER SERVING Calories: 140 | Fat: 13.2g | Protein: 1.8g | Sodium: 117mg | Fiber: 0.4g | Carbohydrates: 1.8g | Sugar: 1.2g

Macadamia Knowledge

There are an estimated seven species of macadamia nuts around the world, but only two species are edible. The majority of macadamia nuts come from Australia, but the nuts that come from Hawaii are often described as the best-tasting.

Pumpkin Fat Bombs

For a richer taste, swap out the coconut oil in this recipe for unsalted butter. Keep the amount of coconut butter the same.

INGREDIENTS | SERVES 12

½ cup coconut butter, softened

¼ cup coconut oil, softened

⅛ cup pumpkin purée

1 teaspoon pumpkin pie spice

¼ teaspoon vanilla extract

8 drops liquid stevia

⅛ teaspoon salt

1. Mix all ingredients together in a small bowl and stir until combined.

2. Pour into an 8" × 8" baking pan and spread out mixture evenly. Refrigerate for 30 minutes and then cut into 12 squares.

PER SERVING Calories: 113 | Fat: 11.0g | Protein: 0.7g | Sodium: 27mg | Fiber: 1.4g | Carbohydrates: 2.9g | Sugar: 0.7g

Go for the Gourd

Pumpkin is rich in fiber, containing 7 grams per cup, but it's not considered a low-carbohydrate food. Pumpkin can be incorporated into a ketogenic diet, but always watch your portions.

Sunbutter Balls

This recipe could also be called the Cravings Killer, as it can help to curb your sugar cravings naturally!

INGREDIENTS | MAKES 12 FAT BOMBS

6 tablespoons mascarpone cheese

3 tablespoons sunflower seed butter

6 tablespoons coconut oil, softened

3 tablespoons unsweetened shredded coconut flakes

An Italian Delight

Mascarpone is an Italian soft cheese best known for being used in the famous tiramisu. It is actually the perfect ingredient for fat bombs; it's creamy, delicious, and contains zero carbs!

1. In a medium bowl, mix mascarpone, sunflower seed butter, and coconut oil until a smooth paste forms.

2. Shape paste into walnut-sized balls. If mixture is too sticky, place in refrigerator 15 minutes before forming balls.

3. Spread coconut flakes on a medium plate and roll individual balls through to coat evenly.

PER 1 FAT BOMB Calories: 121 | Fat: 12.4g | Protein: 1.3g | Sodium: 17mg | Fiber: 0.4g | Carbohydrates: 1.3g | Sugar: 0.5g

Chocolate Caramel Fat Bombs

This is a creamy, chocolaty fat bomb with the flavor of caramel. The flavor is pretty darn close to candy!

INGREDIENTS | MAKES 12 FAT BOMBS

6 tablespoons coconut oil

6 tablespoons heavy cream

2 ounces sugar-free baking dark chocolate

2 tablespoons caramel extract

2 tablespoons confectioners Swerve

1. In a small saucepan over very low heat, add all ingredients, stirring until completely melted. Pour into 12 silicone molds.

2. Refrigerate until hard. Remove from mold. Serve immediately or store in refrigerator for up to 1 week.

PER 1 FAT BOMB Calories: 112 | Fat: 10.7g | Protein: 0.3g | Sodium: 3mg | Fiber: 0.5g | Carbohydrates: 4.7g | Sugar: 0.5g | Sugar alcohol: 2.3g

White Chocolate Pecan Fat Bombs

This classic fat-bomb recipe is easy and incredibly delicious. Walnuts would be a great substitution if you're out of pecans.

INGREDIENTS | MAKES 8 FAT BOMBS

¼ cup pecans

4 tablespoons cocoa butter

4 tablespoons coconut oil

¼ teaspoon vanilla extract

5 drops stevia glycerite

Be Choosy with Nuts

When buying nuts, opt for raw, unsalted varieties rather than roasted, salted, or sugared versions. Raw nuts generally contain no added ingredients, while roasted, flavored nuts can contain unhealthy oils and sugar.

1. Chop pecans coarsely with a knife or process quickly in a food processor so they don't get too fine.

2. In a small saucepan over very low heat, add cocoa butter and coconut oil, stirring until completely melted, about 3 minutes.

3. Remove from heat and stir in pecans, vanilla extract, and stevia.

4. Pour into 8 silicone molds.

5. Refrigerate until hard.

6. Remove from mold. Serve immediately or store in refrigerator for up to 1 week.

PER 1 FAT BOMB Calories: 140 | Fat: 15.0g | Protein: 0.3g | Sodium: 0mg | Fiber: 0.3g | Carbohydrates: 0.5g | Sugar: 0.2g

Dark Chocolate Peppermint Fat Bombs

These fat bombs are modeled after the very famous British chocolates After Eight, which are wafer-thin dark chocolates filled with peppermint cream.

INGREDIENTS | MAKES 8 FAT BOMBS

4 tablespoons coconut oil

4 ounces sugar-free baking dark chocolate

¼ teaspoon peppermint extract

5 drops stevia glycerite

1. In a small saucepan over very low heat, add coconut oil and chocolate, stirring until completely melted, about 3 minutes.

2. Remove from heat and stir in peppermint and stevia.

3. Pour into 8 silicone molds.

4. Refrigerate until hard.

5. Remove from mold. Serve immediately or store in refrigerator for up to 1 week.

PER 1 FAT BOMB Calories: 124 | Fat: 11.5g | Protein: 0.5g | Sodium: 0mg | Fiber: 0.9g | Carbohydrates: 8.1g | Sugar: 0g | Sugar alcohol: 6.2g

Dark Chocolate Espresso Fat Bombs

Who doesn't love the flavors of chocolate and coffee together? This fat bomb will give you energy without even touching the caffeine!

INGREDIENTS | MAKES 8 FAT BOMBS

2 tablespoons cocoa butter

2 tablespoons coconut oil

2 ounces sugar-free baking dark chocolate

¼ teaspoon coffee extract

5 drops stevia glycerite

1. In a small saucepan over very low heat, add cocoa butter, coconut oil, and chocolate, stirring until completely melted, about 3 minutes.

2. Remove from heat and stir in coffee extract and stevia.

3. Pour into 8 silicone molds.

4. Refrigerate until hard.

5. Remove from mold. Serve immediately or store in refrigerator for up to 1 week.

PER 1 FAT BOMB Calories: 124 | Fat: 11.5g | Protein: 0.5g | Sodium: 0mg | Fiber: 0.9g | Carbohydrates: 8.1g | Sugar: 0g

Chocolate Amaretto Fat Bombs

Have you ever tried the Italian liquor amaretto? These fat bombs will remind you of the delicious flavor but without the alcohol and the sugar.

INGREDIENTS | MAKES 8 FAT BOMBS

¼ cup almonds

2 tablespoons cocoa butter

2 tablespoons coconut oil

2 ounces sugar-free baking dark chocolate

¼ teaspoon amaretto extract

5 drops stevia glycerite

1. Chop almonds coarsely with a knife or process quickly in a food processor so they don't get too fine.

2. In a small saucepan over very low heat, add cocoa butter, coconut oil, and chocolate, stirring until completely melted.

3. Remove from heat and stir in almonds, amaretto, and stevia.

4. Pour into 8 silicone molds.

5. Refrigerate until hard.

6. Remove from mold. Serve immediately or store in refrigerator for up to 1 week.

PER 1 FAT BOMB Calories: 118 | Fat: 11.2g | Protein: 1.2g | Sodium: 0mg | Fiber: 1.0g | Carbohydrates: 4.9g | Sugar: 0.2g

Peanut Butter Cream Cheese Fat Bombs

These decadent fat bombs combine the sweetness of cheesecake with the saltiness of peanut butter for an all-around treat!

INGREDIENTS | MAKES 12 FAT BOMBS

1 cup coconut oil
½ cup butter
½ cup crunchy peanut butter
2 tablespoons cream cheese
10 drops liquid stevia
¼ cup crushed unsalted peanuts

1. Place coconut oil, butter, peanut butter, cream cheese, and stevia in a small saucepan over medium heat and stir until melted.

2. Sprinkle crushed peanuts evenly in each well of a 12-cup mini muffin pan lined with cupcake wrappers. Pour peanut butter mixture over peanuts.

3. Place in freezer until hardened, about 30 minutes.

4. Store in refrigerator up to 1 week.

PER 1 FAT BOMB Calories: 314 | Fat: 31.4g | Protein: 3.4g | Sodium: 115mg | Fiber: 0.8g | Carbohydrates: 3.1g | Sugar: 1.4g

Hazelnut Truffles

*These truffles have the flavoring of your favorite hazelnut spread,
and are just as delicious as the real thing.*

INGREDIENTS | MAKES 9 FAT BOMBS

2 ounces unsweetened baking chocolate

1 tablespoon butter

1 tablespoon cream cheese

6 tablespoons finely chopped toasted hazelnuts, divided

2 tablespoons confectioners Swerve

2 drops stevia glycerite

½ teaspoon liquid hazelnut flavor

Balls or Shapes?

You can use fun silicone molds to make your truffles into shapes like hearts or seashells. Just pour the ganache straight from the saucepan into the molds and then refrigerate until solid. When ready, remove from the mold and roll into coating agent.

1. In a small double boiler over medium-low heat, melt chocolate while slowly stirring.

2. Add butter, cream cheese, 3 tablespoons hazelnuts, Swerve, stevia, and hazelnut flavor to chocolate and mix well until incorporated.

3. Remove from heat and keep stirring about 10 seconds.

4. Cool at room temperature about 1 hour until ganache has solidified.

5. Scoop ganache with a spoon and form 9 little balls. You might want to wear plastic gloves to help the chocolate not stick to your hands.

6. Place remaining chopped hazelnuts on a medium plate and roll truffles through to coat evenly.

PER 1 FAT BOMB Calories: 87 | Fat: 7.6g | Protein: 1.7g | Sodium: 146mg | Fiber: 1.5g | Carbohydrates: 4.7g | Sugar: 0.4g | Sugar alcohol: 2.0g

Dark Chocolate Raspberry Truffles

A delightful mix of sweet raspberry flavor and bitter dark chocolate—what a heavenly combination!

INGREDIENTS | MAKES 9 FAT BOMBS

3 ounces unsweetened baking chocolate

2 tablespoons heavy cream

1 tablespoon butter

2 tablespoons confectioners Swerve

2 drops stevia glycerite

½ teaspoon liquid raspberry flavor

3 tablespoons crushed freeze-dried raspberries

Freeze-Dried Raspberries

Freeze-dried raspberries are a genius invention for cooking. They are relatively low in carbohydrates for a fruit and give a big punch of flavor.

1. In a small double boiler over medium-low heat, melt chocolate while slowly stirring.

2. Add cream, butter, Swerve, stevia, and raspberry flavor to chocolate and mix well until incorporated.

3. Remove from heat and keep stirring about 10 seconds.

4. Place saucepan in refrigerator about 1 hour until ganache has solidified.

5. Scoop ganache with a spoon and form 9 little balls. You might want to wear plastic gloves to help the chocolate not stick to your hands.

6. Place crushed raspberries on a medium plate and roll truffles through until thinly coated.

7. For best consistency, keep refrigerated if room temperature exceeds 70°F.

PER 1 FAT BOMB Calories: 85 | Fat: 7.1g | Protein: 1.5g | Sodium: 13mg | Fiber: 1.7g | Carbohydrates: 5.1g | Sugar: 0.4g | Sugar alcohol: 2.0g

Salted Caramel and Pecan Truffles

This truffle is a quite indulgent one. Keep it for those moments when you feel you need a special treat.

INGREDIENTS | MAKES 9 FAT BOMBS

2 ounces unsweetened baking chocolate

1 tablespoon butter

1 tablespoon cream cheese

2 tablespoons confectioners Swerve

2 drops stevia glycerite

½ teaspoon liquid caramel flavor

½ teaspoon sea salt

3 tablespoons chopped pecans

1. In a small double boiler over medium-low heat, melt chocolate while slowly stirring.

2. Add butter, cream cheese, Swerve, stevia, caramel flavor, and salt to chocolate and mix well until incorporated.

3. Remove from heat and keep stirring about 10 seconds.

4. Place saucepan in refrigerator about 1 hour until ganache has solidified.

5. Scoop ganache with a spoon and form 9 little balls. You might want to wear plastic gloves to help the chocolate not stick to your hands.

6. Place chopped pecans on a medium plate and roll truffles through to coat evenly.

PER 1 FAT BOMB Calories: 73 | Fat: 6.4g | Protein: 1.2g | Sodium: 146mg | Fiber: 1.3g | Carbohydrates: 4.2g | Sugar: 0.2g | Sugar alcohol: 2.0g

Standard US/Metric Measurement Conversions

VOLUME CONVERSIONS

US Volume Measure	Metric Equivalent
⅛ teaspoon	0.5 milliliter
¼ teaspoon	1 milliliter
½ teaspoon	2 milliliters
1 teaspoon	5 milliliters
½ tablespoon	7 milliliters
1 tablespoon (3 teaspoons)	15 milliliters
2 tablespoons (1 fluid ounce)	30 milliliters
¼ cup (4 tablespoons)	60 milliliters
⅓ cup	90 milliliters
½ cup (4 fluid ounces)	125 milliliters
⅔ cup	160 milliliters
¾ cup (6 fluid ounces)	180 milliliters
1 cup (16 tablespoons)	250 milliliters
1 pint (2 cups)	500 milliliters
1 quart (4 cups)	1 liter (about)

WEIGHT CONVERSIONS

US Weight Measure	Metric Equivalent
½ ounce	15 grams
1 ounce	30 grams
2 ounces	60 grams
3 ounces	85 grams
¼ pound (4 ounces)	115 grams
½ pound (8 ounces)	225 grams
¾ pound (12 ounces)	340 grams
1 pound (16 ounces)	454 grams

OVEN TEMPERATURE CONVERSIONS

Degrees Fahrenheit	Degrees Celsius
200 degrees F	95 degrees C
250 degrees F	120 degrees C
275 degrees F	135 degrees C
300 degrees F	150 degrees C
325 degrees F	160 degrees C
350 degrees F	180 degrees C
375 degrees F	190 degrees C
400 degrees F	205 degrees C
425 degrees F	220 degrees C
450 degrees F	230 degrees C

BAKING PAN SIZES

American	Metric
8 × 1½ inch round baking pan	20 × 4 cm cake tin
9 × 1½ inch round baking pan	23 × 3.5 cm cake tin
11 × 7 × 1½ inch baking pan	28 × 18 × 4 cm baking tin
13 × 9 × 2 inch baking pan	30 × 20 × 5 cm baking tin
2 quart rectangular baking dish	30 × 20 × 3 cm baking tin
15 × 10 × 2 inch baking pan	30 × 25 × 2 cm baking tin (Swiss roll tin)
9 inch pie plate	22 × 4 or 23 × 4 cm pie plate
7 or 8 inch springform pan	18 or 20 cm springform or loose bottom cake tin
9 × 5 × 3 inch loaf pan	23 × 13 × 7 cm or 2 lb narrow loaf or pâté tin
1½ quart casserole	1.5 liter casserole
2 quart casserole	2 liter casserole

APPENDIX A

Shopping List

Fats and Oils

- Butter
- Coconut oil
- Coconut butter
- Olive oil
- Olives
- Avocados
- Avocado oil
- Coconut flakes (unsweetened)
- Full-fat coconut milk

Protein

- Poultry: chicken, turkey, duck (free-range is best)
- Meat: beef, veal, venison, bison, lamb (grass-fed is best)
- Pork: pork loin, ham, pork chops (humanely treated, pastured is best; make sure ham contains no sugar)
- Eggs
- Bacon
- Sausage
- Deli meat: prosciutto, pepperoni, turkey, roast beef, ham (make sure there is no added sugar)
- Fresh fish: cod, salmon, halibut, mackerel, herring, sardines, tuna, anchovies (wild-caught is best)
- Shellfish: shrimp, crab, lobster, scallops, mussels, oysters, clams
- Canned tuna
- Canned salmon

Dairy Products

- Heavy cream
- Sour cream
- Ricotta cheese
- Cottage cheese
- Cream cheese
- Cheddar cheese
- Parmesan cheese
- Pepper jack cheese
- Mozzarella cheese
- Asiago cheese

Fruits

- Blackberries
- Blueberries
- Raspberries
- Granny Smith apples
- Lemons

Vegetables

- Bell peppers
- Cucumbers
- Broccoli
- Eggplant
- Spinach
- Baby kale
- Cabbage
- Cauliflower
- Lettuce (iceberg and romaine)
- Onions
- Garlic
- Scallions
- Shallots

- Mushrooms
- Celery
- Brussels sprouts
- Asparagus
- Zucchini
- Spaghetti squash
- Canned whole tomatoes
- Fire-roasted diced tomatoes

Nuts, Nut Butters, and Seeds

- Almonds
- Almond butter
- Cashews
- Cashew butter
- Pecans
- Pistachio nuts
- Macadamia nuts
- Chia seeds
- Peanuts
- Peanut butter
- Walnuts
- Pumpkin seeds
- Sunflower seeds

Condiments

- Pickles
- Mustard
- White vinegar
- Apple cider vinegar
- Hot sauce
- Sweeteners and extracts
- Erythritol (granulated and powdered)

- Stevia (liquid and granulated)
- Vanilla extract
- Almond extract
- Orange extract
- Peppermint extract

Miscellaneous

- Pork rinds
- Dark chocolate
- Unsweetened cocoa powder
- Whey protein powder (sugar-free–low net carbohydrates)

APPENDIX B

Resources

BOSTON CHILDREN'S HOSPITAL
300 Longwood Avenue
Boston, MA 02115
(617) 355-7970
www.childrenshospital.org

Boston Children's Hospital has a Pediatric Epilepsy Center that provides support for children with epilepsy. Their program is rated as a Level 4 Epilepsy Center by the National Association of Epilepsy Centers because they deliver an extremely high level of care that includes the use of the ketogenic diet.

CHILDREN'S HOSPITAL LOS ANGELES
4650 Sunset Blvd.
Los Angeles, CA 90027
(323) 660-2450
www.chla.org

Children's Hospital Los Angeles specializes in pediatrics and uses the classic ketogenic diet and modified ketogenic diet as part of their epilepsy treatment program.

KETO CALCULATOR
http://keto-calculator.ankerl.com/

Easily calculate your macronutrient ratios for the ketogenic diet with this online diet calculator.

THE CHARLIE FOUNDATION
515 Ocean Avenue
#602N
Santa Monica, CA 90402
(310) 393-2347
www.charliefoundation.org

The Charlie Foundation for Ketogenic Therapies provides information and dietary therapies for people with epilepsy, other neurological disorders, and cancer.

THE INSTITUTE FOR FUNCTIONAL MEDICINE
505 S. 336th Street
Suite 600
Federal Way, WA 98003
(800) 228-0622
www.functionalmedicine.org

The goal of The Institute for Functional Medicine is to reverse chronic disease and advance knowledge by providing information and education about functional medicine.

THE ULTRAWELLNESS CENTER
DR. MARK HYMAN
55 Pittsfield Road
Suite 9
Lenox Commons, Lenox, MA 01240
(413) 637-9991
www.ultrawellnesscenter.com

Dr. Mark Hyman is one of the leaders in functional medicine. He founded The UltraWellness Center in Lenox, Massachusetts, and has authored several books.

Index

Note: Page numbers in **bold indicate recipe category lists.**